Citizens and Cities

Citizens and Cities
Urban Policy in the 1990s

Dilys M. Hill
Reader in Politics
University of Southampton

HARVESTER
WHEATSHEAF

New York   London   Toronto   Sydney   Tokyo   Singapore

First published 1994 by
Harvester Wheatsheaf
Campus 400, Maylands Avenue
Hemel Hempstead
Hertfordshire, HP2 7EZ
A division of
Simon & Schuster International Group

Typeset in 10/12pt Times
by Dorwyn Ltd, Rowlands Castle, Hants

Printed and bound in Great Britain by
Biddles Ltd, Guildford and King's Lynn

British Library Cataloguing in Publication Data

A catalogue record for this book is available from
the British Library

ISBN 0-7450-1294-9

1 2 3 4 5   98 97 96 95 94

CONTE[NTS]

Chapter 2. URI. Topic.

Chapter 3 & 4. Topic 2. URI

CHAPTER 1

INTRODUCTION

When the city is valued, it is valued as the theater of diversity, the center of a cosmopolitan culture, the breeding ground of freedom and tolerance . . .

But these virtues are the virtues of the marketplace or of the city as 'hotel' . . .

What is lost, then, in this vision of the city as a shopping center is the sense of a people joined together in a perception of common ends; who found their common life on procedures they regard, by and large, as just. . . . What is lost, in a word, is the sense of the city as polity.[1]

In this book the term city refers not to size *per se* but to the urban condition in the sense of that to which urban policy is addressed. This is not to ignore the fact that scale and location are important when one is addressing quality-of-life issues. The city is also a powerful idea: a synonym for the problems of urban living in the late twentieth century and the changes which have occurred over the past twenty years as governments have sought, through a series of largely piecemeal measures, to address those problems. In one sense, the city is the focus of concern for the 'urban crisis', interpreted in a variety of ways: as physical dereliction, multiple deprivation, fiscal inadequacy, the decline of manufacturing employment, the flight of population and business to the suburbs and small free-standing towns, and crime and disorder. Focusing on the urban experience in this sense raises wider questions of city and region, and of the impact of international restructuring of capital and labour.

In another sense the city is a synonym for unsettling changes in values and attitudes: dependency, changing family structures, the decline of civility and civic pride. Not all the attributes are negative; the city is also the arena of intellectual and cultural dynamism, of constant cycles of revival which at their extreme are marked by gentrification and 'yuppie' lifestyles. None of these concerns is new. Over the last two centuries the fear of disorder and of physical and moral decline has gone hand in hand with positive measures to combat them; and with a search for ways of harnessing philanthropy and mutual assistance as well as mobilising state intervention.

The use of the city as a framework for analysis has also sought to define the problem in more narrow terms; as the 'inner city' as the location of the most severe and concentrated problems. In practice many of the most desolate areas of our cities are not adjacent to the city centre but can be found on the large public-sector housing estates of the postwar period. In either case these areas represent the 'other', places and lives outside the experience of the governing and professional – and academic – classes. Again, however, the term is used not only as the focus of urban regeneration but also as a synonym for values and behaviours: moral and attitudinal deficiencies, alienation and anomie. The urban question as formulated in inner-city terms has evolved over the past twenty-five years from a concentration on the problem of persistent poverty to an emphasis on economic rejuvenation. Policy responses, in turn, have moved from welfare issues and social policy to financial and land-use initiatives – and the containment of disorder. A common feature of policy responses has been greater selectivity, with the aim of targeting benefits and initiatives within an existing resource base rather than through a search for universal remedies.

The several ways of defining urban policy – as planning, as the locus of activity in space (addressing the inequalities of spatial action) or as social policy – are part of a wider ideological agenda. In the 1990s the underpinning rationale of policy has been the move to centralisation and privatisation, to markets and quasi-markets and the expansion of consumer choice. Although the move to privatism has been a persistent theme of this agenda, urban policy has been criticised for its lack of consistency, its piecemeal nature, and its lack of coordination at central as well as local level. While the move to the enabling local authority emphasises its strategic role, this is dependent on managing a network of relationships in the public, private and voluntary sectors rather than having sole control of a public agenda. But the strategic role of local authorities has been made problematic by the nature of funding. While the fragmented implementation of urban regeneration has brought additional, targeted funds, mainstream expenditure has been reduced and overall spending limited by the government's setting of assessments and capping of budgets.

The urban arena is used in this book as the setting for citizen involvement, and for the exploration of the meaning of community. Community may be based on the shared experience of place, on attitudes and loyalties, or on common interests. Individuals are members of a number of communities in these different senses, all potential avenues for political participation. Community, however, is a contested notion. From one perspective, community implies citizens working together for common ends, underpinned by shared values. To those on the right, particularly the neoliberal right, such concepts of community are misleading and potentially authoritarian. Common purposes arising from a community of common aspirations is a naive assumption, since society is marked by contractual relationships and anonymity.[2] Obligations will arise, only if people choose to belong to groups and accept their rules, not as the result of a mythic and arguably coercive 'community'. Community then becomes a limited and defensive cooperative activity, as in 'Neighbourhood Watch' schemes.

To those on the left, by contrast, community is part of a socialist ethic of fraternity and cooperation which, far from being misplaced in the late twentieth century, has a renewed resonance in combating market individualism. The criticism of community, however, is not confined to ideological differences between right and left. The concept of community, it is argued, lacks theoretical rigour. It is a notion which is overused but underdefined, too general to have analytical value. It is also overladen with emotional attachments, an assertion of what should be rather than what is.

Whatever the perspective, some concept of the community as the shared experience of place provides the justification of the locality as the arena for the exercise of citizenship. It is at the local level that the opportunities for involvement in self-government are most widely available. Marquand states it succinctly: 'For citizenship is nothing if it is not public. The notion of the citizen implies a notion of the city – of the polis, of the public realm, of public purposes, publicly debated and determined.'³ But community participation need not necessarily take the form of representative democracy. It can incorporate populist ideas, particularly notions of neighbourhood democracy. Nor does local self-government mean a monolithic or coercive pattern of involvement. As Oldfield puts it: 'self-government can refer to any public tasks and activities that a community wishes to engage in. Local initiatives can thus respond and cater to particular "publics" that are narrower in scope than the entire community.'⁴

The concept of citizenship embraces a range of positions. Citizenship as status denotes individuals with rights and duties constitutionally guaranteed to all members of a society. But citizenship must also recognise that individuals are political and social beings with a role to play in society. In this sense the 'citizen' is the democratic aim as opposed to the existing reality of 'subject'. Arguably, citizenship reconciles individualism and social justice, since the possession of civil and political rights without social rights reduces citizenship to a façade. In this debate the tension is between the neoliberal assertion of the market and the free individual, and the civic republican tradition with its emphasis on participation in a *polis* fashioned by its members.

Citizenship is not, however, primarily grounded in the 'active citizen' of volunteerism or the multiple interests of liberal pluralism. Citizenship is about power and its distribution, about the framework of public and thus collective decisions, and accountability for those decisions. This affects the debate on citizens and cities in two ways. One is that the exercise of citizenship may be so circumscribed that some individuals are effectively excluded. In the 1980s and 1990s there has been a debate on whether an 'underclass' exists outside the civic community. For this underclass, suffering from social and political isolation, the result is a significant erosion of citizenship rights.

The second impact that a given distribution of power has on the exercise of citizenship is the effectiveness of the local arena as a location of significant decisions. To what extent, that is, are local authorities still capable of authoritative governance? Over the past fifteen years the function of local authorities has changed from direct delivery of services to a more enabling role within a marketplace of provision. The result has been an emphasis on the local council's strategic position within a network of local agencies, public, private and voluntary. At the same time there has been increased support for devolved decision-making to neighbourhood or areal level, proposed on both democratic and managerial grounds.

That citizenship is about power, and the local arena is a legitimate setting for the exercise of citizenship, is thrown into sharp focus by the unrest and disorder that cities have suffered in recent years. Again exclusion is a major factor, particularly that arising from continued problems of racism. In this setting the city, particularly the disadvantaged neighbourhoods of the inner city and large peripheral estates, is conceptualised not as space but as marginality.

The changing role of local authorities has been accompanied by a refocusing of urban policy from broadly planning and social objectives within a universalistic welfare state framework to a much more marked emphasis on economic regeneration. Economic regeneration is selective and targeted. It focuses on physical dereliction and unemployment, and seeks to promote private investment in city redevelopment through financial incentives and deregulation, initiated by the centre and carried out in public–private partnerships over which government has a controlling oversight. But although initiatives are targeted, they remain piecemeal; by 1992 there were thirty-four different urban policy iniatives covering five central government departments.

Regeneration initiatives have highlighted the fragmented nature of urban policy and the changing role of local authorities in a network of public–private partnerships. These themes also characterise the delivery of major services. The compulsory contracting out of a wide range of local services and the opting out of schools from local authority control mark a change from direct provision by the local authority to a market or quasi-market of service delivery. In this market-place individual choice is seen both as ensuring improved standards and as more effectively democratic. For the right, accountability to the individual consumer is direct and meaningful in ways that periodic local elections, marked by low turnout, do not match. Individual choice and consumer accountability are promoted by greater rights to information, to complaints procedures, and to published standards through national performance indicators.

These objectives are those set out in the Citizen's Charter and the numerous individual service charters to which it has given rise. To critics the basis of these moves is individual consumerism; the Citizen's Charter is a charter for consumers, not citizens. The Citizen's Charter offers no conception of rights that could be codified and enforced. If, to the right, the ideas behind charterism are to expose services to greater competition through the disciplines of the marketplace, to the left the need is to enhance and justify public services, together with much wider access to information. Both share the tools of quality auditing, customer contracts, and redress. The concern for quality in services still leaves unanswered the issue of power; that is, who has power to take decisions, to assess standards of service and to evaluate outcomes. Bringing political democracy back in remains a pressing if, as yet, neglected objective.

The search for greater consumer influence on services should not overshadow the Mill tradition of the educative role of local government in sustaining representative democracy. The relationship between citizens and cities is still encapsulated in the 'noble aspiration' of local government, as Rhodes puts it: 'In particular, it is a means for emancipating the individual and creating a free society through citizen participation.'[5] The agenda for the 1990s is to redefine a normative theory of local government which can specify, as King argues, what powers are available to local authorities and what initiatives they can pursue.[6] The normative theory which appears to be emerging is based on the enabling authority. The enabling authority, however, is a contested concept between right and left. To the right, local government fosters and regulates small-scale agencies that provide services. To the left, local government provides community governance, producing an overall strategy, representing the needs of the community and promoting a watchdog and advocate role.

The chapters in this book develop these themes of urban policy in the 1990s. Chapter 2 addresses the issues of citizenship. It examines the liberal–individualist and civic–republican traditions, and their revival in the 1990s. The chapter concludes that citizenship is not just a status inherent in individuals in the nation-state but a complex of obligations and practices in which people have rights as individuals but also participate as social beings. Chapter 3 explores the interrelated themes of community and participation. To exercise the rights and duties of citizenship within a community means to have the opportunity and the will to participate. Effective participation depends on appropriate structures and processes, and on access and information.

Chapter 4 examines the reality of life in the political community in which individuals as citizens claim equal rights. The strains in contemporary society have focused concern on those people who, it is claimed, have lost their attachment to civil society: an 'underclass' whose social and political participation has been eroded, and who are excluded from full citizenship. Chapter 5 considers the proposition that if the local arena affords a positive setting for the exercise of citizenship, then effective local government must control meaningful decisions. It looks at the role and functions of local government, the debate on enabling and providing, and the case for a power of general competence for local authorities.

Chapter 6 looks at the obverse of the praised values of community and citizenship. Disorder, unrest and crime are, it is argued, as consistent features of urban life as common purpose and fraternity. The chapter examines the disorders of the 1980s, the relations between different areas and groups, and the mechanisms of policing and police–community relations. To reverse incivility and unrest calls for regeneration, with the aim of encouraging participation; strengthening innovation and dynamism associated with city life and culture; and halting physical and economic decline. Chapter 7 addresses these issues, both as they concern the 'inner city' and as they give rise to the criticism that urban policy in Britain remains fragmented, lacking in coherence and cohesion of purpose and implementation. What, exactly, is 'the problem', and is the goal policies for places or policies for people?

Chapter 8 looks at urban policy that focuses on a particular aspect of policies for people, at the consumer in the market-place as a variant of 'citizenship'. The chapter addresses the issues of service delivery in the local context of a mixture of consumer choice, regulation, and the management of quality. It examines the debate over customer, consumer and citizen in relation to three major areas of legislative change in the 1980s and 1990s: those of education, housing and community care. It argues that the importance of democratic politics must be reaffirmed as the legitimate base for choices, if equity as well as standards is to be realised.

Chapter 9 draws these themes together. It concludes that urban policy must be directed to local governance, 'bringing local democracy back in', and promoting the individual as citizen as well as consumer of the urban experience.

Notes

1. H. Arkes, *The Philosopher in the City* (Princeton, NJ: Princeton University Press, 1981), p. 3.
2. R. Plant, *Social Justice, Labour and the New Right*, Fabian Pamphlet 556 (London: The Fabian Society, February 1993), pp. 15–16.
3. D. Marquand, 'Subversive language of citizenship', *The Guardian*, 2 January 1989.
4. A. Oldfield, 'Citizenship: an unnatural practice?', *Political Quarterly*, vol. 61, 2, April–June 1990, p. 183.
5. R.A.W. Rhodes, 'Developing the public service orientation: or let's add a soupçon of political theory', *Local Government Studies*, vol. 13, 3, May/June 1987, p. 71.
6. D.S. King, 'The New Right, the New Left and local government', in J. Stewart and G. Stoker (eds), *The Future of Local Government* (London: Macmillan, 1989), p. 202.

CHAPTER 2

CITIZENSHIP: ISSUES AND DEFINITIONS

Introduction

The aim of this chapter is to examine the concept of citizenship as it reflects life in the *polis*, the public realm in which individuals debate and resolve public purposes. In the ancient world, citizenship meant participation in the city-state, its obligations and duties. The subsequent development of the concept has highlighted both the autonomy and agency of individuals, and their common purpose and action as social beings. This chapter examines the liberal–individualist and civic–republican traditions of thinking about citizenship and the search for civility and fraternity which would provide the motivation for life in public society. This theoretical discourse has been revived in the 1980s and 1990s by the emergence of the 'active citizen' – strictly speaking, itself a tautology – in political debate. There has been a re-examination of the meaning of citizenship, and the structures and institutions which underpin it. The conclusion is that citizenship is not just a status inherent in individuals in the nation-state but a complex of obligations and practices.

Citizenship recognises people's rights as individuals *and* their life as social beings, including their continued affirmation of the social dimension. That is, citizenship is both status, derived from membership of a collectivity (in the modern era, the state), and a system of rights and obligations that incorporates justice, equality and community. Two further sets of differentiation are usually made in respect of citizenship: between formal and substantive rights possessed by individual citizens, and between procedural rights and actual outcomes. Citizens, that is, may possess formal rights, but lack the means to exercise those rights. Similarly, there may be procedures which are open and equal, but there is no guarantee that individuals are entitled to a particular outcome. The assertion that a further distinction should be made between negative and positive rights; that is, between civil and political rights on the one hand and social and economic rights on the other, has been extensively analysed by Plant and others, and will not be readdressed here.[1]

Citizenship and its rights provide the legitimation of life in the modern *polis*. To be fully effective, citizenship needs supporting procedures, institutions and arenas in which it can be acted out in practice. These arenas are multilayered, including the expression of local opportunities, initiatives and mutual ties. Although local government does not determine citizen status, it does provide the arena in which many rights are exercised. To this end it has retained discretion over decisions, supported by a local mandate. Local government is thus more than the mere agent of central government, implementing decisions made elsewhere.

This chapter explores these themes, beginning with the history and development of the notion of citizenship. It then considers the Marshall inheritance, derived from T.H. Marshall's position that citizenship embodies social as well as civil and political rights. In the 1980s, however, an alternative formulation was proposed by leading British Conservatives based on the 'active citizen', the free individual contributing to society through voluntary action and philanthropy. To be active, however, requires the empowerment of the citizen through procedures, institutions and arenas. Chapter 2 concludes that effective citizenship must encompass autonomy, agency *and* practice.

Citizenship: history and development

For Aristotle, to be human is to be political. In the third book of the *Politics* he formulates citizenship as participation in or membership of the *polis*, confined to those (excluding women and slaves) who took part in the exercise of power and the defence of the city-state. Citizenship was action, and constituted the life of virtue. In medieval times citizenship entailed a duality of loyalty – to Church and state – but also affirmed the fraternity of guild member and burgher in city life. Indeed, the notion of the city was a key element in the development of Western thought on freedom, the individual, and civility. As Turner states: 'To leave the countryside in order to enter the city was typically connected with the process of civilization; to become urban was to "citizenize" the person.'[2] Fraternity was also a keynote of French revolutionary thought on citizenship – and incorporated the status of *citoyenne* as well as *citoyen*.[3]

The civil and political rights of citizenship that evolved in the eighteenth and nineteenth centuries, however, were challenged by Marx as inadequate in a capitalist society which rendered large sections of the population inherently and permanently powerless. There were fundamental divisions between classes and class interests, ultimately founded in property rights and the ownership of capital, which could not be removed by appeals to the common values of citizenship. While capitalism had created the framework within which citizenship could develop, in practice it used the so-called equal status of citizens to maintain the fundamental class divisions of society. The bourgeoisie remained the controlling elite; the civil and political rights of citizenship could not disguise the real position of the majority of the population as subjects. It can be argued that these inequalities between capital and labour remain, and that struggle and conflict are still a part of the realisation of citizenship. The nineteenth century in Britain also saw, however, a strong moral ethos of public service and civic spirit, including local government based on unpaid, but increasingly elected, public involvement.

Modern democratic society defines citizenship universalistically in terms of the nation-state. But in the twentieth century, following T.H. Marshall, there has been a concern with the social rights of citizenship. And for contemporary thinkers, the debate is essentially about how to realise the good life in society, how to find 'a normative theory of social membership'.[4] The need in the late twentieth century is to restore *civitas* and provide the motivation for engagement in public affairs. Life in civil society and political community depends on the exercise of a civility that goes beyond mutual tolerance into active support for processes and structures that constitute the public realm; what Shils calls 'the virtue of civil society'.[5]

Three strands of thought emerge from the historical evolution of the concept and dominate contemporary debate: the liberal-individualist traditition, the civic–republican tradition, and, following Marshall, the social rights of citizenship, founded on the principle of equality. In the liberal–individualist tradition the individual is an autonomous being, capable of moral agency and bearing rights. That is, individuals can be said to have rights to the conditions necessary to human action, to agency.[6] Citizenship is a status; the rights attaching to status are those of freedom from interference. And while citizens are free to choose their governors, their involvement in public life is a matter of choice rather than an inherent quality of citizenship. Liberal individualism tolerates an abdication from politics which is in marked distinction from the civic–republican tradition where, by definition, citizenship is practice.[7] The liberal–individualist citizen claims rights as against the state and owes duties to it, primarily to pay taxes and defend it. The individual also has the duty to respect the rights of others, but no wider obligations to society as such, other than those entered into on a contractual basis.[8] The liberal tradition formulates the citizen in procedural terms, with citizens sharing a belief in the rules that govern living together in society, rather than having a shared belief in a substantive common good. Such a notion of the common good runs counter to the pluralism of liberal democracy.

The liberal–individualist tradition asserts the nature of citizenship as status, rights inhering in the individual free from hindrance by others or by the state. This position has been reaffirmed in recent years by the new right, an ideological standpoint which has significantly challenged claims to social welfare rights. From this perspective the real world in which we live is that of a liberal contractual society based on individualised market and commodity relations.[9] But the atomistic perspective has been criticised by Marquand as reductionist individualism, denying common purposes and a common good.[10] Marquand argues, by contrast, that we live in society because we are social beings; we do not choose our purposes in rational isolation but through a constant process of communication with other society members.[11] From the viewpoint of the left, this concept of the common good lies at the heart of citizenship and embodies those needs, rights and opportunities which everyone must have in order to pursue their goals. Freedom, that is, is a necessary condition for autonomy but, for that very reason, it cannot be separated from the capacity to pursue ends, from resources and opportunities.[12]

It is mutuality of purpose that underlies the civic–communitarian tradition which emphasises that individuals are citizens only as members of a community. This tradition holds that it is a shared commitment to practice which makes individuals citizens.[13] The civic–republican tradition's concern with practice has its roots in Machiavelli's *virtù*, following the Roman ideal of virtue (*virtus*), above all in the obligation of military service to defend the republic, which in turn was allied to values of public-spiritedness. In this tradition the citizen's public commitment is to deliberate on common purposes, then to take action to secure them. These are inherent duties, and not to fulfil them is to cease to be a citizen.[14] If in liberal individualism the key element is freedom from the state, in civic republicanism it is the shared experience of participation in the political community which is crucial.

Oldfield traces the history of civic republicanism through the work of four key thinkers: Machiavelli, Rousseau, Hegel and Tocqueville.[15] Throughout this tradition runs the recognition that individuals are not only bearers of rights but performers of duties; as social beings their life in the community is dependent on both the recognition of common goals and a willingness to act to achieve them. Civic republicanism has attracted interest in recent years in a renewed search for civic virtue to set against the emphasis on self-interest and individual rights of new right conservatism.

Critics argue, however, that there are two major difficulties in the civic–republican tradition which pose serious doubts over its claims to generate the true nature of citizenship. The first problem is the individual's autonomy, that rights-based agency which is at the heart of liberal individualism. How may individuals be melded in the community spirit without endangering that autonomy; are not the communitarian ethos and individualism inherently opposed? As Turner puts it: 'The paradox is that, while citizens are required to be individuals in order to exercise conscience and choice, the institutions which make citizenship possible promote equality and bureaucracy.'[16] The individual, that is, should not be sacrificed to the citizen. This tension remains.

The second reservation over the civic–republican perspective follows from the first. What force or value can be found which will motivate individuals to engage in the practice of citizenship, to take part in political affairs, to value and defend the good of the community? Historically, political thinkers saw this difficulty as needing an underpinning value system – a religion – which would enable people to realise that their common good was their individual good. Modern communitarians hope that if individuals are empowered and provided with the structures and institutions which enable them to participate in political life, the problem of commitment will be overcome. It is this institutional support which motivates and provides commitment, enabling individuals to reach moral and political autonomy. Doubts still remain, however. As Oldfield puts it, citizenship still appears 'an unnatural practice',[17] one which needs to be instilled through education and a set of values or social mores.

Intimately bound up with this argument about how to generate commitment to the duty to practise citizenship has been the focus on fraternity. Fraternity is that bond which Aristotle identified as 'concord', a form of friendship appropriate to citizens:

> But we do attribute concord to states, when the citizens have the same judgment about their common interest, when they choose the same things, and when they execute what they have decided in common. In other words, concord is found in the realm of action . . .

and again:

> We see, consequently, that concord is friendship among fellow citizens, and that is indeed the common use of the term. For its sphere is what is in the common interest and what is important for life . . .[18]

This Aristotelian notion, echoed by Rousseau, sees these bonds as ties between good (that is, those with civic virtue) individuals who share commitments. Without such fraternity, the *polis* cannot be sustained. From the French Revolution onwards, political thinkers have explored this notion of fraternity. They have emphasised the reliance on common values through patriotism and loyalty, the socialisation through shared experiences of family and work, the 'neighbourliness' that inheres in daily life. But fraternity as common purpose in the tradition of the French Revolution has faced challenges from the resurgence of liberal individualism in modern conservative thought and practice. Thus the need to restate the bonds of fraternity, and the means whereby it can be expressed, remain central to contemporary debate; as I argue below, the volunteerism of 'active citizenship' does not by itself constitute such fraternity. Fraternity essentially inheres in feelings of belonging, of common purpose, and in action to achieve it, in solidarity.

The Marshall inheritance

The obligations and duties of citizenship dominate the debate on citizenship which has its roots in the work of T.H. Marshall, particularly his *Citizenship and Social Class*, published in 1950. Marshall defines the three elements of citizenship as civil, political and social rights which have developed over time. Civil rights emerged in the eighteenth century and political rights in the nineteenth, with social rights as the twentieth-century cumulation of fully effective citizenship. While many authors take Marshall as their starting point in the citizenship debate, there have been two critical reassessments. The first relates to what appears to be the evolutionary nature of the development of the rights of citizenship, and ambiguity over the extent to which conflict between classes in capitalist society was a necessary part of the achievement of rights.[19] Not only have rights been born from conflict and struggle, from revolution and demands from below as well as concession and legislative extension from above, they remain liable to change. A second, and related, criticism is the claim that although social rights enable citizenship to be exercised effectively, these rights are not an inherent element of citizenship. That is, social rights facilitate citizenship, they do not constitute it.[20]

Citizenship in Marshall's writings is a status held by all those in full membership of a community; that is, citizens are equal. By the social element of citizenship Marshall meant 'the whole range from the right to a modicum of economic welfare and security to the right to share to the full in the social heritage and to live the life of a civilised being according to the standards prevailing in the society. The institutions most closely connected with it are the educational system and the social services.'[21]

In the development of the Marshallian themes it has been argued that civil and political rights can be effectively combined

with social rights. Citizenship, while it confirms individual autonomy and privacy, claims rights against the state for the provision
of the conditions for its exercise. In the twentieth century the
incorporation of social rights into the status of citizen created a
'universal right to real income which is not proportionate to the
market value of the claimant'.[22] The grounding of citizenship as
civil, political and social rights produces citizenship both as status
and as a set of rights. The rights and duties of citizenship work
both ways. That is, while citizens have duties to the community of
which they are members, citizenship rights give them claims
against the state, the obligation of the state to its members. This
does not mean that social rights would be individually enforceable,
but that the state has an overall general duty to provide services
available to all citizens.[23]

Thus citizenship propounds rights. It also evokes corresponding
duties, particularly the duty to pay taxes, to be educated, and to
undertake military service. But Marshall goes beyond this to stress
that there is a general duty to serve the community where one can,
and a duty to work. While the national community may be too
remote to act as the driving force in evoking citizenship, the local
community and the working group may provide the necessary
vitality. It is interesting to note that Marshall's developmental
thesis claims that the historical source of social rights was membership of a local community and of functional associations, which
was eroded and replaced in the nineteenth century by the Poor
Law. This theme of localism will be taken up again later in this
chapter.

A major criticism of Marshall's position is that although social
rights are claimed to be part of citizenship, some rights are still
very unequally distributed between men and women, and between
groups defined in terms of ethnic or cultural identities.[24] Marshall's argument that social citizenship tended to reduce certain
inequalities is challenged as at best unsubstantiated, both as historical explanation and as contemporary fact. The counterargument is
that social equality cannot be achieved through the development
of citizenship, and social rights can never be more than secondary
rights of citizenship.[25] In this context it is necessary, as Bottomore
stresses, to differentiate between formal rights and substantive
rights. Citizens may have formal rights but lack the means to
exercise them. The exercise of substantive rights is affected by

poverty, which has a major effect on the quality of citizenship experienced by poor people.[26] Poverty excludes people from the full rights of citizenship, diminishing their social and political participation. They become isolated and excluded: a point which will be dealt with further in Chapter 4. Nor are class inequalities the whole story in the struggle for citizenship. The past twenty years have seen the growth of social movements (women's, environmental) which still believe that full citizenship has yet to be realised. The feminist criticism of liberal capitalism, in particular, is that it compartmentalises society in ways that exclude women from full participation, and thus from citizenship.[27]

The problem is not just that the existence of the social rights of citizenship is challenged by continuing inequalities, but that new right conservatives, in both Britain and the United States, have seen welfare not as a social right of citizenship but as evidence of dependency. If, for the left, citizens are apathetic because the system offers them too little opportunity for active involvement beyond minimalist voting and expressions of feelings of loyalty, then to the right it is the stultifying effects of the welfare state that produce passive and dependent citizens. Since the late 1970s the content of the 'citizenship of entitlement' has in practice been reduced.[28] Against this can be set the argument that welfare rights are necessary to maintain the participation of all as equal voices in the conversation of public life.[29]

While the controversy between right and left over social rights continues, contemporary research has shown the extent to which British respondents actually do focus on the social rights of citizenship. The British give social rights primacy, but justify this position in the liberal and individualist language of contract – an interesting mix of the liberal–individualist and civic–republican forms. Modern democracies are neither societies of strangers, as liberal contractualism implies, nor the communities of friends of civic republicanism, but a combination of both.[30] This appears to support the argument that welfare rights are integral to a contemporary sense of citizenship.[31]

The legacy of Marshall's approach can thus be seen as the priority generally given to the social rights of citizenship, since these are the 'necessary prerequisites of individual agency'.[32] Two elements of this tradition are given particular emphasis. Marshall stressed that citizenship is a process which has evolved over time and incorporates social elements – an approach which, the Speaker's Commission on Citizenship believed, finds accord in the thinking of British people.[33] The second element is that the emphasis on civil, political and social rights and the entitlements to which they give rise is matched by a concern with obligations and duties. If the citizen has duties – at a minimum, to obey the law and pay taxes – then the state has obligations to provide the entitlements which constitute rights. This is not to be seen as some kind of bargain between the individual and the state, a quid pro quo: both elements exist in their own right.

The Marshall tradition, however, still gives rise to questions about the nature of capitalist society within which citizenship operates. If the core of social citizenship is the right to welfare, then this right in modern societies is founded not only on wealth-creating market economies and their attendent taxation systems but on bureaucracies which, in delivering services, are delivering rights.[34] We shall return to the problem of bureaucracies and service delivery, and the contemporary interest in the citizen as consumer, in Chapter 8. More critical than this reservation, however, is the assertion that citizenship is either impossible under capitalism because of continued class inequalities or that, alternatively, social citizenship requires equality and is therefore incompatible with individualism, since this is curtailed by welfare's bureaucratic base.[35]

The active citizen

The active citizen, evoked in 1988 by the Home Secretary, Douglas Hurd, in a speech at Tamworth (where Robert Peel had introduced his Manifesto in 1835), seems far removed both from the revived republican tradition and from the concern with social welfare rights as a fundamental of effective citizenship. Although it was endorsed by Margaret Thatcher at the 1988 Conservative Party Conference, Hurd's concept, while it reflected the mixture of self-help and voluntarism of the Thatcher ideology, made little practical impact. Its successor in the Conservative canon has been the consumer of the Citizen's Charter, based on notions of redress, not rights. Plant's analysis of social rights shows how the Conservative right has rejected the extension of the social rights of citizens in favour of the role of the market in extending choice and individual liberty. Modern Conservatives are opposed to the idea that citizenship confers a status independent of economic standing.[36]

The Conservative promotion of 'active and responsible citizenship' did, however, help to fuel the debate on what citizenship does involve, including the observation that encouraging active citizens in the Hurd sense might raise questions about the extent to which the British had rights they could effectively claim against the state or whether, as Charter 88 continued to assert, rights needed to be made more constitutionally secure, notably in a Bill of Rights.

Writing in autumn 1989, Douglas Hurd defined active citizenship as 'the free acceptance by individuals of voluntary obligations to the community of which they are members'. Such freedom can flourish only within communities of shared values, common loyalties and mutual obligations that provide a framework of 'order and self-discipline'.[37] Hurd's thesis stressed local communities as nurseries of civic life, advocated Neighbourhood Watch as an example of revived neighbourliness, and promoted the spirit of voluntarism. These themes had also been emphasised by John Patten, then one of Hurd's Home Office ministers, a year earlier.[38] Self-help, a robust enlightened self-interest and individual freedom, allied with individual giving (in both cash and service), were at the heart of the idea.

But this picture leaves an uneasy feeling that the activism of voluntary service involves a depoliticisation of the citizen.[39] Nor is it clear how self-reliance and personal responsibility automatically lead to good-neighbourliness and generosity. Instead, the 1980s have been criticised as extolling a materialistic individualism which was far removed from sustained community commitment. On the contrary, Conservative governments had, it was argued, rested on a philosophy of market sovereignty and individual striving, strongly opposed to collective action. Now, critics believed, the new-found activism appeared little more than charitable giving and support for law and order.

Such a vision cannot provide, as Conservatives hoped, a viable alternative sense of community to the state-centred community of entitlements and rights. It also poses a false picture of charitable giving. In practice, only about one-seventh of charitable receipts come from fund-raising and donations; the rest is raised from fees and charges, much of it from central and local governments paying for services (the fees for residential care, for example). Other critics went further. If the active citizen is the enterprising and self-reliant individual, helping the poor through charitable giving and voluntary service, then it seems that their counterparts must be the unenterprising. Voluntary action casts the recipients not as rights-based claimants but as dependants and subjects rather than citizens. This is inevitably so, argues Ignatieff, since the essential element of active citizenship is property, without which the citizen is a passive dependant on handouts and collective services.[40] Yet others drew attention to further, and increasingly worrying, consequences of the enthusiasm for voluntarism. Voluntary action can appear to exonerate the community from collective responsibility. And in practice it places the burden very heavily on women, making it much harder for them to participate in community affairs – a vital element of true citizenship.[41]

The passively good active citizen also appears to lack that spirit of robust enquiry, questioning and scepticism which is essential to a democratic polity. And there is something paradoxical about a Conservative ideology which emphasises the elevation in the economic sphere of the enterprising individual who yet has a relatively passive role within political institutions; a consumer sovereignty not matched by changes in political arrangements.[42] Indeed, it has been argued that a situation has been reached whereby privatised forms of social provision could be seen as an alternative form of modern citizenship.[43] Through such privatised services the individual acts as consumer–citizen, exercising free choices, self-help and self-reliance.

At the same time there has been concern to envisage a richer conception of the good life, based on a belief that civil society amounts to more than the collective self-interest of the kind expressed in Neighbourhood Watch schemes. Civil society is that which is neither the state nor private; it has been conceptualised as that combining of individual choice and associational plurality which fosters our involvement in both small decisions and larger purposes. Two things stand out about this perspective. The first is the concern that civil society is somehow a different, or opposed, concern to that of the political community. The answer to this concern is that the classic solution to the search for the good life was, after all, that it consisted of life in the political community, the citizen in the *polis*.

The second concern in this debate is about the nature of associational life. Both the right and the left argue for an enrichment of that life. For the right, the need is to detach the individual from reliance on the state and encourage the private, the voluntarily entered into, life of enhanced neighbourliness. For the left, the need is to re-establish the means and processes of true fraternity, acted out in the public arena and supported by collective services. The left's answer to the individualism and voluntarism of the right's 'active citizen' has been to press for the ideals of the political community and the common good. Inherent in this perspective is the affirmation of equality in participation, and the importance of civic action. What is important is citizen access to political decision-making, not the individual consumer in the market or the philanthropic volunteer. The goal is not a passive citizenry but an actively participant one. As Barber puts it: 'civic activity educates individuals how to think publicly as citizens even as citizenshp informs civic activity with the required sense of publicness and justice'.[44] This participative conception of citizenship is fostered at the local level, since for most people this is the most accessible arena for action.

The debate between right and left on the nature of associational life, and the problem that citizen participation can be self-interested and manipulative as well as collective, focuses on the nature of civil society. For Shils, civil society lies beyond the individual's circle of family and immediate locality, but short of, albeit related to, the state. Civil society is pluralist, made up of complex and autonomous institutions, and marked by civility in the conduct of members of society to each other.[45] Within the plurality of civil society, voluntary associations and their associated freedoms are essential. These freedoms depend on individuals respecting each other as members of the same society, even if they are opponents; in this sense civility is not mere courtesy but the virtue of civil society, an affirmation of the common good.[46] This is clearly far removed from the voluntarism of 'active citizenship'.

The premises of active citizenship as the dutiful and caring citizen giving money and service are also rejected as inadequate by the movement for constitutional reform. In Britain the concept of citizenship is a complex one: we are subjects of the Queen rather than citizens. There is no comprehensive constitutional list of entitlements, nor is there a list of duties (though citizens have a duty to respect the law). Legally, citizenship is connected with immigration, and it is the British Nationality Act 1981 which defines categories of citizenship. In practice, as citizens in a constitutional monarchy, we owe allegiance to the Crown in the form of the Sovereign. The constitutional settlement is based on the supremacy of the Crown in Parliament in which, traditionally, there are no legal limits on what Parliament can enact.[47] Thus, as the Speaker's Commission recognised, there are no rights in the United Kingdom; individuals are, rather, free to do that which is not prohibited by law.

Within the constitutional debate, Charter 88 ('an informal, open community of people of different opinion, faiths and professions'[48]) bases its demands on the individual rights of civil and political liberties. Specifically, these demands include electoral reform, a written constitution, a Bill of Rights (a demand not endorsed by the Speaker's Commission on Citizenship or by the Conservative and Labour parties, but advocated by the left-of-centre Institute for Public Policy Research) and a Freedom of Information Act. Charter 88 has been critical of the Hurd concept of the active citizen, seeing it as a diversion from the real need for constitutional reform which will protect individual rights and the institutions of pluralist democracy.

The Charter 88 proposals have attracted criticism for their emphasis on individual rights rather than a wider concern with social rights. The Freedom of Information proposals, while they are welcome, do not fully address the wider problems of powerlessness and alienation, and their roots in the lack of real arenas in which to learn and participate. Obligations and values are both underplayed in the Charter 88 conception. What is missing is that understanding of citizenship as embodying universalism, egalitarianism and secularism. As Turner puts it: 'Modern citizenship presupposes some notion of equality, and emphasis on universalistic criteria and a secular system of values to reinforce claims and obligations.'[49]

At the same time, however, it is evident that the Charter 88 debate resonates with a wider mood. That there is support for constitutional change of a strong democratic and participative kind is demonstrated by the survey carried out by MORI for the Joseph Rowntree Reform Trust in 1991. This showed that there was considerable popular support for a Freedom of Information Act and a Bill of Rights, while 50 per cent supported some form of proportional representation.[50]

The active citizen ultimately founders, however, not just on the wider constitutional debate, but on the limited assumptions of the notion as expressed by Douglas Hurd and others. The civic–republican tradition shows clearly where the weakness lies. The citizen of the republican ethos is active in the true sense because his or her citizenship is the practice of involvement in a community, deliberating and deciding that which is public. As Stivers puts it, there are four attributes in any real conception of the active citizen: authoritative action, consideration of the public interest, learning, and relationship. That is: 'In acting together for the public interest, citizens form a political community, a *polis*, which is the space or arena within which participants achieve common aims, handle conflict, constitute and carry forward shared values, and in so doing, lead a virtuous life.'[51]

Empowering the citizen

It can be argued that the 'active citizenship' advocated by Conservatives, the unexceptional and well-meaning recommendations of the Speaker's Commission (including codification of the law relating to legal citizenship, basic social entitlements, encouragement of voluntary work, and citizenship education not merely for schoolchildren but for judges and a wide range of public servants), and demands for constitutional reform remain largely beside the point in the current situation. Citizenship in practice in the Aristotelian tradition needs positive action to make it effective. If the expressed feelings of powerlessness and alienation are to be addressed, real attention will have to be given to the procedures, institutions and arenas which promote citizen action. Moreover, to be effective in these processes and arenas, the individual needs, in Heater's words, 'the participatory equipment of political knowledge, skills, judgement and initiative' – including, where necessary, those of protest and opposition.[52]

The meaning of empowerment in the citizenship debate varies over the political spectrum. For the Conservatives, individuals are empowered by action through the market, and the emphasis has been on the consumer, on choice, redress, and compensation. These actions, it is claimed, give individuals increased power over service providers and over the quality of services. In this schema the greater power of the individual is matched by an improved accountability which comes from the discipline of the market and its freedom of choice. For Labour, there has been in practice, in recent years, a similar concern for the consumer and the quality of services. But beyond this, Labour's Gordon Brown has argued, the individual needs information, far greater rights to be consulted, and wider participation in democratic institutions – together with a reinvigorated notion of public service as a reflection of shared concerns.[53] Implicit in this kind of reasoning is the belief that empowering the citizen must be matched by the greater account-ability of democratic institutions and the service providers within them.

Empowering people implies notions of both protest as a form of action and of the 'public' – the realm within which such action is envisaged. Citizenship positively incorporates values of dissent and protest rather than mere passive obedience: vigorous defence of our freedoms in this direction is a necessary part of empower-ment. As Barber argues, the key to conflict resolution in partici-patory democracy is the transformation of private interests into publicly defensible values in unrestricted debate.[54] To pursue this aim there must be an effective concept of the public within which the good life can be realised. In this context the fivefold perspec-tives of Frederickson are suggestive: the public as interest groups (the pluralist perspective); the public as consumer (public choice perspective); the public as represented (legislative perspective); the public as client (service-providing perspective); and the public as citizen (modern citizenship perspective).[55] The key to em-powerment, then, is a notion of the public which focuses on effec-tive participation in democratic institutions and on an expanded notion of civil society, with shared concerns for the common good.

An important part of the public realm within which the em-powered citizen is frequently seen as operating is the local arena. Perhaps the most radical suggestions on this aspect of self-government have come from Barber. In his view, an institutional framework for 'strong democracy' would include: neighbourhood assemblies; televised town meetings and a civic communications co-operative; civic education and equal access to information; repres-entative town meetings, office holding by lot, and lay justice.[56] More pragmatically, in Britain both right and left have emphasised the local domain, and the non-partisan Speaker's Commission on Citizenship endorsed 'decentralised local administration and a variety of active organisations'. Douglas Hurd, in his presentation of the active citizen, quotes Burke approvingly: 'To be attached to the subdivision, to love the little platoon we belong to in society, is the first principle . . . of public affections. It is the first link in the series by which we proceed towards the love of our country, and of mankind.'[57] To say that activity should take place at local level is not, however, the same as advocating local government in the traditional sense. Hurd himself attacked established local bureaucracies, and Conservative governments since 1979 have challenged many of the existing practices and service provisions of local authorities in favour of the private sector and voluntarism. What emerges is a 'caring' rather than an 'active' image of the citizen–consumer.

By contrast, left and liberal perspectives on localism stress citizenship as civic equality. Democratic local self-government teaches the individual how to exercise true citizenship in the equal making of decisions. Inspiration for this view has come not only from opposition to the centralising trends of Conservative governments but also from the dynamism of a rediscovered pluralism and initiatives from below emerging from the break-up of the old state socialist political systems in Central and Eastern Europe. The local arena is the logical setting for the solution to immediate problems, and for the provision of services which people use on a daily basis. New movements and issues have also been evident in this return to the grass roots. The emphasis on localism goes beyond a belief in local government and traditional associations to reflect contemporary interest in environmentalism and other social movements, characterised by a stance of 'think global, act local', in which citizenship rights must be expanded by a continuing struggle for equality of gender and race, and for conservation and more equitable distribution of the earth's resources.

Key elements in this participative democracy are power sharing through decentralised decision-making and a pluralism of associations in which people can become actively involved. As a result of these activities, citizenship as the acknowledgement of the public alongside the private good is fostered. This kind of citizenship cannot be nurtured by consumer choice, by exercising the 'exit' option of which Hirschman speaks,[58] but by positive involvement not merely to monitor standards but to hold public providers to account.

At the same time it is clear that entwined in these beliefs, on both left and right, has been a sense that local 'community' is eroding. Urban redevelopment, migration to ever-widening suburbs, the emphasis on home pursuits are all, it is sometimes claimed, a threat to a sense of community. The right's caring voluntarism, the work of the various Prince of Wales's charities and of organisations such as Business in the Community, the left's concern with reactivating local politics – all point to a belief that fresh efforts are needed if the claims for local activism are to have any meaning.

To emphasise the locality, however, is to raise again the three issues referred to above. The first issue is the need for competent individuals, motivated to be active citizens. The second is the need for radical enquiry and protest which nevertheless still endorses representative democracy. The third dimension is what Walzer calls 'critical associationalism', in which individuality and privacy can co-exist with the civic virtue of citizenship.[59] Analysis of these issues suggests that there are two key objectives. First, the fostering of the civic–republican tradition of citizenship will itself provide, through the real opportunities provided by improved democratic institutions and processes, the necessary encouragement and motivation. More information, greater 'empowerment', are essential to this objective. The improved scale and vitality of participation, it is hoped, will allow representative democracy to be challenged critically, not undermined. The second objective is to realise a more actively organised civil society in which associations are not mere handmaidens but partners; consulted but also, increasingly, providers of goods and services, while public authorities act more as enablers responsible for policy planning, finance and monitoring. Later chapters return to these important issues, including the pressing issue that, in Britain, giving local authorities greater autonomy itself poses fundamental questions. If decentralised authorities have autonomy, then variation will exist between localities, and this could challenge the principle of equal citizenship.

Conclusion

In this chapter the contemporary debate on citizenship has been explored from both the liberal–individualist and civic–republican perspectives. The main conclusion to be drawn is that citizenship must encompass autonomy, agency *and* practice. While the liberal–individualist tradition emphasised autonomy and civil and political liberties, civic republicanism has stressed communitarianism and the practice of citizenship. This communitarianism is informed by ideals of civility, fraternity and concord, the bonds of citizenship. The civic–republican tradition asserts a common good to facilitate the real exercise of individual liberty. To this Marshall adds social rights and the recognition of citizenship as the status bestowed on those who have full membership of the community: citizens are equal. While the Marshall position that social rights are now part of twentieth-century citizenship gained broad acceptance, this has been challenged both by new right theorists who dismiss welfare 'rights' as dependency and by those who, like Barbalet, believe that while social rights facilitate citizenship, they do not constitute it. The pivotal view, however, seems to be that welfare rights are integral to the contemporary sense of citizenship, as revealed both by research into the public's understanding of citizenship and by the imprimatur of the Speaker's Commission.

Citizenship evoked in defence of rights has to be matched by duties. In the individualism of the liberal tradition, these are contractual duties of obedience to and respect for law and order. Beyond this, any further obligations may be voluntarily entered into, but they are not strict duties of citizenship. In the communitarianism of the civic–republican tradition, citizenship is realised by practice, by duties to defend the community (militarily if need be) and to exercise civic virtue by participation.

The focus on the 'active citizen' in the late 1980s again raised issues of definition, and of how citizenship could be realised. Criticisms of the right's view of the centrality of caring voluntarism led to a renewed emphasis on action and common purpose, on the Aristotelian tradition of active citizenship as constituting the good or virtuous life. Thus alongside the search for citizenship has gone the exploration of the concept of civil society and the good life, of Walzer's 'critical associationalism', and a concern for a civility which goes beyond good manners to a mode of political action. From a different perspective, the need to go beyond the conception of the right's 'active citizen' was demonstrated by the debate on the need for constitutional reform, its exemplification by Charter 88, and growing recognition on the left that constitutionalism had to be taken seriously.

Both right and left consider that promoting citizenship – however they define it – means giving greater powers to individuals. While empowerment also means different things from different standpoints, there is a common emphasis on community, on a variety of definitions of localism, and on the need to generate the will to engage in action. Such motivation arises both from enlightened self-interest and from shared values and common loyalties. But it is also argued that institutions and processes which encourage and promote participation themselves provide the motivation, the will, which the practice of citizenship requires. Others sound a note of warning. Individual freedoms should not have to be bought with the obligations of citizenship, and individual privacy is as important as participation in the common cause. The promotion of a strong participatory idea of citizenship should not be at the expense of individual liberty. This is not, however, to retreat into the liberal position that the essence of individual liberty is the negative right of absence of coercion. The idea of commonality, of political community, is the framework that ensures liberty and its exercise. As Mouffe puts it, what binds people together is the common recognition of a set of ethico-political values; this allows for both pluralism and the respect of individual liberty.[60]

The search for a revitalised citizenship has also stressed that a major part of its practice takes place in the locality, both within decentralised administration and in active associational life. Much of the argument in support of localism, however, takes it for granted that there is a correspondence between community and locality, and that participation is both possible and virtuous. In modern society, the assumed identity between locality and community is at best too facile and at worst positively misleading, while participation can be used either as a panacea displacing responsibility for severe socioeconomic problems on to consumers and carers, or as a rallying cry for activist politics which can raise issues of conflict and sectionalism. It is to these problems that Chapter 3 now turns.

Notes

1. See, for example, R. Plant, 'A defence of welfare rights', in R. Beddard and D.M. Hill (eds), *Social, Economic and Cultural Rights:*

Progress and achievement (London: Macmillan, 1992), pp. 22–46.
2. B.S. Turner, 'Outline of a theory of citizenship', in C. Mouffe (ed.), *Dimensions of Radical Democracy* (London: Verso, 1992), p. 49.
3. B.S. Turner, *Citizenship and Capitalism: The debate over reformism* (London: Allen & Unwin, 1986), p. 18.
4. B.S. Turner, 'Further specification of the citizenship concept: a reply to M.L. Harrison', *Sociology*, vol. 25, 2, May 1991, p. 217.
5. E. Shils, 'The virtue of civil society', *Government and Opposition*, vol. 26, 1, Winter 1991, pp. 429–41.
6. A. Gewirth, *Human Rights: Essays on justification and applications* (Chicago: University of Chicago Press, 1982).
7. A. Oldfield, *Citizenship and Community: Civic republicanism and the modern world* (London: Routledge, 1990).
8. A. Oldfield, 'Citizenship: an unnatural practice?', *Political Quarterly*, vol. 61, 2, April–June 1990, pp. 177–87.
9. D. Selborne, 'Who would be a socialist citizen?', in G. Andrews (ed.), *Citizenship* (London: Lawrence & Wishart, 1991), p. 100.
10. D. Marquand, *The Unprincipled Society* (London: Fontana, 1988), p. 214.
11. *ibid.*, p. 217.
12. See R. Plant, *Citizenship, Rights and Socialism*, Fabian Tract 531 (London: The Fabian Society, October 1988); K. Hoover and R. Plant, *Conservative Capitalism in Britain and the United States: A critical reappraisal* (London: Routledge, 1989).
13. Oldfield, 'Citizenship: an unnatural practice?', p. 178.
14. *ibid.*, p. 181.
15. Oldfield, *Citizenship and Community*.
16. Turner, *Citizenship and Capitalism*, p. 109.
17. Oldfield, 'Citizenship: an unnatural practice?'.
18. Aristotle, *Nicomachean Ethics*, transl. M. Oswald (New York: Bobbs-Merrill, 1962), pp. 256, 257; and see Oldfield, *Citizenship and Community*, p. 9.
19. Turner, *Citizenship and Capitalism*.
20. J.M. Barbalet, *Citizenship: Rights, struggle and class inequality* (Milton Keynes: Open University Press, 1988), p. 67.
21. T.H. Marshall and T. Bottomore, *Citizenship and Social Class* (London: Pluto Press, 1992), p. 8. T.H. Marshall, *Citizenship and Social Class*, was first published by Cambridge University Press in 1950.
22. *ibid.*, p. 28.
23. R. Plant, 'Social rights and the reconstruction of welfare', in Andrews (ed.), *Citizenship*, p. 57.
24. A. Phillips, 'Citizenship and feminist theory', in Andrews (ed.), *Citizenship*, pp. 76–88; M.L. Harrison, 'Citizenship, consumption and rights: a comment on B.S. Turner's theory of citizenship', *Sociology*,

vol. 52, 2, May 1991, pp. 209–13; Marshall and Bottomore, *Citizenship and Social Class*.

25. Barbalet, *Citizenship: Rights, struggle and class inequality*, pp. 59, 72.
26. Marshall and Bottomore, *Citizenship and Social Class*, p. 70.
27. Phillips, 'Citizenship and feminist theory'; R. Lister, 'Citizenship engendered', *Critical Social Policy*, vol. 11, 2, Autumn 1991, pp. 65–71; M. Dietz, 'Context is all: feminism and theories of citizenship', in Mouffe (ed.), *Dimensions of Radical Democracy*, pp. 63–85.
28. D. Oliver, 'Active citizenship in the 1990s', *Parliamentary Affairs*, vol. 44, 2, April 1991, pp. 157–71.
29. G. Parry, 'Conclusion: paths to citizenship', in U. Vogel and M. Moran (eds), *The Frontiers of Citizenship* (London: Macmillan, 1991), p. 173.
30. P.J. Conover, I.M. Crewe and D.D. Searing, 'The nature of citizenship in the United States and Great Britain: empirical comments on theoretical themes', *Journal of Politics*, vol. 53, 3, August 1991, pp. 800–32.
31. D.S. King and J. Waldron, 'Citizenship, social citizenship and the defence of welfare provision', *British Journal of Political Science*, vol. 18, 1988, pp. 415–43.
32. Vogel and Moran (eds), *The Frontiers of Citizenship*, p. xi.
33. The Speaker's Commission on Citizenship, *Encouraging Citizenship* (London: HMSO, 1990), pp. 4–5.
34. Turner, *Citizenship and Capitalism*, p. 108.
35. *ibid.*
36. Plant, 'Social rights and the reconstruction of welfare', p. 52.
37. D. Hurd, 'Freedom will flourish where citizens accept responsibility', *The Independent*, 13 September 1989.
38. J. Patten, 'Launching the active citizen', *The Guardian*, 28 September 1988.
39. D. Heater, 'Citizenship: a remarkable case of sudden interest', *Parliamentary Affairs*, vol. 44, 2, April 1991, pp. 140–56.
40. M. Ignatieff, 'Citizenship and moral narcissism', in Andrews (ed.), *Citizenship*, p. 26.
41. Oliver, 'Active citizenship in the 1990s', p. 164.
42. V. Bogdanor, *Democratising the Community* (London: Federal Trust for Education and Research, June 1990), p. 1.
43 Harrison, 'Citizenship, consumption and rights', p. 212.
44. B. Barber, *Strong Democracy: Participatory politics for a new age* (Berkeley, CA.: University of California Press, 1984), p. 152.
45. Shils, 'The virtue of civil society'.
46. *ibid.*
47. For a general discussion of these issues, see J.P. Gardner, 'What lawyers mean by citizenship', in The Speaker's Commission on Citizenship, *Encouraging Citizenship*, Appendix D.
48. *Charter 88*, as reprinted in Andrews (ed.), *Citizenship*, pp. 207–11.

49. Turner, *Citizenship and Capitalism*, p. 22.
50. T. Smith, 'Citizenship and the British Constitution', *Parliamentary Affairs*, vol. 44, 4, October 1991, p. 435.
51. C. Stivers, 'The public agency as polis: active citizenship in the administrative state', *Administration and Society*, vol. 22, 1, May 1990, p. 88.
52. D. Heater, *Citizenship: The civic ideal in world history, politics and education* (London: Longman, 1990), pp. 198–201.
53. G. Brown, 'Empowerment to the people', *The Guardian*, 10 March 1992.
54. Barber, *Strong Democracy*, p. 135.
55. H.G. Frederickson, 'Toward a theory of the public for public administration', *Administration and Society*, vol. 22, 4, February 1991, pp. 395–417.
56. Barber, *Strong Democracy*.
57. Hurd, 'Freedom will flourish'.
58. A.O. Hirschman, *Exit, Voice and Loyalty* (Cambridge, MA.: Harvard University Press, 1970).
59. M. Walzer, 'The civil society argument', in Mouffe (ed.), *Dimensions of Radical Democracy*, pp. 89–107.
60. C. Mouffe, 'Democratic citizenship and the political community', in Mouffe (ed.), *Dimensions of Radical Democracy*, pp. 225–39.

CHAPTER 3

COMMUNITY AND PARTICIPATION

Introduction

Three interrelated themes are explored in this chapter. The first theme concerns the definition of community, and the varied ways in which it has been used to explore social reality. While citizenship has traditionally been seen as exercised within a community to which people had attachments, the concept of community itself is the subject of controversy. The second theme relates to the argument that to exercise the rights and duties of citizenship within a community means to have the opportunity and will to participate. The third theme examines the ways in which effective participation is dependent upon the existence of appropriate structures and processes, and on access and information to them for individuals, groups and movements.

As Chapter 2 showed, both traditionally and in the contemporary debate citizenship is conceptualised within a community to which people have attachments, and in which they share values and interests. Active citizenship and mutual obligation are, it is argued, dependent on the diffusion of power. But the definition of community, and its relation to locality as opposed to sectional or social interests, is disputed. It is a descriptive and an evaluative term with both positive and negative connotations. It can be used to evoke a way of life which is lost, or as a mechanism of social control, or to describe an arena of both conflict and consensus. Equally disputed is the relevance of community to the complexities of modern society, with its increasingly sophisticated mass communications and information technology. From this perspective community may be viewed as a decline into nostalgia, or as only a limited and partial element in people's lives. As Mabileau, Moyser, Parry and Quantin suggest, people are moved by ties that transcend locality, such as class, status or profession; and by interests that are defined as 'communities' in non-spatial ways, such as those of academics or chess-players.[1] Alternatively, whereas in the 1960s and 1970s sociologists rejected the term community as conflating spatial boundaries with ways of life (a form of social determinism), subsequent work has sought to regain sensitivity to place and locality as a significant dimension of social relationships.[2] The debate on community, its relation to locality and interests, has also taken place alongside increased political and managerial concern with area and neighbourhood as the focus for service delivery, consultation and democratic activism.

Although disagreement over the meaning of community continues, there is more general agreement that to exercise the rights and duties of citizenship means to have the opportunity and will to participate, both as individuals and as groups. The meaning of participation has also given rise to lively analysis. In recent years research has revealed the extent to which political participation continues to be constrained by economic and social factors, and by issues of access and information. Effective participation, that is, depends to a large degree on the expectations of local people, the processes of local government, and the attitudes of social and political groupings.

The model of democratic society within which the debate on community and participation currently takes place is one where local and global factors interact. While at international level power shifts to regional and transnational organisations, both public and private, there are also attempts to sustain or rejuvenate the locality as the setting for participatory, not just representative, democracy.

Community, place and locality

Community has been used broadly to describe different aspects of the relations between institutions and locality, including geographically defined populations, collectivities of people sharing values, ideas or lifestyles, and social interaction. That is, space, characteristics and interaction dominate the community literature. For Plant, an important element is the recognition that people's perception of community cannot be divorced from their stance on other values. While a traditionally minded conservative would view an hierarchical, deferential village as a community, a socialist might stress that a community can exist only in an egalitarian society.[3] The idea of community is thus related to the individual's ideological stance on other aspects of life, such as equality, liberty and fraternity.[4]

People do not merely inhabit space, but, as social interactionists such as Karp, Stone and Yoels have emphasised, attach meaning to it. Communities are purposive for their members. Communities exist through human communication; they are not merely territorial units but consist in the links that exist between people sharing common interests in a network of social relationships.[5] People interact in the course of their everyday social and economic lives; therefore, their experience of community is both spatial and social. This interactionist perspective is variously called a community of attachment, or a spirit or sense of community. The notion of the community of attachment has its roots in Tönnies' 'ideal type' of community – *Gemeinschaft* – whose three pillars were the family, the neighbourhood, and friendship. This was to be contrasted with modern society – *Gesellschaft* – whose ties were marked by much looser and anonymous patterns of contractual relationships.[6] *Gemeinschaft* embodies normative assumptions: that community is to be valued because it embodies important identities and commitments which are absent from much of modern life. These ideal types find a resonance in the debate over the nature of late-twentieth-century individualistic market capitalism which, as Marquand and others have argued, erodes what remained of the old communalism.[7] Difficulties arise, however, in pursuing ideas of socialist alternatives. As Kenny has put it, how is the stress on equality and social solidarity to be reconciled with differences in interests and identities, or the community of place (and the emphasis on the left on the special nature of the working-class community, for example) with the normative dimension of what society ought to be or look like?[8]

Place, then, does not deterministically shape residents' way of life. The central notion of community is, rather, that people have something in common. While that commonality might be grounded in a territorial area, the shared interests can take many forms: religion, ethnicity, culture and language, as well as wider-ranging links of vocation or profession, or the looser ties of leisure pursuits. And research carried out for the Department of the Environment reveals that many people had a very mixed perception of territory, identifying with different kinds of area, with groups of people, and with generalised images of place.[9] Indeed, locality may play a wholly subsidiary role, as Webber suggests in his idea of 'communities without propinquity'. By this he means that rather than individuals being mainly involved with those among whom they live – spatial cohesion – the meaning of community, especially for professional and middle-class groups, is found in shared interests and values.[10] This is similar to the perspective of network theorists, in which it is linkages among people with common interests, not territoriality, that is the core of community.

These views have been not gone unchallenged, on two grounds. First, localities exist as political units, and thus act as a focus for political action. Second, the apparent need for a sense of place for many people means that territoriality cannot be discounted. As a result, as Walmsley says, people often have a strong sense of belonging to their local area, and wish that sense of belonging to be recognised in the political sphere.[11] The need for a sense of place refers to the way in which individuals relate to an area over time, and to its importance particularly for the less mobile – the elderly, the poor, the young, and the sick. This in turn highlights the problem that whereas many individuals can opt for a preferred lifestyle, others have little choice over where to live – and the ghetto can be the setting for anomie or a destructive, rather than an enhancing, subculture.[12] At the other extreme, individuals may take a wholly instrumental view of the locality, based, for example, on the value of the housing and the quality of the schools, without investing it with more sustained commitments.

Thus locality remains problematic. While some people will have a clear stake, others have much looser sense of attachment. For this latter group, travel-to-work or travel-for-leisure areas delimit locality and will vary, clearly, for those with access to a car and those without.[13] Nor is community necessarily defined by administrative or political boundaries; it is dependent on people's attitudes. It is thus both a descriptive and an evaluative term.[14]

Locality is also used ambiguously in relation to ethnic and religious communities who may be defined in part by terrritory – for example, concentrations of minorities in inner cities – but also by their assumed common lifestyles and values – as, for example, in 'the Asian community' or 'the Greek-Cypriot community'.

The claim for the continued relevance of 'community' was highlighted in the government's *Policy Guidance to the Local Government Commission* on the restructuring of local government areas.[15] The Guidance stressed that the identity, accessibility, responsiveness and democracy of each proposal should be assessed, by means of a 'Community Index', to show how they met the government's central criterion of community. Identity encompassed how well the reform proposals reflected community identities and loyalties; accessibility related to the acceptability of services under any proposed new local government regime; responsiveness addressed the question of the opportunity for local government to reflect community preferences; and democracy considered the continued existence of local government units accountable to their constituent communities.[16] Interestingly, under the 'democracy' element of the Community Index, the Guidance includes the ability to influence: 'the opportunity for representative groups to make an effective input into the decision making processes of councils is an important facet of the democratic system'.[17]

While these guidelines were acceptable in principle, doubts were expressed over the government's commitment, given that increased central control had itself called into question the future of local government. Doubts have also been expressed about the sustainability of community in modern materialistic society, marked as it is by individualism and more domestic-centred lifestyles. Community as an organising concept has also been scrutinised critically by feminist and anti-racist groups, and by radical movements, who see it as potentially marginalising and divisive. That is, a strong sense of local attachment may be based on exclusion, on a narrow assumption of 'natural community' that fosters intolerance.[18]

Over the past quarter-century these complexities of place and community have been explored by research studies, three of which offer important insights: the survey conducted for the Redcliffe-Maud Commission on local government in England, Hampton's study of Sheffield, and the comparative study of political participation in Britain and France by Mabileau, Moyser, Parry and Quantin. The Redcliffe–Maud survey looked at residents' perception of a 'home' area, and concluded that community involvement centred on three factors: social attachment (length of residence, number of friends and relatives in the area); interest in local affairs; employment and leisure activities.[19] The Royal Commission was primarily concerned with 'home' areas with which people identified, in the context of local government reform in which questions of size, efficiency and 'remoteness' were important elements.

Hampton followed the Royal Commission's approach in his work on Sheffield, and the questions were couched in the same terms in the two surveys. Both were concerned with perception rather than with objective indicators, and both sought to show how people related to local government units through their community involvement. In Sheffield the 'home area' was very localised, rarely larger than a ward, and certainly not coterminous with the local authority area. Similar findings were evident in the national survey, though in smaller towns around half of the respondents did identify with the authority as their 'home' area, and there was a general tendency for those with higher educational levels to relate to a rather wider area. Interestingly, community recognition was not more prevalent among the manual working-class respondents (though evidence from a Welsh mining village in the Mabileau survey suggests that certain working-class communities still retain powerful meanings (see below); and the sustainability of working-class communities continues to find support[20]).

The attachment which Hampton's study reveals was essentially a social sense of community, connected only very tenuously to a sense of civic consciousness derived from common experience of Sheffield. Hampton concludes that a distinction must be drawn between a person's attachment to an area and the conditions that enhance civic consciousness; they are not automatically related.[21] People's recognition of a very localised community as the basis for their social life, as revealed by the Redcliffe–Maud and Wheatley Commissions, and by Hampton, might form the basis for neighbourhood management – or, as Boaden, Goldsmith, Hampton and Stringer argue, for the development of the concept of parish councils – but it could not form a viable basis for the local government reforms of the 1970s.[22] And its place in the restructuring of the 1990s remains problematic.

The third major study of community comes from two studies by Mabileau, Moyser, Parry and Quantin, and Mabileau, Moyser and Day. The former examined local politics and participation in Britain and France; the later examined participation and democracy in Britain. As part of the Mabileau, Moyser, Parry and Quantin work, a case study of two British areas (Penrhiwceiber, a Welsh mining village and Stockwell, an inner-city area in the London Borough of Lambeth) used an index to analyse the idea of community.[23] This community index combined a cognitive (whether the area was believed to be a community) and an affective (whether strongly attached to it) indicator. The authors found that community incorporated both spatial boundedness and communality. Communality included the sharing of needs, problems and interests; mutual support; the mutual regard of individuals as equals; and a sense of togetherness and fellowship.[24] Perception of the area in very communitarian terms was limited to a quarter of respondents, and was highest in the Welsh mining village.

The Malibeau, Moyser and Day study of Britain showed that high communitarians did have a positive attitude to their local political world. But while basic community feeling was associated with positive attitudes towards the local polity the authors conclude that communitarian theory remains 'not proven' – people may have benign feelings towards community life without being stimulated into action.[25] The study's use of extensive survey analysis of six areas[26] showed that length of residence was most conducive to the community spirit, and possession of a sense of community, or being well integrated into the locality, reflected the different experiences and social locations of residents. But, as with Hampton's findings in Sheffield, there was no clear-cut relation between community identification and political involvement. Those with strong attachment to their area, who saw it in community terms, were not led in a participatory direction in the way communitarian theory would suggest – indeed, it was the least communitarian who appeared to be the most active.[27] It was, rather, those who were active in the locality by joining groups and having a wide circle of friends who translated this social activity into public participation. As the authors point out, it is possible that what was being identified was less the effect of 'place' than the propensity of certain types of people to interact socially.[28]

What these different sets of research findings reveal is that the meaning of community resides in both its spatial and its social dimensions, but the relation of community to action remains at best unproven. The nature of these relations varies according to the location itself, the social characteristics of residents, the meaning of community they hold, and their hierarchy of values.

Decentralisation and neighbourhood

The debate on definitions has been made more complex by the use of 'community' as a label for a variety of services delivered on a localised basis or to particular groups: thus community work, community development, community care, community policing, community architecture. Confusion arises because these labels obscure what the basis of action consists in (for example, the actual or assumed interaction of place and poverty), or describe desired objectives (cohesive groups, neighbourliness) rather than objective criteria. In broad terms the central theme is, as the Barclay Report on social work put it, 'a very general movement away from centralism and towards a belief in ordinary people'.[29]

Professional workers in public services, for their part, see the community dimension as implying a decentralised form of organisation with a significant devolution of decision-making power. From this perspective local communities are not only the arena of problems and needs, but also the source of positive resources such as informal caring.[30] These aspects of community, however, are arguably as much the channel for social control as for the empowerment of local people. The difficulty is the reality and appropriateness of such uses of the community focus. In this context community approaches may be used as a means of developing alternatives to state provision, fostering individual independence, or democratising hierarchical bureaucracies. But this raises the question of 'off-loading' state responsibilities, of minimum universal standards and of equity in service provision in which poor people, disadvantaged areas and women (as informal carers) may suffer disproportionately. Nevertheless, arguments for people-centred community-based initiatives continue to be put forward.

Both the social policy and sociological literature have a de-centralist tradition. Within social policy, decentralisation has service-delivery, consultative and self-government aspects operated through a variety of neighbourhood mechanisms. In the sociological literature, neighbourhood and community have traditionally been closely linked. The neighbourhood has been seen as filling a wide range of needs for its residents, including acting as an area for social interaction, a component of social status, a source of services, an environment for self-fulfilment, and a protected area.[31] And in both the rebuilding of cities in the immediate postwar period, and the urban renewal of the 1960s, planners championed the neighbourhood as creating, not merely sustaining, community.[32] The problem, however, is that there is no automatic correspondence between the neighbourhood boundaries as perceived by residents, the administrative areas of local services, and the network of interpersonal relationships. For some, neighbourhood does reflect both social networks and sense of attachment, but for others it remains, in Janowitz's phrase, a 'community of limited liability' within a range of much wider experiences.[33]

Attempts to define and delimit neighbourhoods have used a range of indicators, not all of them compatible. These have included residents' identification with an area, level of social interaction, territorial name and/or physical distinctiveness, and the extent to which there is a 'neighbourhood effect' on voting and political action.[34] In spite of these difficulties of definition, the decentralisation of services, and neighbourhood-based activism, continue to exercise interest. Powers and functions may be decentralised to an agency office, to a 'mini-town hall' covering a group of services, to a local group, or to some form of representative committee or forum. A notable example of such an approach was the anti-poverty programmes of the late 1960s and early 1970s, including the Educational Priority Areas set up following the Plowden Report of 1967, the Urban Programme and the Community Development Project of 1969, and the General Improvement Areas and Housing Action Areas set up by the Housing Acts of 1969 and 1974 respectively. The Community Development Project – based originally on what were to become disputed theoretical bases of social pathology and 'cycles of deprivation', and on areal solutions to problems – ended in controversy.

The Community Development Project (CDP) is important, since it highlights the controversy surrounding the use of area as the basis of policy. The CDP, set up in 1969 by the Home Office, operated through twelve local projects, each with an action team and a research team. The CDP concluded that policy targeted at deprived areas was misguided. Poverty was the consequence of society-wide structural inequalities, not of localised conditions, and its resolution raised fundamental issues of the distribution of power in society. Although they were controversial at the time, these conclusions became largely accepted, particularly the recognition that neighbourhood and short-term projects cannot provide permanent solutions on their own.[35]

From the late 1970s onwards a number of specifically neighbourhood-based initiatives were launched, primarily by Labour councils in London and the major conurbations, and revolving around housing and personal social services. In 1980 Walsall set up a system of thirty-three Neighbourhood Offices (later reduced to thirty-one); in 1982 Labour gained control in the London Borough of Hackney and began to introduce its 'Going Local' programme; and in the mid-1980s Labour-controlled Islington decentralised housing, social services, environmental health and welfare rights provision into twenty-four neighbourhood offices on a 'mini-city hall' basis, with associated neighbourhood forums. These and similar schemes elsewhere had varying degrees of success. Flatter forms of organisational structure emerged, together with greater devolution of personnel and budgetary powers, and some movement towards a more participatory form of management.[36] But there was initial resistance from trade unions, professional workers and some councillors over issues of relationships, responsibilities and accountability.

Neighbourhood decentralisation is thus a multidimensional activity in which – as Hambleton shows – the issues are the degree to which power is decentralised, the degree of service integration at local level, and the extent to which management reform is combined with political change.[37] Greater democratisation of services, with the use of area committees of councillors, was introduced in many of the neighbourhood schemes. Perhaps the most radical of these initiatives was the one in the London Borough of Tower Hamlets, established by the Liberal Party when it took control in 1986 and reaffirmed when it returned to power in

1990. Under this scheme the majority of the council's central committees and departments were disbanded, and functions devolved to seven autonomous neighbourhood areas. But decentralisation was a top–down exercise, and while each of the seven neighbourhoods appointed a Neighbourhood Chief Executive and had its own bureaucracy, the centre continued to determine overall budgets. Management decentralisation was accompanied by neighbourhood committees of councillors with decision-making powers, and consultative committees and user panels. Lowndes and Stoker conclude that while service delivery was enhanced by decentralisation, issues of direct versus participatory democracy still remain unresolved.[38] The Tower Hamlets model, however, remains one of the most radical schemes. It has attracted attention among practitioners and academics – and has encouraged Liberal Democrats to push reasoned alternatives to 'centralised' bureaucracies.

While administrative decentralisation continues to be developed, formal neighbourhood political action has been much more sporadic. The publication of the Skeffington Report, *People and Planning*,[39] at the end of the 1960s, and the formation of the Association for Neighbourhood Councils in 1970, seemed to offer an alternative, bottom–up approach to political participation. This approach was based on notions of local areas as communities of self-interest – and, in some perspectives, of self-government. Both the Labour Party and the Liberal Democrats have supported such action. The Labour Party, particularly in the major cities, took a variety of initiatives (representative neighbourhood bodies; neighbourhood offices) and in the 1980s also pursued, in response to what was seen as the centralism of Conservative governments, a form of local socialism involving tenants' and other groups.[40] The Liberal Democrats' advocacy of local action goes back to the 1970s, when the then Liberal Party adopted, in Liverpool and other areas, a grass-roots 'community politics' approach. Community politics of this kind is usually concerned with services within an area or to a particular group, and involves area organisations generating demands and seeking to meet them through their own action, or by putting pressure on public agencies.

Although they are frequently associated with attempts to seek more radical social change, these forms of participation have had limited success. They have tended to give way to neighbourhood involvement which is incorporated into decentralised management schemes and other 'top–down' approaches.[41] Grass-roots activism, however, has not entirely disappeared. In the early 1990s an example of the American 'citizen organising' concept was founded in Bristol. Originally based on local church congregations, the Communities Organised for a Greater Bristol (COGB) is a partnership of church congregations and local associations committed to building 'a more just, sustainable and participatory city and environment' in the face of what it saw as people's feelings of powerlessness. It sought an input into the Bristol local plan, and eventually prepared its own alternative. It also saw its role as providing training in effective organising under the aegis of a national body, the Citizen Organising Foundation.[42] By the summer of 1992 a number of other cities were establishing similar broad-based organisations based on the 'citizen organising' idea.

Both the administrative and political approaches to decentralisation were re-examined by both the right and the left from the late 1970s onwards. There was increasing criticism of the defects of large-scale bureaucracies. The remedy, the right argued, was deregulation and privatisation, not 'bottom–up' participatory approaches within existing structures. The Marxist left, for its part, criticised neighbourhood-based movements because they lacked the legitimacy of representative and accountable institutions, and because they were potentially divisive of working-class solidarity. To all critics, the key administrative issues were the extent to which the area bureaucracies were mere replicas of those at the centre, how resources were allocated between areas, and the mechanisms of access and control. These questions have been made more complex by the increased requirement placed on local authorities to contract out services through Compulsory Competitive Tendering (CCT), potentially removing them from neighbourhood influence. In addition, there were doubts over how the rights of the people who did not take part, the non-participants, were to be protected and represented.

In the 1990s decentralisation will work, as Deakin has argued, only if local people want it and it delivers tangible goods. Even then, difficulties arise in that local government is not the only actor on the local scene; there are also agencies of central government, quangos such as Development Corporations, and private bodies with power over people's lives, such as building societies and banks.[43] Area structures or groups are rarely able to challenge the decision-making structure of local government. Neighbourhood-based action is also limited in its ability to address a number of important issues. One of these is whether decentralisation acts for or against the interests of those who do not relate primarily to a territorial community, particularly ethnic groups. And there is disquiet over questions of equity and deprivation, and the expectations (as expressed by Conservative governments, for example) that family, neighbourliness and voluntary action are sustainable responses to what are, in practice, structural economic changes. The neighbourhood community that is, is an adjunct to, not a replacement for, national and local government initiatives and services.

The outcome of decentralisation has nevertheless been judged positive, especially where it cuts across paternal or authoritarian patterns of management, and departmental isolation. It has also become part of the argument on the quality of services and the need for greater participative democracy (see Chapter 8). It challenges both the rigidities of traditional bureaucracies and the individual consumerist bias of markets. From this perspective neighbourhood councils, tenants' cooperatives, tenants' forums, women's and ethnic groups increase the potentiality for a renewal of civil society. These groups are vital to participatory democracy, but they have to guard against becoming like the bureaucracies they seek to challenge. But if funds are to be put into the hands of local residents to allow them to take decisions and share power, then some form of elected and accountable neighbourhood committees seem inevitable.

While much of this neighbourhood participation is informal, more structured forms exist in parish councils in England and Wales, which have limited statutory powers and can precept on the districts for funding. Parish councils have an important right to be consulted on planning applications. In Scotland, the 1973 Local Government (Scotland) Act provided for community councils to act as a forum for local opinion; they, like community councils in Wales, have a purely consultative role. In England, the Local Government Act 1972 allowed for town councils in former borough or urban districts, albeit with similar powers to those of the parish councils. There are some 8000 parish and town councils in

England, with over 70 000 councillors (three times the number of district and county councillors) and with a wide variation in their activities. But while ministers have expressed support for local councils, they resisted calls to introduce them into the 300–400 unparished parts of England, even though the *Policy Guidance to the Local Government Commission* instructs the Commission to take account of 'the scope for delegations to parish councils'.[44] At the same time, however, the government did not advocate a wide increase in parish council powers. It was more important that their consultative role was taken more seriously, and there might be possibilities for increasing their role as agents of principal councils; for example, in accepting additional responsibilities for the management of local facilities.[45]

Participation

The belief that the local community is a proper arena for the exercise of citizenship has a long history. Traditionally, the argument has been that a local level of decision-making, with local bodies responsible for addressing problems and implementing solutions, itself stimulates citizen involvement. The classic theorists, from Alexis de Tocqueville and John Stuart Mill onwards, stressed the educational and experiential meaning that participation has for individuals. Communitarian theorists have argued, as we saw in Chapter 2, that citizenship entails participation: not to take part is to abrogate citizen rights.

Arnstein's 'ladder of participation' suggests levels of involvement which move from non-participation (manipulation), through degrees of consultation and information which are essentially 'tokenism', to more active forms of citizen involvement, culminating in a degree of power through citizen control.[46] The key to participation is involvement, either directly or indirectly, in the making and implementation of decisions.[47] Richardson rejects the power debate. The problem is not simply that of a power struggle between two opposing sides but, rather, issues of strategies (including those of access and resources) in the decision-making process. Outcomes are not predetermined by power positions; they are varied, and arguably unpredictable.[48] The majority of such participation is instrumental in nature, to protect interests or achieve particular ends, and thus based on rational assessments of costs and benefits. This is not true, however, in all cases. People's actions may be motivated by altruism, a feeling of 'community spirit', or in reaction to actual or potential threats. Thus involvement may be seen as having two sides: people's predispositions, and reaction to the immediate situation.[49]

At a practical level, local involvement remains a minority activity. Survey research indicates that interest in local politics is not high, and is strongly correlated – as is voting – with age, education and owner-occupation.[50] Under 10 per cent of people attend council, committee or public meetings. Involvement in local groups and voluntary work is higher. The Volunteer Centre UK's 1991 survey showed that during the previous twelve months over half the adult population had volunteered at least once, with the highest participation being among the 35–44 year olds.[51] In Lynn's 1990 survey, 15 per cent of respondents were active members of a local group, and nearly a third had done some sort of voluntary work in the previous twelve months. Substantial minorities of people had some kind of contact with local council offices, and almost half expressed the wish to complain about specific services, though only a quarter actually did so. Complaints were generally made at council offices, but one in six respondents made their complaints to a councillor – though hardly any at all to the local government ombudsman, and very few to the local MP. Asked what they would do if the council proposed action of which they strongly disapproved, the majority responded that they would contact the council offices, a councillor or an MP. Despite their own choice of contact with council offices, they believed, revealingly, that the most effective form of action was through the in MP or the media.[52] Contacts with the council could be improved, as they are being improved in some areas, by local authorities allowing a form of question time at area committee level, some full committees, and even council meetings.[53]

Research into local public participation in Britain and France by Mabileau, Moyser, Parry and Quantin shows that the social characteristics of those who take part run in the expected direction. The more educated individuals participate most, but this is modified by class and by age. Those with professional and managerial backgrounds are the most, and the poor least, involved. The middle aged are most active, the young least. The non-participants are young, manual working class, and those with the least education. Most interestingly, however, are the findings which show that it is people's level of political interest, including psychological identification with a political party, that is important to public participation. These predispositions have a far stronger impact than wealth or education. From their research findings Mabileau, Moyser, Parry and Quantin devise seven categories of participants: inactive, just voters, party campaign specialists, complete activists, protesting specialists, contacting specialists, and group specialists. The first two categories are by far the largest, accounting for over two-thirds of their respondents; active citizen involvement ranges from 10 to 25 per cent of the sample, with the assumption that active amateur politicians are well under 10 per cent.[54] The general conclusions of the research are that it is possible to show predispositional factors to public involvement: high educational qualifications, psychological attachment to a political party, and not being young. Crucially, however, there is no linear relationship between class and activism. Other factors intervene, particularly membership of formal groups or associations and a high level of political interest.[55]

One measure of actual participation has been voter turnout in local elections, which ranges from around 40 per cent in conurbations to 50 per cent in English and Welsh non-metropolitan districts, though claimed voting levels are much higher, at around 60 per cent. These responses, like those for actual voting, are correlated with age, education, occupation and owner-occupation.[56] Research by Rallings and Thrasher shows the relation between turnout and size. Not only is turnout higher in district than in county elections, it is higher in smaller than in larger wards, and the authors posit that the optimum balance between size, contests between the parties and participation is achieved where the electorate is between 2500 and 6000 people.[57]

In this context it is interesting to note the findings of the Widdicombe Committee. The Widdicombe Committee (the Committee of Inquiry into the Conduct of Local Authority Business [Chairman, David Widdicombe QC]) examined the varying pattern of single- and multi-member wards and local council elections by thirds or for the whole council. The Committee recommended that a more uniform system of single-member wards and whole council elections would provide strong links between members and constituents, and might encourage a higher turnout. The difficulty here is what the size of the wards would be, and whether the move to single-member wards would reduce the number of councillors, already low by European standards. In the United Kingdom there is about one councillor to every 2200 citizens, compared to one to between 250 and 450 citizens in most Western nations. The reason for this is not that other countries have larger councils, but that they have far more.

The other weakness of electoral participation arises from the voting system. The distortions that occur in local elections as a result of the first-past-the-post system, particularly that of exaggerated majorities, has led to calls for alternative voting systems. These have been considered by Stewart and Game, who conclude that a central consequence of any form of proportional representation voting system would be a very substantial increase in the proportion of hung councils, though there is some evidence that turnout might improve.[58]

Major participants: councillors and organisations

Major research carried out in the 1980s, both for the Widdicombe Committee and by Mabileau, Moyser, Parry and Quantin, enables us to compare the characteristics of local participants with those of councillors. Both studies show similar findings. The majority of councillors are middle aged (between 45 and 64), male, better educated, and come from relatively high-status occupations. By comparison, younger people are underrepresented, and although the number of women involved has increased, they still constitute only around one-third of councillors.[59] Studies have also shown that there is a consistent and persistent underrepresentation of non-whites in elected councils. So although councillors have characteristics in common with local activists, they are a local elite compared with the population as a whole. Within this elite there may be an inner core: councillor turnover has increased since 1974, and Widdicombe suggested that this might be resulting in two distinct classes of members, with an inner group devoting considerable time and energy to council work and an outer circle who come and go fairly quickly.[60]

More recent research into the problems of turnover shows that about a third of councillors drop out from the council at each local election, and most of them will have served only one or two terms. The main difficulties stem from trying to reconcile work and family commitments with council work. One result is the over-representation of those who can make the heavy time commitment: the retired, the self-employed and the unemployed.[61] Councillors also differ from the general population in having wide connections to local groups, though other local elites have even stronger attachments. Councillors' perceptions reinforce their position. They are in touch with local people, and believe that their priorities are shared by them.[62] But they have a decided view of the nature of local groups; research has consistently found that councillors judge groups on whether they are seen as legitimate, representative, helpful, or the reverse of these approved characteristics.[63]

Local participation, of course, does not take place in a vacuum. Structures and processes, and their power-holders, shape involvement. Local elites are not passive; they can set initiatives and mobilise support. This support will come not just from party followers but also from major interests in the area, and from the voluntary sector. Research has also shown that councillor activity falls into a number of distinct categories, including acting as brokers of demands, being orientated towards different concerns such as the local electoral area (the ward), constituents' welfare problems, or with a primary focus on city-wide strategy and policy.[64] The distinctive role is the representative one, since it is this which distinguishes councillors from members of other local agencies. Widdicombe found that the role of members as local representatives was taken very seriously, as were attachments to area, to community and to the ward.[65] Stewart and Game, however, argue that the full potential of the councillor's representative role has not been developed. Many councillors remain too locked into a committee routine and the cycle of meetings; the problem then is that their role becomes defined by the organisation – committees and services – rather than by the communities they represent. The remedy is to lessen the domination of the committee system in its traditional form, and provide direct support for the representative role through improved information, area committees and other mechanisms.[66]

In taking up these different roles, councillors are influenced by their party loyalties and the committee and council structures within which they work. But they are also crucially influenced by their interlocking memberships of a wide variety of groups. Within this network they both reflect and mobilise demands; that is, they are not merely passive channels for issues but positive articulators of them. They provide citizens with a voice, but they also act as the voice of the community.

A major part of the community framework within which councillors operate is the network of local organisations. The voluntary sector plays a significant role in fostering participation, since it both contributes to local services and feeds demands into parties and local councils. Since the 1970s there has been an upsurge in voluntary organisations and interest groups. As a result, local authorities have had to come to terms with a more diverse, articulate and assertive public, while local groups have had to examine their activities to reflect the new demands.[67] Research into local interest groups distinguishes among a number of categories: sectional interests, among which producer and trade-union groups dominate; cause or promotional groups centred on common objectives; single-issue groups; organisations catering for particular social groups (ethnic minorities, women[68]) or those with a territorial focus (tenants, residents). These categories may overlap. At the local level, perhaps the most helpful analysis has been provided by Stoker's fourfold classification of groups: producer or economic; community (including those concerned with amenity, tenants', women's and ethnic interests); cause; and voluntary sector.[69]

On the basis of this kind of classification, it is possible to see how groups come to have either an outsider or an insider status. Local authorities judge groups as helpful or unhelpful, with the result that access can be granted on a highly selective basis. From this perspective Stoker and Wilson conclude that local councils' different strategies for dealing with local groups can be categorised as arm's-length management; sponsorship; or encapsulation.[70] And while there is statutory provision for cooption on to committees (see below), compulsory consultation has been confined to the areas of economic regeneration and local taxation under the Local Government and Housing Act 1989 and the Local Government Finance Act 1988.[71] The result of these various factors is that councillors seek to manage a complex scenario of interest-group activity while organisations, for their part, aim both to influence the agenda and to achieve insider status. Both are high-risk strategies.

The participation of local organisations in the political community has commonly been described as a partnership between local government and the voluntary and not-for-profit sectors. But cooperation has costs as well as benefits, and can lead to incorporation, with its problems of loss of an independent critical role and potential distancing from supporters. The result may be a lack of trust and even the alienation of a group from its members, especially with local black groups and in conditions of financial stringency. A further difficulty is that groups that gain access to political processes do not necessarily gain equal access to setting the agenda. Where no channels exist through which groups feel that they can make their views known, conflict and confrontation may be preferred forms of participation.[72]

In all cases, the central issues are control over the agenda (which can still lie in the hands of the professionals), priorities in the use of resources and their distribution, and the group's claim to legitimacy; that is, to represent the view of their members and to act 'responsibly' in the eyes of the authority. There are also crucial issues of access and support. To be effective, groups need structures and opportunities for involvement, skills support and other practical help, otherwise existing inequalities in input will merely be reinforced. In many cases, paternalism continues to mark the relationship and decision-making remains highly centralised, with group inputs seen as an adjunct of, not a replacement for, representative democracy.

From the perspective of the voluntary sector, more groups are demanding a direct input into decisions. There are also more channels in the local arena for them to exploit. The growth of quangos, for example, has meant that other organisations are influential local actors and potential sources of funds and assistance – Urban Development Corporations and the Inner City Task Forces, for instance, have a strong record of cooperation with voluntary organisations.[73] In addition, there has been a growth of political mobilisation among minority groups on ethnic and religious lines. Much of this activity is self-sustaining, but problems arise over funding, and not all groups believe that the way forward is incorporation into existing class-based political institutions.[74]

The input of organisations can be viewed from a wider perspective, however, which analyses their involvement not through a partnership model but within the framework of conflict and resistance. The focus on social movements, as these groupings are known, stems from the work of Castells and others, and is concerned with struggle, not cooperation. In *The Urban Question* (1977), Castells defined groups that were organised around collective consumption – that is, around the public provision of goods and services – as urban social movements, a description essentially centred on class and party struggles, but later modified to a broader base. Lowe widened this to define social movements as 'organisations standing outside the formal party system which bring people together to defend or challenge the provision of urban public services to protect the local environment'.[75] Though Castells's original work stressed the urban setting of such movements, centred on goals of collective consumption, cultural identity and political action,[76] the attachment to the local has been criticised as, at best, not proven. More generally, social movements have been seen as an extension of single-issue politics largely outside the old party system, concerned, for example, with green issues or women's rights. Elements of this perspective continue to be important in urban analysis, but the main emphases remain those of the partnership and direct-input models.

Taking part: provisions for access

Taking part in the local political community, as individuals, groups, movements or elected representatives, operates within the frameworks of both representative and participatory democracy. Although they are often seen as complementary aspects of democratic society, there is considerable tension between the two formulations. In its starkest form, in the work of Schumpeter and Sartori, representative democracy effectively consists in periodic competition between political elites for popular electoral support. In this analysis, wider citizen involvement is potentially destabilising. Pateman, by contrast, has argued for a broad-based participatory democracy in which individual involvement in decision-making takes place within the family, the workplace and other societal institutions, as well as in the political arena.[77]

In both formulations, however, participation depends on access, and on easily available information about local matters. There are

many informal channels of access: through social and organisational networks; making contacts with councillors individually
(through ward 'surgeries' for example); engaging in specific actions
(for example, protests, petitions). At a more structured level, access can arise through consultative and collaborative arrangements. These can include tenants' and residents' groups in the area
of housing management, neighbourhood groups, including elected
neighbourhood forums, groups set up to advise on particular facilities (in the leisure area, for example) and ethnic minority and
women's groups. Two forms of statutory provision for access,
which have been in existence since the late 1960s, have been important, though their current impact is open to question. These are
the provisions for citizen input into the planning process under the
1968 Town and Country Planning Act (though the Act itself did
not include the word participation) – the actual processes for
which were set out in the 1969 Report of the Skeffington Committee, *People and Planning* – and the opportunity for individuals to
sit as coopted members on a range of council committees, originally established at the end of the nineteenth century under the
Local Government Act 1894.

In the case of the planning system, although the Skeffington
Report stressed that full participation meant the public sharing in
the plan-making process, and a wide range of activities were explored in the 1970s, actual practice has been more limited. In
effect, planning participation has been broadly consultative in nature, eliciting people's views through surveys, exhibitions, community forums and advisory panels. While such consultations have
made a contribution, particularly in the early years of structure
planning, their impact has rarely been more than marginal. The
Skeffington Report saw participation as an agent of change that
would give people significantly greater control over planning decisions; in practice, this has not happened. In large part this has been
due to the changes introduced by the Conservative government in
1981, when DoE Circular 23/81 discouraged planning authorities
from providing more than the statutory minimum, on the grounds
that the planning process was time-consuming and costly.

At the district planning level, the provisions for public enquiries
have attracted the involvement of individuals, single-issue groups
and protest movements, often in a highly publicised way. The district level arena became increasingly important in the 1980s as

changes in planning law gave more powers to the districts, who were responsible for producing district-wide local plans, and to whom planning applications went. In 1991 the Planning and Compensation Act required decisions on planning applications to be made in accordance with mandatory local plans, now termed development plans (most of which, it is hoped, will be in place by 1996), with the aim of reducing appeals and thus speeding up the planning process. In effect, the provisions for consultation and participation are considerably reduced.[78] This could have significant limiting effects on the input from groups and protest movements.

Although the outcome of the Skeffington proposals has been disappointing, in the period since the mid-1970s, 'community architecture' has played a similar – albeit reduced – role to the Skeffington provisions. In the United States community architecture grew out of advocacy for the poor and minorities. In Britain there have been a variety of local design services (for example, COMTECHSA, the Community Technical Services Agency in Liverpool) by which voluntary professionals provide architectural and planning services free to non-profit community groups.[79] The aim has been to help local groups to determine the needs of their community, and gain some degree of control over the environment, in the face of complex legislation and bureaucratic council procedures.

Beyond the provisions for participation in the planning system, more formal involvement in the work of local councils arises through the use of cooption on to council committees. The power to coopt was originally granted in the Local Government Act 1894, and has gradually expanded during the twentieth century. The rationale for cooption has been that it brings in expertise and local knowledge (as in the case of education) and can enhance the involvement of underrepresented groups such as ethnic minorities, women and council tenants. In the 1980s, however, the government was concerned that cooption might be being misused to increase the involvement of majority party sympathisers, and the Widdicombe Committee's terms of reference covered the cooption of non-elected members. The Committee found that the practice had in fact declined significantly since the Maud Committee enquiry in the mid-1960s: there were about 6000 such members on local authorities compared with some 16000 in 1965. The decline was greater than the fall in the number of local authorities consequent on the 1972 Local Government Act reform. Cooption was more common in London boroughs than in shire districts, and covered both statutory and informal arrangements.

Certain legislation requires cooption – in the fields of education, and police committees (except in Scotland), for example – and more informal arrangements have grown up in housing and social services, while cooption to women's and race relations committees was found almost entirely in Labour-controlled authorities. In practice most local authorities have little or no cooption, and Widdicombe found that cooption to central coordinating committees such as policy and resources was extremely rare.[80]

The Widdicombe Committee recommended that only councillors should have the right to vote on decision-making committees; coopted members should take the form of non-voting advisers, a view with which the government concurred. The government's response to Widdicombe was to require, through the Local Government and Housing Act 1989, that only councillors were to be voting members of decision-making committees. Exceptions were allowed, however, not just for education and the police but for committees dealing with localised estate management and leisure facilities. But while cooption may be in decline as an input into local decision-making, the alternative of individual participation (as parent governors, for example) has increased. The participation of parents and teachers in school governing bodies was established by the Education (No. 2) Act 1980. The 1986 Local Government (No. 2) Act increased the role of parent governors, and the Local Education Authority lost its right to a majority on school governing bodies. The powers of governors, and the provision for opting out, were extended by the Education Reform Act 1988 and the Education Act 1993; these provisions will be dealt with below, in Chapter 8.

Making citizenship effective: the sources of information

If participation in the life of a community is dependent on processes and access, they in turn are dependent on two-way channels of information. Research for the Widdicombe Committee revealed that people were reasonably well informed about local authority matters, and had a higher level of awareness than earlier surveys had suggested.[81] Survey data published in 1992 reaffirmed these findings. Knowledge of local government and services was fairly high, though this was correlated with status, education, age and owner-occupation.[82] The sources of this knowledge are varied. Local authorities' consultation processes provide information and publicity, and an opportunity to express demands. There are rights to present petitions to the local council, and to inspect local authority accounts. More openness in local council business was introduced by the Public Bodies (Admission to Meetings) Act 1960 (a private member's bill introduced by backbench MP Margaret Thatcher). The 1960 Act provided a right of access by press and public to full council meetings, but not to committee or subcommittee meetings; it also applied to health authorities and some other public bodies. Access to committees was guaranteed under the Local Government Act 1972 and by the Local Government (Access to Information) Act 1985, which provided that, with certain specified exceptions, council, committee and subcommittee meetings are open to the press and the public, who may also inspect reports, background documents and council minutes. There are fears, however, that exclusions could increase as local authorities operate more and more of their services through commercial contracts.

Local authorities also provide information for local taxpayers through the statements sent out with the local tax demand. Some do more, providing details of service performance and targets (see below, Chapter 8). A 1992 survey showed that an expanding area of information provision is that offered through 'one-stop shops' or information bureaux, the majority established after the 1985 Local Government Access to Information Act.[83] There are also provisions covering the right to see personal files (the Data Protection Act 1984 for computer-held material; the Access to Personal Files Act 1987 for written files); there are appeals procedures for parents under the Education Act 1980, and for dealing with curriculum complaints under the Education Reform Act 1988. Local authorities engaging in economic development are required, by Section 33 of the Local Government and Housing Act 1989, to consult local commercial and industrial bodies, and there are similar requirements to consult in relation to the preparation of Inner Area Programmes.

In addition to the material provided by local councils, the voluntary sector makes a major contribution through law centres and Citizens' Advice Bureaux, and health authorities are also required to provide information to users. But the main debate surrounding the issue of informed participation has centred on local authority publicity and public relations, and on the role of the local media. Local authority public relations (including the production of civic newspapers) has expanded significantly since the 1970s, and has become the object of controversy. In the mid-1980s the government sought to curtail what it saw as partisan propaganda by certain local councils opposed to government policy. The Secretary of State for the Environment called on the Widdicombe Committee to issue an interim report on publicity. The Widdicombe recommendations would have allowed councils to support or oppose legislation, and to inform the public generally about local government. The government, however, went beyond the Widdicombe recommendations: it restricted councils to issuing material related to the specific functions and services of local government under Section 27 of the 1988 Local Government Act (amending Section 2 of the 1986 Local Government Act) and prohibited publication of any material designed to affect public support for a political party.

The main avenues for publicity and information about community affairs, however, are the press and broadcasting. Here the parameters of community, access and information are interrelated in complex ways. One difficulty has been how the media reflect particular communities. In practice, the local press and local broadcasting normally cover areas wider than individual towns and cities (or parts of them). Relatedly, in the postwar period there has been an increasing concentration of ownership both within and between the press and broadcasting media, and there are fears that this gives rise to a uniformity or commonality of feature and editorial material; for example, across local newspapers in the same group.

The amount of space given to local news, and the media's ability to devote specialised journalist expertise to local matters, raise issues of the depth of coverage and the ability, and willingness, of these information sources to offer critical appraisals of public affairs. Too often, it is argued, journalists, particularly in the local print media, rely too heavily on official press releases, and present an uncritical picture of the political scene. The concentration of ownership in the media and the danger of blandness constitute one set of difficulties. The growth of free newspapers presents a further problem. The success and circulation of the free press point to two difficulties. One is that of the continued viability of local newspapers in the face of great competition for advertising. The other is of the role of editorial and feature articles within free newspapers where there are few journalists and space is constrained.

The local press, however, still has extensive coverage in Britain. There are some seventy-three regional and local daily and evening newspapers, but these include separate listings for papers in the same group. There are several hundred local papers, published weekly or twice-weekly. Within the press, as in television and radio, there has been increasing consolidation of ownership, in all sectors – regional and local dailies, local weekly and free newspapers – and between press and broadcasting, which raises issues of how important locality continues to be in coverage.

Much local press coverage forms a local monopoly, and enjoys a substantial readership. The result is, in the view of Franklin and Murphy, that the local press does not merely reflect news and information but has a high potential for setting the agenda of discussion of local matters. The result of monopoly ownership is an acquiescent press with little effective scrutiny; this view is disputed by the press itself, which cites the range of free papers and local radio as countervailing forces.[84] Franklin and Murphy also suggest that local authority public relations officers play a catalytic role, with the local press, particularly the free newspapers, depending heavily on press releases from the local authority and information handed out by local organisations. The overall picture then becomes one of presenting a view of a stable and largely conflict-free community in which the local press does not act as a scrutinising or informing mechanism of any vitality.[85]

In addition to the growth of free newspapers, information sources have increased significantly since the 1960s with the development of local news and features programmes within the regional television output, and with the advent of local radio. For television, regional news amounts to a minimum of two and a half hours per station per week for ITV, with a comparable situation for the BBC; however, these news programmes have been adjudged 'dull, conservative, formulaic'.[86] Local radio, for its part, has undergone a number of changes which also raise issues of the nature of community, and channels of information between public and official bodies. Initially, it had been hoped that local radio would reflect defined communities and have a high commitment to public affairs broadcasting. In reality, few stations cover 'communities' in this way. Outside the major cities the stations generally serve a wider area than a single town, and in many cases they have a county or subregional coverage.[87] And while local commercial radio does normally choose to carry news, it is not legally required to do so, and output is largely music-based.

This situation has, in turn, been affected by the Broadcasting Act 1990 and the expansion of commercial local radio, both into new areas and into more specialised outputs. The government's preceding White Paper emphasised that local services would not be required to comprise education, information and entertainment, though they could follow a public service pattern if they wished. It also emphasised that the rationale for this expansion was that it would 'create an environment in which community radio, based on a combination of local identity and cultural diversity, will be able to fulfil its potential'.[88] In this sense, community radio is conceived as serving smaller areas and particular tastes, including those of minority communities.[89]

The Radio Authority set up by the 1990 Act has the duty to do all it can to secure the provision of a range and diversity of local services in the commercial sector. Section 104 (2)(b) of the 1990 Act again reflects a 'community' aspiration, requiring licence applicants to show that their proposal would 'broaden the range of programmes available by way of local services to persons living in that area or locality'. Currently, there are thirty-nine local BBC stations serving England and the Channel Islands, and seven in Scotland. Wales has both Radio Wales and local programmes on Radio Clwyd, together with the Welsh-language station Radio Cymru; similarly, Northern Ireland has Radio Ulster and local programmes on Radio Foyle. In practice, in all parts of the United Kingdom, the 'community' focus is essentially a local input into a subregional broadcasting system which does not, by its nature, provide (nor does its remit require it do so) a continuous two-way channel of information within the political community.

The BBC's consultation paper *Extending Choice*, published in 1992, is committed to the continuation of local radio. The BBC's stations will be all-speech at peak times, and speech-based throughout the rest of the day. News, information and serving minority audiences will be priorities.[90] The coverage of commercial radio is far larger;[91] there are around 110 stations in all (the numbers depend on how some of the stations in a group or operating on split frequencies in adjacent areas are counted), of which twelve are in Scotland, six in Wales and three in Northern Ireland. The government's hope in promoting the expansion was that local commercial radio would cover areas currently not served by independent local radio – locations with relatively high ethnic minority populations, and major metropolitan areas capable of supporting a number of competing commercial stations. The eventual target is for up to 300 new local services by the end of the 1990s, which will probably be mainly of the incremental services type. Incremental services are those broadcast in addition to, and within the areas of, conventional Independent Local Radio (ILR) contractors.

Stations of the incremental services type have pioneered broadcasting directed at small communities, for example, RTM in Thamesmead, or at particular groups, for example, Sunrise Radio for Asian listeners in West London, WNK and LGR for Afro-Caribbean, Asian, Turkish, African and Greek listeners in the Haringey area, or at wider communities of interest, for example, Jazz FM in London. At the other end of the scale, five new regional commercial radio stations will begin operating in 1994.[92] But alongside this diversity of output targeting has gone a continued process of concentration of ownership within the Independent Radio system, and a dominance of some half a dozen larger media companies; there is no ILR station which is not partly owned by a larger company. And truly 'community'-level broadcasting is dependent on a mix of public and private backing for small community radio stations, supported by the efforts of the Community Radio Association.

Conclusion

The idea that local democracy is rooted in something called 'community' has, as Mabileau, Moyser, Parry and Quantin show, a long history in Western thought.[93] Essential elements of the theory are that communities are natural, not artificial, units and should, ideally, be small. Small size encourages concern for the area and leads to higher levels of participation, especially where the community exercises some degree of control over local decisions. Ranged against this communitarian approach is the assertion that participation reflects social interactions which have nothing to do with a sense of community but are primarily the pursuit of sectional interests. In this debate the theory of community as local interaction appears more persuasive. Although life in modern society is 'delocalised', most people do live and work within relatively defined areas. The services they receive as residents of particular places also have to be localised and particularised. In this setting local government has been the leading actor, and political and administrative structures have significant meaning for citizen action.

While a place for local involvement can still be sustained, normative theories of participation have proved more problematic. Although participation may be the essential element of communitarian definitions of citizenship – in Barber's words, 'community grows out of participation and at the same time makes participation possible'[94] – the passivity or apathy of individuals presents difficulties. On the one hand, democratic theorists have argued that lack of interest is to be expected; it is a reflection of satisfaction with the existing political order, and a natural preference for the life of family, work and leisure. Such satisfaction, and relative low levels of participation, ensure the stability of democracy. To others, opportunities to take part are limited; apathy is the result of the marginality of politics (often to periodic voting) and inaccessible structures and processes. Some, like feminist theorists, go further: if political involvement is marginal, this is not because people are naturally apathetic but because elites structure reality to exclude many groups. Counteracting passivity and what Berry calls the privatised lives led in liberal democracies requires education, above all, education through actual involvement.[95] For many people such involvement arises for instrumental reasons – achieving particular ends, often on a limited or an *ad hoc* basis – and is dependent not merely on opportunity but on information.

A current concern with citizen involvement in the community has stressed the idea of empowerment, particularly in the context of consumer choice. Individuals are involved as users rather than as citizens. The enabling council and the empowered citizen are part of the debate on the nature of the modern state, and will be explored further in Chapters 5 and 8. What is of interest here is a concern that empowerment may be replacing participation as the focus of action in the community. Individuals are 'empowered' (with the resources of access and information) to claim their rights as consumers; councils become 'enabling' bodies responsible for the good governance of their communities, but not necessarily the providers of all services. A similar emphasis may be seen in the work of Clarke and Stewart, when they speak of empowering the public as community: giving people the right to participate through direct involvement, which entails creating new democratic structures such as neighbourhood forums or councils.[96]

The reality of the relationship between community and individuals must be, as Berry emphasises, that of joint participation in a shared good. Then community truly becomes constitutive of the identity of individuals.[97] To argue this view of citizenship, however, is to reaffirm the equal status of all in the political community. In reality, not only do many people choose not to exercise their citizenship beyond the minimal action of period voting, but it can be argued that there are groups within the population who are not merely apathetic but excluded. The assertion goes further. Those who are marginalised or excluded from full participation in civic life are more than atomised individuals or small groups. It is argued that the excluded form a separate stratum of society, an 'underclass', which is denied full citizen status. This problem will be addressed in Chapter 4.

Notes

1. A. Mabileau, G. Moyser, G. Parry and P. Quantin, *Local Politics and Participation in Britain and France* (Cambridge: Cambridge University Press, 1989), p. 191.
2. G. Day and J. Murdoch, 'Locality and community: coming to terms with place', *The Sociological Review*, vol. 41, 1, February 1993, pp. 82–111; P. Cooke (ed.), *Localities: The changing face of urban Britain* (London: Unwin Hyman, 1989).
3. R. Plant, 'Community: concept, conception and ideology', *Politics and Society*, vol. 8, 1978, pp 79–107.
4. G. Parry, G. Moyser and N. Day, *Political Participation and Democracy in Britain* (Cambridge: Cambridge University Press, 1992), p. 302.

5. D.A. Karp, G.P. Stone and W.C. Yoels, *Being Urban: A sociology of city life*, 2nd edn (New York: Praeger, 1991).

6. F. Tönnies, *Community and Association* (London: Routledge & Kegan Paul, 1955).

7. D. Marquand, *The Unprincipled Society* (London: Jonathan Cape, 1988).

8. M. Kenny, 'Facing up to the future: community in the work of Raymond Williams in the fifties and sixties', *Politics*, vol. 11, 2, October 1991, pp. 14–19.

9. A. Hedges and J. Kelly, *Identification with Local Areas: Summary report on a qualitative study* (London: Department of the Environment, 1992).

10. M.M. Webber, 'Order in diversity: community without propinquity', in L. Wingo (ed.), *Cities and Space* (Baltimore, MD: Johns Hopkins University Press, 1963), pp. 23–56.

11. D.J. Walmsley, *Urban Living: The individual in the city* (London: Longman, 1988) p. 62.

12. *ibid.*, pp. 63, 123.

13. J. Urry, 'Conclusion: places and policies', in M. Harloe, C.G. Pickvance and J. Urry (eds), *Place, Policy and Politics: Do localities matter?* (London: Unwin Hyman, 1990), p. 189.

14. Mabileau, Moyser, Parry and Quantin, *Local Politics and Participation in Britain and France*, p. 185.

15. Department of the Environment, *Policy Guidance to the Local Government Commission* (London: Department of the Environment, June 1992).

16. Annex A, para. 3.2. MORI conducted area surveys for the Commission covering identity, including both administrative and subjective dimensions of attachment, and contact with local councils; see B. Gosschalk and J. Pearson, 'In search of identity', *Local Government Chronicle*, 28 May 1993, p. 16.

17. Department of the Environment, *Policy Guidance to the Local Government Commission*, Appendix (ii), p. 32.

18. See, for example, the discussion in K. Young, *People, Place and Power – Local democracy and community identity*, Belgrave Paper No. 8 (Luton: The Local Government Management Board, 1993).

19. Royal Commission on Local Government in England, 1966–9 (the Redcliffe–Maud Commission), Research Study No. 9, *Community Attitudes Survey: England* (London: HMSO, 1969), pp. 143–5.

20. See, for example, J. Seabrook, *The Idea of Neighbourhood: What politics should be about* (London: Pluto Press, 1984).

21. W. Hampton, *Democracy and Community* (London: Oxford University Press, 1970), pp. 100–01; 120–21.

22. W. Hampton, *Local Government and Urban Politics* (London: Longman, 1987), pp. 34–5; N. Boaden, M. Goldsmith, W. Hampton and P.

Stringer, *Public Participation in Local Services* (London: Longman, 1982).

23. G. Parry and G. Moyser, 'Community, locality and political action: two British case studies compared', in Mabileau, Moyser, Parry and Quantin, *Local Politics and Participation in Britain and France*, pp. 190–214.
24. *ibid.*, pp. 192–3.
25. Parry, Moyser and Day, *Political Participation and Democracy in Britain*, pp. 338–44.
26. The six areas were Carmarthen (Wales); Machars (Scotland); Oswestry; Penrhiwceiber (Wales); Sevenoaks; the Spotland area of Rochdale; and the Stockwell area of Lambeth. The same areas were used in the Mabileau, Moyser, Parry and Quantin study.
27. Mabileau, Moyser, Parry and Quantin, *Local Politics and Participation in Britain and France*, pp. 210–12.
28. *ibid.*, p. 211.
29. Barclay Report, *Social Workers: Their roles and tasks* (London: Bedford Square Press for National Institute for Social Work, 1982), p. 204. See also the discussion in P. Wilmott (ed.), *Local Government Decentralisation and Community* (London: Policy Studies Institute, 1987).
30. H. Butcher, 'The "community practice" approach to local public service provision – an analysis of recent developments', *Community Development Journal*, vol. 21, 2, April 1986, pp. 107–15.
31. G. Menahem and S. Spiro, 'Urban neighborhoods and the quest for community: implications for policy and practice', *Community Development Journal*, vol. 24, 1, January 1989, pp. 29–39.
32. For the history of the role of town planning in these matters, see A. Ravetz, *The Government of Space: Town planning in modern society* (London: Faber & Faber, 1986).
33. M. Janowitz, *The Community Press in the Urban Setting* (Chicago: University of Chicago Press, 1967).
34. See, for example, the discussion in Walmsley, *Urban Living.*
35. J. Green and A. Chapman, 'The British Community Development Project: lessons for today', *Community Development Journal*, vol. 27, 3, July 1992, pp. 242–57.
36. R. Hambleton and P. Hoggett, 'The democratisation of public services', in P. Hoggett and R. Hambleton (eds), *Decentralisation and Democracy: Localising public services*, Occasional Paper 28 (Bristol: School for Advanced Urban Studies, University of Bristol, 1987), p. 53. For an insight into the Walsall initiative, see Seabrook, *The Idea of Neighbourhood.*
37. R. Hambleton, *Consumerism, Decentralization and Local Democracy*, Working Paper 78 (Bristol: School for Advanced Urban Studies, University of Bristol, 1989), p. 6.

38. V. Lowndes and G. Stoker, 'An evaluation of neighbourhood decentralisation, Part 1: consumer and citizen perspectives', *Policy and Politics*, vol. 20, 1, 1992, pp. 47–61; 'Part 2: staff and councillor perspectives', vol. 20, 2, 1992, pp. 143–52. Issues of borough-wide housing policy, and the clash of communities in a decentralised regime, also remained problematic in Tower Hamlets, as the by-election win of a BNP candidate in Millwall in September 1993 highlighted.

39. Committee on Public Participation in Planning (the Skeffington Committee) *Report, People and Planning* (London: HMSO, 1969).

40. J. Gyford, *The Politics of Local Socialism* (London: Allen & Unwin, 1985).

41. A. Cochrane, 'Community politics and democracy', in D. Held and C. Pollitt (eds), *New Forms of Democracy* (London: Sage/Open University Press, 1986), pp. 51–77.

42. *Communities Organised for a Greater Bristol* (Bristol: COGB, mimeo, September 1992).

43. N. Deakin, 'Formal structures and their relationship to community', in A. Walker, P. Ekblom and N. Deakin, *The Debate about Community: Papers from a Seminar on 'Community in Social Policy'*, Discussion Paper 13, (London: Policy Studies Institute, February 1986), pp. 31–40.

44. *Policy Guidance to the Local Government Commission*, para. 18.

45. *The Role of Parish and Town Councils in England: A consultation paper* (London: Department of the Environment, nd [1992]), paras 42, 46, 47, 50.

46. S.R. Arnstein, 'A ladder of citizen participation', *Journal of the American Institute of Planners*, vol. XXXV, 4, July 1969, pp. 216–24.

47. See, for example, S. Verba and N. Nie, *Participation in America: Political democracy and social equality* (New York: Harper & Row, 1972); L. Milbrath, *Political Participation* (Chicago: Rand McNally, 1965). Milbrath categorises individuals according to their degree of involvement as 'apathetic', 'spectators' and 'gladiators'.

48. A. Richardson, *Participation* (London: Routledge & Kegan Paul, 1983).

49. Mabileau, Moyser, Parry and Quantin, *Local Politics and Participation in Britain and France*, pp. 4, 35.

50. P. Lynn, *Public Perceptions of Local Government: Its finance and services*, Department of the Environment (London: HMSO, 1992). The survey was carried out in 1990.

51. *The Individual and the Community: The role of the voluntary sector* (London: Home Office, February 1992), pp. 6, 29.

52. Lynn, *Public Perceptions of Local Government*, pp. 54–60, 61–9.

53. J. Gyford, *Questioning the Council: An experiment in public participation* (Luton: Local Government Management Board, January 1993).

54. Mabileau, Moyser, Parry and Quantin, *Local Politics and Participation in Britain and France*, pp. 52–3, 55.
55. *ibid.*, p. 85.
56. Lynn, *Public Perceptions of Local Government*, pp. 48–9.
57. C. Rallings and M. Thrasher, 'Democracy needs a health audit', *Local Government Chronicle*, 13 March 1992, pp. 20–21.
58. J. Stewart and C. Game, *Local Democracy – Representation and elections*, Belgrave Paper No. 1 (Luton: Local Government Management Board, 1991), pp. 14–19.
59. J. England, 'The characteristics and attitudes of councillors', in *The Local Government Councillor*, Research Volume II, in Committee of Inquiry into the Conduct of Local Authority Business (Chairman, David Widdicombe QC) *Report*, Cmnd 9799, (London: HMSO, 1986) pp. 9–123; Mabileau, Moyser, Parry and Quantin, *Local Politics and Participation in Britain and France*, pp. 158–60.
60. *The Conduct of Local Authority Business*, Research Volume 1, *The Political Organisation of Local Authorities*, Cmnd 9798, pp. 48–51.
61. A. Bloch, *The Turnover of Local Councillors* (York: Joseph Rowntree Foundation, 1992). These findings have been reinforced by work currently being carried out by C. Game and S. Leach at INLOGOV, 'The recruitment, retention and turnover of elected councillors', mimeo, 1993.
62. Mabileau, Moyser, Parry and Quantin, *Local Politics and Participation in Britain and France*, pp. 161, 169.
63. P. Saunders, *Urban Politics: A sociological interpretation* (London: Hutchinson, 1979); K. Newton, *Second City Politics* (Oxford: Clarendon Press, 1976).
64. J. Gyford, *Local Politics in Britain* (London: Croom Helm, 1976 and 1984); K. Newton, *Second City Politics*.
65. *The Conduct of Local Authority Business*, Research Volume 1, *The Political Organisation of Local Authorities*, p. 58.
66. Stewart and Game, *Local Democracy*, pp. 33, 37–8.
67. J. Gyford, *Citizens, Consumers and Councils: Local government and the public* (London: Macmillan, 1991), p. 41; see also Gyford, 'Diversity, sectionalism and local democracy', in Committee of Inquiry into the Conduct of Local Authority Business, Research Volume IV, *Aspects of Local Democracy*, Cmnd 9801 (London: HMSO, June 1986), pp. 106–31.
68. The role of women's committees set up in some Labour-controlled local authorities, with the aim of expanding participation, is explored in J. Lovenduski and V. Randall, *Contemporary Feminist Politics: Women and power in Britain* (Oxford: Oxford University Press, 1993).
69. G. Stoker and D. Wilson, 'The lost world of British local pressure groups', *Public Policy and Administration*, vol. 6, 2, Summer 1991, p. 22.
70. *ibid*, pp. 23, 31.

71. Although the introduction of the national business rate has made such consultations less important, the requirements of the 1988 Act remain. See Gyford, *Citizens, Consumers and Councils*, pp. 87–8.

72. L. Susskind and M. Elliott, 'Paternalism, conflict and coproduction: learning from citizen action and citizen participation in Western Europe', in D. Soen, F.A. Lazin and Y. Neumann (eds), *Cities, Communities and Planning in the 1980s* (Aldershot: Gower, 1984), p. 165.

73. *The Individual and the Community*, p. 7.

74. See, for example, J. Solomos and L. Back, 'Black political mobilisation and the struggle for equality', *The Sociological Review*, vol. 39, 2, May 1991, pp. 215–37.

75. M. Castells, *The Urban Question* (London: Edward Arnold, 1977), *The City and the Grassroots* (London: Edward Arnold, 1983); S. Lowe, *Urban Social Movements* (London: Macmillan, 1986), p. 3.

76. Castells, *The City and the Grassroots*.

77. For the two perspectives, see J. Schumpeter, *Capitalism, Socialism and Democracy* (London: Allen & Unwin, 1943); G. Sartori, *Democratic Theory* (Detroit, IL.: Wayne State University Press, 1962); C. Pateman, *Participation and Democratic Theory* (Cambridge: Cambridge University Press, 1970).

78. See Department of the Environment, 'Consultation papers: new development plans system' (London: DoE, 4 September 1991).

79. See, for example, M.C. Comerio, 'Design and empowerment: 20 years of community architecture', *Built Environment*, vol. 13, 1, 1987, pp. 15–27; L. Mottram, 'Reclaiming the role of the community – CTAC at Chell Heath', *Town and Country Planning*, vol. 60, 1, 1991, pp. 14–15.

80. *The Conduct of Local Authority Business*, Research Volume 1, *The Political Organisation of Local Authorities*, p. 149.

81. *The Conduct of Local Authority Business*, Research Volume III: *The Local Government Elector*, Cmnd 9800 (London: HMSO, June 1986).

82. Lynn, *Public Perception of Local Government*.

83. B. Dawson with C. Brigham and M. Mylles, *One Stop Shops* (Luton: Local Government Management Board, nd. [*circa* 1992]).

84. K. Whetstone, 'Fearless watchdogs that refuse to be muzzled', *The Independent*, 6 November 1991. Keith Whetstone is a former president of the Guild of British Newspaper Editors.

85. B. Franklin and D. Murphy, *What News? The market, politics and the local press* (London: Routledge, 1991), pp. 6, 23, 65–74, 195; B. Franklin, 'Watchdog or lapdog? Local press/politician relations in West Yorkshire', *Local Government Studies*, vol. 17, 5, September/October 1991, pp. 15–31. See also H. Cox and D. Morgan, *City Politics and the Press* (Cambridge: Cambridge University Press, 1974); B. Franklin, *Public Relations Activities in Local Government* (London: Charles Knight, 1988).

86. J. Dugdale, 'On a lighter note, the local news', *The Guardian*, 3 May 1993.

87. For the history of local radio, and the mid-1980s government-proposed experiment for community radio, subsequently cancelled in 1986, see P.M. Lewis and J. Booth, *The Invisible Medium: Public, commercial and community radio* (London: Macmillan, 1989), Chapter 6, 'Serving Neighbourhood and Nation: British Local Radio', pp. 89–114.

88. *Broadcasting in the '90s: Competition, choice and quality. The government's plans for broadcasting legislation*, Cm 517 (London: HMSO, November 1988), para. 8.5, p. 38.

89. Home Office, *Radio: Choices and opportunities. A consultative document*, Cm 92 (London: HMSO, February 1987), para. 6.7.

90. *Extending Choice* (London: BBC, November 1992).

91. Estimates of audience size suggest that on an average day, just under 6 per cent of the UK population hear BBC local radio, compared with 16 per cent for independent local radio. The daily reach of commercial radio is expanding noticeably. See E. Cowie, 'Trends in radio listening 1991', BBC Broadcasting Research *Annual Review of BBC Broadcasting Research Findings 1992* (London: John Libby/BBC Broadcasting Research Department, 1993), pp. 9–15. In August 1993 the Radio Advertising Bureau estimated that independent local radio had a 33.4 per cent share of radio listening hours, compared to BBC local radio's 11 per cent: M. Wroe, 'Commercial radio wins record audience', *The Independent*, 3 August 1993.

92. The regions are the North-West; Severn Estuary; North-East; Central Scotland; West Midlands. They are likely to be popular-music-based.

93. Mabileau, Moyser, Parry and Quantin, *Local Politics and Participation in Britain and France*, p. 234.

94. B. Barber, *Strong Democracy: Participatory politics for a new age* (Berkeley, CA: University of California Press, 1984), p. 152.

95. C.J. Berry, *The Idea of a Democratic Community* (Hemel Hempstead: Harvester Wheatsheaf, 1989), p. 53.

96. M. Clarke and J. Stewart, 'Empowerment: a theme for the 1990s', *Local Government Studies*, vol. 18, 2, Summer 1992, pp. 18–26.

97. Berry, *The Idea of a Democratic Community*, p. 106.

CHAPTER 4

EXCLUDED FROM CITIZENSHIP

Introduction

Chapter 3 explored the nature of participation and community in the contemporary debate on the foundations of citizenship. This chapter, by contrast, explores constraints on the realisation of that citizenship. Life in the *polis* embraces all citizens, and individuals, as citizens, claim equal rights in the political community. Modern societies may be stratified by class and divided by group and interest, but the status of individuals as citizens embraces everyone; that is, the civil community is inclusive. At the same time, strains in modern industrial society arising from structural economic changes, long-term unemployment and increasing income disparities have focused concern on those people who, it is claimed, have lost their attachment to civil society. The proposition is that there now exists an 'underclass' that is cut off from political participation and thus effectively excluded from full citizenship. The extent of the poverty of such a group, and particularly its long-term detachment from the world of work, means that people in this position are not so much the bottom stratum of the class system as outside that system altogether.

In this chapter the position of the poorest in society, and their relation to social and political life, is examined. We consider the argument that within the wider poverty context there is an 'underclass' which is potentially excluded from the community, and from full citizenship. There are four core concerns: the definition of the underclass; the arguments about the inclusivity of shared goals; the disparities between groups and classes, and the extent to which these are increasing; the renewed focus on citizen rights and obligations as this is translated into the work–welfare debate.

Exclusion has a sociospatial, as well as an economic and political, dimension. It is argued, particularly in the United States, that poverty has isolated the poor in geographical areas of cities that the rest of society defines as peripheral.[1] Once these people are trapped in the ghetto, social mobility and the denial of aspirations may lead to violence, further labelling such areas as deviant from mainstream society. The result is a reinforcement of the stereotyping in which deprived areas are seen as slums characterised by high levels of social pathology; there is little official attempt to improve life in the community, and the public shun such areas.[2]

There are, however, significant reservations over what constitutes the underclass, and how it may be defined. The definition may be based variously on long-term relations to the labour market and on dependence on state benefits, on cultural and behavioural patterns grounded in ghetto isolation and poverty, and on marginalised groups such as immigrants or ethnic minorities in inner cities. An agreed definition, and thus proof of the actual existence, of an underclass remains as elusive as ever. In part the problem has arisen from the differing emphases offered by left and right, and differences between American and British perspectives. Although social scientists may resist the use of the word 'underclass' as both methodologically unsafe and politically stigmatising, the term has become common currency, with the media using it to signify values and behaviour as well as economic status.

The existence of an excluded minority runs counter to the general proposition that individuals in the political community share a common citizenship. It also negates the notion of community as membership, as shared communal experience, or the notion of membership 'one of another': those in the underclass are not like the rest of us. But social divisions, evident when Titmuss was writing on the social divisions of welfare (whose three major categories were social welfare, fiscal welfare and occupational welfare[3]) in the 1950s, continue to mark out the poor and the poorest from the rest of society. And LeGrand and others have demonstrated the extent to which it has been the middle class which has benefited from the mixed economy of welfare; that is, in the use made of social services such as health and education, and in access to occupational and fiscal welfare (pension schemes, tax relief on mortgages and other tax allowances). The result has been that while some workers have enhanced their position, social divisions have widened rather than narrowed.

Those who are most disadvantaged by these divisions remain excluded from the labour market, live in deprived areas, and are trapped in welfare dependency. To Mann, this means that they 'are, in terms of their day-to-day experience, in the same social position as the paupers of the 1840s, the "residuum" of the 1880s and the "unemployables" of the 1930s'.[4] But if the poorest can be labelled as an underclass, then there is a temptation for governments to operate coercive and selective social policies towards them, based on separate standards and criteria from those applied to people awarded the status of 'full' citizens. Citizen-voters become separated from the non-citizen class of paupers. By contrast, inclusivity would argue that income, education and housing are basic rights, so poverty must be addressed as a denial of human rights. More generally, as Lawson has argued, 'poverty' policy has become separated from broader labour market and economic issues. The taxpaying public become content to leave responsibility for the poor to the state, and increasingly attribute poverty to individual and behavioural causes.[5]

If, as this chapter argues, the definition of an underclass has to be founded on long-term relations to the labour market rather than primarily on culture and behaviour, then the extent of income disparities becomes a key element. Between 1979 and 1990–1, average incomes grew by around 35 per cent. But the number with less than half the average income more than doubled, from 5 to 12 million people, with the most rapid increase among unemployed and single-headed households. That is, around a fifth of the UK population was living in poverty by 1989. The real income of the bottom 10 per cent of the 1990–1 income distribution had fallen, compared with 1979, by 14 per cent (after housing costs). The *share* of total income for all the lower income groups also fell between 1979 and 1990–1. Moreover, poverty due to unemployment, has continued to increase over this period. What we have seen, that is, is that although incomes in general grew after 1979, the widening income distribution has meant that the poor have gained little and the very poorest are absolutely worse off.[6] Lone parents continue to be overrepresented in the bottom 10 per cent –

as too, in 1990–1, do couples with children (on the basis of net income after housing costs).

Two aspects of these disparities are important: the widening gap between those at the very top of the income scale and the rest; and the widening difference between the employed and the unemployed. Assessing the extent of these questions has been made more difficult by the way in which the government's definitions of unemployment and poverty since 1979 have become the subject of controversy. While evaluating disparities has been made more difficult by the controversy over the statistics on unemployment and poverty, judgements on certain aspects of social policy have highlighted absolute deterioration in the support systems consequent on the withdrawal of benefits for 16–18 year olds, the substitution of the Social Fund for the previous system of single payments for essential household items, and the fall in the real value of child benefit since 1979.

Within this debate on universalism versus exclusion, the nature of citizen rights and duties has been re-examined in relation to social benefits. The detachment of significant minorities of individuals from mainstream work and family values creates, it is argued, a culture of dependency which is damaging both to families and to society. Politicians of both the right and the left have begun to re-examine the relation between work and welfare, and to stress the obligations which individuals should be required to fulfil in return for state benefits. The belief that citizenship entails obligations as well as rights is not new; as we saw in Chapter 2, T.H. Marshall's definition of social citizenship embodied reciprocal relations between the individual and the state. At the level of policy, the Beveridge Report envisaged that training and work would be conditional requirements set against the provision of long-term unemployment benefit: 'complete idleness even on income demoralises'; and the correlation of state benefits was enforcement of the citizen's obligation to work.[7]

What is new is the way in which debate on work–welfare schemes has become entwined with concern over the cultural and behavioural traits of individuals and groups. Leading American commentators such as Murray and Mead have drawn attention to what they perceive as a dependency culture in which dysfunctional families (characterised by lone parents, poor work histories, low educational attainments, and youth crime) are detached from the work ethic and mainstream social values. The existence of such an underclass, they argue, is not simply the result of economic conditions. Rather, it is the product of long-term reliance on state benefits, poor motivation and lack of obligations: to work, pay taxes, maintain a stable family, become educated to school-leaving level. To break the mould of this dependency the state must enforce obligations through work–welfare schemes such as 'Workfare' and its mix of education, training and work requirements. The poor must become workers, argues Mead, before they can stake larger claims to equality.[8]

These ideas have been fiercely debated on both sides of the Atlantic. Research in the United States by Wilson and others into the underlying causes of deprivation and dependency, and the attitudes which the poor have to work and mainstream social values, questions the primacy of behavioural explanations.[9] The debate in Britain has become similarly controversial over the existence of an underclass mired in a dependency culture, and over the desirability of making work and training obligations a part of benefit schemes.

An underclass?

The concept of an underclass goes back to Marx's reference to a 'surplus population' in capitalist society made up of the unemployed, the unemployable, and a 'lumpenproletariat' of criminals, prostitutes and vagrants. In this century, commentators have used the term to explore a number of separate but related phenomena, including the position of ethnic minorities; major economic changes; and social pathology.[10] In relation to the position of ethnic minorities, commentators have shown how, in the years after 1945, discrimination and racism disadvantaged such groups in the labour and housing markets, with the result that a permanent underclass threatened to emerge. By the 1960s the effect was, as Mann puts it, 'to assign the black population a kind of second-class citizenship'.[11]

In the 1980s the use of the term underclass was a prominent element of both neoconservative discourse on individual and family behaviour, and the debate on structural changes in the economy and the labour market. Over the past two decades economic changes have seen a decline in manufacturing industry, and thus in skilled and semi-skilled jobs. At the same time, the rapid expansion of information technology, and the growth of high-skill service industries, has led to a demand for more highly trained workers. Not all the expansion in service industry has been high-skilled; the most rapid rise in jobs has been in services such as fast food, cleaning, catering and food retailing, where positions are frequently part-time, low-waged, and mainly provide employment for women. In the 1980s the growth of low-paid and part-time jobs in the service industries increased the disparities in pay and working conditions within the labour force, and revived the arguments about the 'poverty trap' dilemma between work and welfare.

By contrast to the concern with economic changes, the American conservative new right has seen the underclass problem as one of welfare dependency and deviant lifestyles. Thus the underclass is distinguished from the poor in terms of individual behaviour. The term underclass, first coined by Auletta in an article in the *New Yorker*, has been used by Mead and Murray to describe the position whereby the welfare state creates and perpetuates an underclass.[12] Work–welfare schemes with their contractual obligations, they argued, would transform dependent individuals into solid citizens and taxpayers, enabling the underclass to join the working class. American liberals, by contrast, rejected the culture-of-poverty definitions of the underclass in favour of explanations based on uneven economic growth and the restructuring of manufacturing industry.[13]

The impact of American writers on the British debate on the underclass was highlighted by the work of Murray, the author of *Losing Ground*, whose views on an emerging British underclass were published in the *Sunday Times* on 26 November 1989.[14] Murray focused on lone parents, crime and persistent unemployment as the indicative factors. He stressed that underclass members are not passive victims but pursue values that are inimical to the wider society. Individuals in the underclass are socially and morally deviant, and are sustained in their behaviour by state welfare systems which do not enforce obligations or self-help. By contrast, Frank Field's book *Losing Out: The emergence of Britain's underclass* (1989) looked at those who are detached from society in terms of socioeconomic change. The emerging underclass was not synonymous with the poor as such; rather, it consisted of those people – the unemployed, lone parents and the very old – who were both separate from the working class and effectively excluded from citizenship.[15] It is inequality, not poverty, that marks out the underclass, in a society which no longer puts social justice at the heart of policy.

The relation of an 'underclass' to the system of social stratification has been at the centre of the debate. To Smith the underclass is a supplementary category to the class system; the underclass are those who fall outside the system because they do not have a stable relationship with legitimate employment. There are three important aspects to this proposition. First, in order for an underclass to exist, it must have stability over time, and not comprise those who are out of work at any given moment. Second, the use of the concept should not be extended to people who belong to a secondary labour market of low-paid, part-time and insecure jobs. Third, though the underclass should properly be defined in structural terms, it is still possible that cultural factors such as family and work values consign some people to it without defining the underclass by reference to such attitudes.[16] Nevertheless, employment restructuring threatens to polarise the full-time secure 'core' worker from the part-time, 'flexible' and insecure worker (by 1990 nearly 22 per cent of the total British labour force was in part-time work). The division between employed and unemployed, or insecurely employed, can become recognised and permanent. The danger then is that substantial numbers of children are born into an underclass with little chance of escaping from it; this challenges the very notion of citizenship. The poorest in society become vulnerable to exclusion and self-exclusion, a form of non-citizenship which is akin to internal exile from their own society.[17]

From the structural perspective, then, the underclass is defined as those families who are detached from stable employment and dependent on state benefits over long periods. A high proportion, though not a majority, will be single-parent families with one or more children. In addition, underclass members are poor, lack educational qualifications, and live in rented accommodation. Most significantly, however, and in contradistinction to American analysis, it cannot be shown that such families are concentrated in specific areas; data presented by Heath question the assertion that the underclass is a community set apart from its neighbours. While members of the underclass are much more likely than employed families to be resident in poor neighbourhoods, even in the poorest neighbourhoods employed family units make up the great majority of residents.[18]

Using labour-force data, Buck's analysis of the long-term unemployed (excluding early retirees, students, and the chronically sick) concluded that on this basis the underclass had grown from 4.2 per cent of the population (1.96 million people) in 1979 to 9.9 per cent in 1986 (4.58 million people). But the existence of an underclass as a long-term phenomenon is more problematic; it depends on the persistence of long-term unemployment over people's entire working lives. That is, as Buck puts it, people may be not so much stable members of an underclass as unstable members of the working class. Similarly, while there is a relation between unstable employment and other factors such as council house tenure, age, ethnicity, education and numbers of children, this relation is not so strong as to mark off a socially segregated group.[19] This last finding is important. The danger of using the term underclass is that the focus on single parents and the long-term unemployed, on the homeless and on crime, may then result in public welfare becoming a residual service targeted on the poor in an exclusionary and punitive manner. Mann takes an even more vigorous view: he argues that the idea of a static underclass cannot be sustained, since the existence of social divisions itself generates resistance and challenge.[20]

In spite of these findings, the popular belief persists that there is a spatial dimension: that housing estate ghettos, cut off from mainstream social life by unemployment, poverty, poor transport and restricted life chances, characterise the underclass dilemma. There is also the belief among commentators on the right, in both the United States and Britain, that structural definitions offer at best only partial explanations. The key issue, they argue, is that the underclass exhibits a distinctive culture which is both self-damaging to families and a threat to society's values. While such a stratum may not be a class in sociological terms, it nevertheless forms a significant group which has no stake in accepted values. The danger then is that society comes to accept (in the sense that even in periods of economic growth, high rates of unemployment are tolerated) a group which is excluded from both the areas and the rights of participation.

For those commentators who stress cultural factors, the key problem is not that there are barriers to employment, self-sufficiency and adequate child-rearing but that people's attitudes and behaviour exclude them from the labour market. Such attitudes and behaviour then produce a family and generational effect, and perpetuate a cycle of dependency. In this cultural focus, particular differences from mainstream society become key concerns. Thus while lone-parent families form less than a majority of the underclass in economic terms, they are a particular focus of attention, as are cultural differences based on race, religion and lifestyle. As we shall see below, neoconservatives have also seen the state benefit system as encouraging and reinforcing non-work and non-traditional families; arguments which, in Britain, appear to remain unproven.

The inclusivity of shared goals

The existence of an underclass violates the assumption that everyone is a citizen, with certain entitlements common to all. Fairness and social justice are central to this belief. As Barbalet has put it: 'A political system of equal citizenship is, in reality, less than equal if it is part of a society divided by unequal conditions.'[21] What is argued here is that such unequal conditions go beyond those inequalities of outcome which are the result of encouraging equality of opportunity. That is, social citizenship encourages a striving towards equality of opportunity, but the unequal outcomes are then seen as legitimate. Illegitimate inequality is that which cannot be justified on the basis of equal citizenship rights.[22]

There is a further set of assumptions here. Social citizenship implies not only that there are entitlements common to all, but that people will share a common experience of universal services provided by a common process. To the extent that this experience is eroded, particularly because of 'welfare residualisation' through work–welfare schemes or 'social housing' confined to the poorest, the common experience of citizenship is undermined. Universality confirms a common citizenship, while 'targeting' may be perceived, both by the beneficiaries and by the public, as marking out a second-class citizenship. Targeting becomes the mark of the residualised; they, in turn, are alienated from the more secure majority. The argument for universal benefits rests on the opposite premises: they are without stigma, cheap to administer, avoid the poverty trap, and are recouped from those who do not need them through the tax system.

The poorest, whether they are seen as an underclass or more broadly defined, face barriers to exercising their rights in a wider sense. The homeless are unlikely to be registered to vote; the poorest have difficulty with access to information and legal review and redress (for benefit claimants, for example); the lack of childcare facilities and labour-saving devices traps women in 'time poverty', making social as well as political participation remote.[23] Isolation becomes characteristic of exclusion. Exclusion from the full rights of citizenship is more acute for ethnic minorities and women, and at the local rather than the national level; not only has there been an increasing 'feminisation' of poverty, but an increasing 'racialisation' also. These trends have been long accepted in the United States, and are now evident in the United Kingdom too. An important issue in Britain has been the extent to which racial violence and harassment have sustained racial inequalities in housing. These attacks, and the threat of them, have been very significant, it is argued, in perpetuating a second-class welfare citizenship for black people.[24]

King and Waldron explore what it is to be a citizen, as opposed to a subject, drawing on Rawls's book *A Theory of Justice*. As they put it: 'A person is a *member* of a society if and only if the design of its basic institutions fairly reflect a concern for his or her interests along with those of everyone else.'[25] And, following Rawls's contractual theory, people cannot, in good faith, agree to live with great deprivation and inequality. In the Rawlsian position, people would consent only to principles which focused concern on the plight of the poorest, that is, to welfare provision. Conversely, the deprived can argue that a society without basic welfare is treating them as less than citizens, since it operates a system to which they could not possibly have consented. Only if citizens have social rights can they genuinely consent to social and political arrangements.[26]

Moreover, multiple deprivation – of income, housing, jobs and life chances – is itself alienating. Where people have limited choices and suffer social isolation, often reinforced by geographical isolation in run-down inner-city areas and peripheral housing estates, their citizenship status is threatened. Individuals in this position cannot easily substitute an individualistic 'consumer' status, seeking redress or taking their custom elsewhere, for their citizenship rights. In practice neither the market nor the local authority may provide the poorest section of society with real choices. Where the local authority and other agencies do provide services directed at the most deprived, these are often fragmented and uncoordinated, and perceived by their users as part of a remote and alien – and alienating – authority structure. This remains true even where the professionals responsible for local services provide the communication link between the underclass and the wider society. These professionals are seen as part of the controlling authority structure even where they lay claim to a role as client advocate or poverty activist. To combat this position of an alienated, multideprived underclass requires an affirmation of inclusive rights and the need to 'restate the case for effective citizenship rights for all, regardless of class, race, gender, age, disability or employment status', as Lister puts it.[27]

Disparities in the enterprise society

The 'underclass' is not the same as the poor. All those in poverty are not necessarily part of a distinctive and excluded group which persists through time and is actually or potentially detached from the labour market. But poverty more widely construed does bear on citizenship status and community membership. Poverty is also growing, as inequality grows; thus the threat to social inclusion deepens.

In the 1980s the agenda of the new right – the retreat of the state as public provider and the promotion of the free market – produced widening inequality. This widening inequality was justified, it was argued, in that the release of entrepreneurial initiative consequent on lower direct taxes would result in rising economic activity. All would benefit as wealth 'trickled down' in the economy, and there would be a general rise in living standards. In practice, this has not happened. Instead, inequality has widened. Parallel to these developments, and arguably a constituent part of the disparities themselves, was the relative deterioration of public services. In the 1980s these disparities became literally more visible in the numbers of homeless on the streets and the decay of services and areas.

Contemporary evidence suggests that while poverty and inequality increased in most Western democracies in the 1980s, it increased most markedly in the United Kingdom, where the number of poor, non-elderly households rose much faster than elsewhere. Comparative research shows that, in 1979, 3.6 per cent of such households and 4.3 per cent of families with children had incomes less than 40 per cent of median household income. By 1986 the rates had doubled to 7 per cent and 8.6 per cent respectively, and more than twice as many single-parent families were in poverty as in Sweden or the Netherlands.[28]

In the UK the increase of poverty and inequality is contested by Conservative governments, who argue that the real income of the poorest households rose in the 1980s. At the same time, other evidence – for example, on infant mortality, non-payment of fuel bills, water supply disconnections, homelessness (the number of households accepted as homeless by local authorities doubled in the decade 1978–89, involving at least 300,000 people[29]) and rising debt – appears to indicate worsening poverty. Baker addresses this seeming paradox, and suggests six possible explanations for the phenomenon: statistics showing rising real incomes are misleading; the growing incidence of financial crisis reflects agency responses, not an increased problem; changes to the benefit structure (from Supplementary Benefit to Income Support) are in part responsible for apparent increases in poverty; people on the lowest income may have once been more prosperous, and are suffering budgetary problems associated with a bigger fall in income; budgeting has become more difficult; the 'credit explosion' has put more people at risk. From this analysis Baker concludes that the rise both in incomes and in hardships is real. The main cause of budgeting problems is the difficulty low-income people have in managing on less than their peers. This is made worse by the fact that few low-income people have savings, and a minor increase in needs or fall in income produces disproportionate effects.[30] These conclusions are supported by other evidence. A 1992 survey of families on very low incomes estimated that more than half were having deductions made from their Income Support benefit for arrears of poll tax or fuel bills, or for repayment of loans from the Social Fund. Almost all were in debt, with the borrowed money going on basic necessities or emergencies.[31]

One aspect of this severe poverty is the increase in the number of one-parent families, with about two-thirds of lone parents being on income support. Between 1979 and 1986 the number of lone-parent families grew by 20 per cent, to just over one million, while the proportion receiving Supplementary Benefit grew from 38 to 60 per cent.[32] These numbers have continued to increase. By 1993 there were some 1.3 million lone parents, 70 per cent of whom were dependent on Income Support.[33] The number of never-married lone mothers has risen sharply. In 1993 they represented 6.4 per cent of all families, compared with 1.2 per cent in 1971 and 3.2 per cent in 1986. Policy attempts to address child poverty have not kept up with these changes. The Social Security Act changes of 1988, which replaced Supplementary Benefit and Family Income Supplement with Income Support and Family Credit, were intended to target resources more effectively on families with children. In 1992, however, the living standards of families on income support were found to be far below the most basic level, with families making up the difference between Income Support and their needs by economising on clothes, shoes or food (particularly for the mothers), though there is evidence that families on Family Credit, which tops up low wages for people with children, are faring better.[34] The poorest also suffer serious hardship because of delays in the housing benefit system, often to the extent of depriving claimants of their legal rights.[35] The result of these situations is that the poorest, particularly lone parents, are trapped in increasing isolation, and their ability to make contacts beyond the home is curtailed. In 1993, the government's 'back-to-basics' emphasis in social policy revived the debate on the implications of lone parenthood for a whole range of social ills: delinquency; irresponsible behaviour; family breakdown; and priority demands for housing. Lone parents – particularly young single mothers – seemed set to attain the scapegoat role they had assumed in the American debate.

The trend of increasing poverty rose markedly after the mid-1980s. In 1979, according to the government's official Households below Average Income statistics, 9 per cent of the population had below *half* the 1979 average income; by 1990/1 the proportion below *half* 1990/1 average income was 24 percent –

more than double.[36] These numbers had risen steeply after 1983, when the UK had the sharpest rise in poverty in the EC. By 1988/9, research using various data bases estimated that nearly 20 per cent of the UK population, between 11 and 12 million people, were in poverty.[37] Those most at risk were the unemployed. The impact of this unemployment has been made worse by the cut in unemployment benefit – in 1979 a married claimant received 35 per cent of average earnings; in 1990 it was 27 per cent, and a greater proportion of that was means-tested.[38] At the same time the tax system has become more regressive, worsening the distribution of disposable income. While the bottom 10 per cent of households saw its real income (after housing costs) fall by 14 per cent between 1979 and 1990/1, the top 10 per cent saw its income rise by 62 per cent.[39] The position here is not that the real wages of the low-paid have fallen, but that wage inequality has risen more sharply in Britain than in continental Europe, and unemployment benefits are lower.

In the decade 1979–89 the effect of the rise in the number of poor people from five million to twelve million was to increase the numbers of children living in poverty to some 3.2 million.[40] The increase in spending on benefits in the 1980s, for its part, was due to the rising number of recipients; the real value of what each individual received barely increased at all. In real terms, benefits had been cut by 20 per cent relative to average incomes.[41] In addition, about half of the current benefit expenditure on families goes to lone parents. Although female participation in the labour market has been rising, lone mothers appeared increasingly reliant on benefits, and the numbers in this group have risen sharply.[42] The proportion of families with dependent children headed by a lone parent, the majority of them women, rose from 8 per cent in 1971 to 14 per cent in 1983 and 19 per cent in 1991. The whole of the increase was accounted for by the increased proportion of families headed by single, divorced and separated mothers. Lone mothers are less well qualified, have a lower income, and are more likely to be living in local authority accommodation than two-parent families.[43]

Two elements of these widening income disparities have caused particular concern: the way benefit changes affected young people, and the substitution of the Social Fund for previous help to families for large-item purchases. The 1988 Social Security Act changes withdrew benefit from most 16 and 17 year olds, with the intention that such young people would be in school, on a Youth Training Scheme, or in work. A bridging allowance to help those for whom there is no immediate training place is available for only eight weeks. Those who are not living at home, or are without parents, can claim Income Support for up to sixteen weeks, after which it ceases. Income Support continues, however, in cases of severe hardship (but the regulations was tightly drawn, and many young people are unaware that they can apply). These young people are particularly vulnerable to the trap having no money, therefore nowhere to live, and therefore no prospect of finding a job or training placement. Availability, and take-up, of training places has fallen below projected levels: numbers of young people have failed to register, and many Training and Enterprise Councils have had long waiting lists for Youth Training Places.[44] The result has been an upsurge in youth homelessness and its attendant dangers, and an increased burden for those families where the young people had to rely on parents who were themselves on benefit but received no extra help, because these children had left school. These most vulnerable young people, often homeless and without work,[45] are a growing part of the underclass; their ability to become included in membership of the community as a shared experience is at risk. The debate on the housing position of young people, and in particular of young single mothers, was taken a stage further by the announcement by the Housing Minister Sir George Young in the autumn of 1993 that the needs of couples would be given priority in council house waiting lists. There were fears that this would mean that councils' obligations to house single-parent families would be ended, with a resulting scapegoating of these groups as 'queue-jumpers' and the turning back of responsibility for their housing needs to their parental families.[46]

The second major disquiet at the impact of growing disparities in income and life chances is over the operation of benefit systems affecting those in deepest poverty. The Social Fund, established by the Social Security Act 1986 and implemented in April 1988, replaced the previous system of single payments by which people on Income Support (which provides only subsistence) could pay for large domestic items. The Social Fund is cash-limited; this affects the success of applications at particular offices, according to budgetary pressure. The single payments were grants paid in addition to the weekly benefit; the Social

Fund is made up of grants and loans, which the individual has to repay out of Income Support. That is to say, the majority of the poorest now have to pay for large items out of their subsistence benefit, and there is evidence of growing indebtedness to the Fund, including multiple loans being paid back by an increasing number of people, causing severe hardship.[47] The reasoning behind the changes was that single payment grants to those on benefit discriminated against people on low incomes who had no such recourse, and had to rely on savings or borrow for unforeseen expenses.[48] The Social Fund, it was argued, would help people to reduce their dependency on benefit, and produce equity with other low-paid people. The Social Fund can be seen, in effect, as a substitute for reassessing real benefit levels to enable poor people to share in the life of those around them.

Living in deepest poverty isolates people from social contacts, from sharing in the common experience of the majority of the population, and from effective membership of the community. The extent to which income disparities have been growing over the past decade is more marked in the United Kingdom than in other Western societies, and particularly affects families with children, among whom lone parents are the most vulnerable. Poverty has a spatial component, marking out inner-city areas and peripheral housing estates as areas of multiple deprivation. As research on the underclass has shown (see above), while it is not spatially determined, since extreme poverty and long-term unemployment are found over a wider geographical area, many poor families live in rundown areas of cities, both at the core and in outlying council house estates. Such disparities are even more marked in the United States. There, research confirms that concentration of poverty within cities has increased, but is not uniform; it affects primarily African-Americans outside the West, and Hispanics in the Northeast.[49] This spatial aspect has been emphasised in the work of Wilson, the author of influential studies of the underclass, who has revised his analysis to substitute for 'underclass' the term 'ghetto poor', whose marginal position in the labour market is uniquely reinforced by their extreme social isolation.[50]

In Britain the problem is that the mitigation of poverty through targeting resources has failed to address the adequacy of benefit levels; as a result, the size of the poorest group has grown rather than diminished. The belief in the early 1980s, supported by new right thinking, was that reduced real benefits would force people into work (by making reliance on benefits less attractive) and reduce their dependency. Dependency on benefits has not diminished, however, and the fear is that as the marginalised grow in number, so a crisis of social citizenship looms.

Rights and obligations

The status of economic and social rights as human rights has been propounded by Plant and others.[51] The debate on work–welfare relations raises the fundamental issue of citizenship, in that welfare benefits become not a question of assistance granted to the needy but an inherent part of the rights of the citizen. As a quid pro quo, those with rights have duties and obligations to the society in which they hold those rights.

Dependency, work–welfare schemes, and a deviant underclass are interrelated elements of the debate on welfare policy, and on the nature of civic society. From the perspective of new right conservative thinking in Britain and the United States, the underclass is defined not as a class in economic terms but as that subset of the poor whose poverty is attributable to their behaviour. The underclass is then defined as the 'undeserving' poor, whose detachment from mainstream work and family values must be addressed by reinforcing work norms, family authority and individual reponsibility. In *Losing Ground* and elsewhere, Murray argues that benefit programmes have created welfare dependency, and are the cause of as much poverty as they have cured. The underclass, in his definition, is that subset of the poor who live off mainstream society, through welfare dependency or crime, without participating in it.[52] For Mead the problem is more one of permissiveness, resulting in growing numbers of single mothers and of non-work among single men, many of them the fathers of welfare children.[53]

Conservative and liberal opinion is divided, however, on why welfare beneficiaries do not seek and keep employment more actively. For liberals, the explanations are structural, centring on a lack of jobs, unsuitable and ill-paid jobs, low educational levels, and poor childcare facilities. For conservatives, the explanations are behavioural, and are due to parental and familial irresponsibility, early school leaving, and defective work habits. As Murray says, commenting on the possible emergence of a British underclass, the term refers not to the degree of poverty but to a type of poverty, characterised by high rates of illegitimacy, non-work and crime.[54]

To conservatives the remedy for these problems is to make some form of Workfare a condition of obtaining benefits. Mead endorses this approach, arguing that it is the passivity of the non-working poor which needs to be reformed, not the economy. Compulsory work should be enforced, not because Workfare will reduce dependency in the short term, but because it makes the welfare experience less passive, and is the best hope of enforcing the work norm.[55] At the core of the debate is the issue of citizenship, that is, who should be considered a bona fide member of the community: 'The question is how passive you can be and still be a citizen in full standing'.[56]

Important issues of the rights and obligations of citizenship are raised by work–welfare schemes. The narrow definition of such schemes – Workfare – refers to the demand that benefit claimants should undertake (unpaid) work in return for welfare benefits. More broadly, the term Workfare refers to a range of work-related activities (job search, education, training, job placement and work experience) which are mandatory rather than voluntary.[57] In the American context, conservatives who favour Workfare argue that it is a reasonable requirement that citizens should provide a quid pro quo for the benefits they receive. Opponents argue that it is far more productive, and more likely to prevent future dependency, to provide better training and education for welfare beneficiaries, since opportunity, not motivation, is the key to employment.

In the United States Workfare is targeted largely at unemployed single mothers receiving Aid For Dependent Children (AFDC) welfare benefits. Under the Family Support Act 1988, education, training and employment were made an explicit element of welfare benefits, and extended to those two-parent families where the principal wage earner, usually the father, was unemployed.[58] But the rate at which the provisions have been implemented varies from State to State, as do the definition of education and training, and the effort required for 'job search'. In Britain in the 1990s there appears to be an interest in work–welfare schemes among politicians in all parts of the political spectrum, from the right's interest in the American programmes to the left's interest in the

Swedish system. Under the latter scheme the unemployed get 80 per cent of former earnings (up to a maximum limit), and after a year they are offered a government training course or a place on a temporary work scheme. Those under 20 are particularly targeted for help. Unemployed people who refuse the training or work placements are deprived of the standard benefits, and paid a bare minimum.

In European countries, as well as in the United States, it is expected that lone mothers should not rely on out-of-work benefits for long periods, but should be encouraged to join the labour market. The state should enforce maintenance from absent fathers, a position taken up in Britain with the operation of the Child Support Agency from April 1993. British policy also emphasises that while lone parents with children up to the age of 16 are not required to be available for work, they are not unduly discouraged from working if they wish to do so.[59] In 1992 the government also reduced the number of hours of work per week which qualify parents to receive Family Credit from twenty-four to sixteen, as a work incentive. The difficulty, however, has been that while the 1988 Social Security Act increased the income disregard to £15 per week, no account is taken of work expenses; this effectively traps those who are unable to obtain free childcare.[60] In addition, the sixteen-hour threshold means that lone parents who work more hours are no longer eligible for Income Support but must claim means-tested Family Credit, but again there is no allowance for childcare. Returning to work is particularly difficult for lone parents, who identify low pay and costly and unobtainable childcare as the main barriers; three-quarters of lone parents have to live on Income Support, and it remains very difficult for them to work their way out of poverty.[61]

A work programme for the long-term unemployed, Employment Action, was introduced in Britain in October 1991. The scheme, which was not compulsory, provided temporary work on community projects through Training and Enterprise Councils, with a target of 60 000 places a year. This total was never met, and the scheme was amalgamated with Employment Training to form a new package, Training for Work. Again, what is demonstrated by these moves is that governments have tried a number of short-term expedients rather than undertaking a long-term re-evaluation of an enduring safety net (though a re-examination of Social

Security and other benefits was anticipated in late 1993). A degree of compulsion does exist, however, in British unemployment provisions. Those 16 and 17 year olds who are offered a place on a Youth Training Scheme will be refused benefit unless they attend. Adults, after two years of unemployment, must attend a Restart course or face a temporary loss of a proportion of their benefit. From April 1993, 'Jobplan workshops' required attendance from those who had been out of work for a year, with similar penalties for non-attendance. The 1993 spring budget announced a new Community Action programme to provide 60 000 part-time community work places for the long-term unemployed. Run by the Employment Service, it was seen as providing a basis for a much larger compulsory work-for-benefit programme if the government decided to introduce one.

More radical suggestions have been made. Ralph Howell, Conservative MP for Norfolk North, suggests replacing unemployment benefits with a tax-free weekly wage of £100, for which the unemployed would perform socially useful environmental and community work. The scheme would be voluntary, except for those under 20. But there is no training element in the scheme, and over the long term the aim is to abolish unemployment and other benefits in favour of bringing all the unemployed into the work scheme.[62] Support on the left for work–welfare schemes is grounded on concepts of social justice, self-worth and self-esteem. Plant has argued that mass unemployment is incompatible with social justice. Where unemployment is a long-term and structural rather than a short-term recessional phenomenon, the state must become the employer of last resort, preferably on the Swedish 'workfare' model. Plant recognises, however, that this does not immediately satisfy the critics of 'dependency', since mass Workfare schemes would not make people independent of state aid but would transfer dependency from the Department of Social Security to the Department of Employment.[63]

A philosophy of reciprocal obligations was also a theme of the charity Full Employment UK's 1991 report, which argued that the long-term unemployed should accept new reponsibilities to contribute to society in return for benefits. Society, in return, should accept the obligation of providing temporary community work.[64] In 1993 Full Employment expanded their ideas (the Jobchart proposals), advocating that the long-term unemployed should be required to work up to three days a week on nine-month contracts. Income Support would be withdrawn, although other family benefits would remain. Full Employment UK claim their research showed that most long-term jobless supported the idea of a two-way obligation between themselves and society.[65] Earlier work on Workfare, commissioned in 1987 by the Department of Employment, also appeared to show that those participating in Community Programme projects found the notion an acceptable one.[66]

The disadvantaged citizen

Between 1979 and 1990 the value of unemployment benefit for a married couple with two children fell by nearly 20 per cent; benefit was withdrawn for 16 and 17 year olds and Income Support for 18–25 year olds was reduced. Underlying these changes has been a move away from policies which acknowledged the external causes of unemployment to those which emphasise individual responsibility and behaviour. To governments, the problem was a culture of dependency with a lack of incentives and responsibilities, which threatened to produce an underclass detached from mainstream values. The notion of dependency in this approach is highly selective. Many groups in society depend on different kinds of benefits from the state, including industry dependent on state grants for restructuring and individuals with state pensions or, more widely, dependent on the health and education systems. What is of concern in the context of targeted social policy, however, has been a mix of lifestyles and attitudes, allegedly persistent and intergenerational, which make up a culture of dependency.

The notion of a dependency culture as it has operated in social policy refers to the belief by Conservative governments in the 1980s, following the ideas of Murray, that the payment of state benefits encourages people to become dependent on them, acts as a disincentive to finding work, and undermines responsible behaviour. Thus the notion combines economic and sociological approaches to disincentives and motivation, and moral judgements about appropriate behaviour.[67] Furthermore, as Dean and Taylor-Gooby remind us, 'dependency culture' and 'underclass' are mirror-images of the same discursive construct, not objective phenomena; what we are deaing with here is symbolism and myth.[68]

Proving that such behaviour exists, and forms a persistent and comprehensive pattern that divorces disadvantaged groups from the social and political community, has been difficult and contentious. A number of studies have examined the values and attitudes of the most disadvantaged. Dean and Taylor-Gooby have shown that survey data on those groups that could be defined as falling within a 'dependency culture' revealed that they in fact shared the work orientation of the mass of the population, held mainstream values that attributed dependency to unemployed people, and endorsed marriage. Single parents showed a greater support for diversity of family patterns and disagreed that single parents are less successful in bringing up children. The disadvantaged groups also took the view that welfare does not undermine self-help or mutual aid; they did not display the appropriate values of a culture of dependency.[69]

Using in-depth interviews of a group of claimants, Dean and Taylor-Gooby also show that claimants, by and large, wanted to come off benefits. Most claimants did not see dependency on social security as a fixed status; they hoped it was a temporary experience.[70] But there was little evidence that the most disadvantaged were reclusive or apathetic, though it was clear that opportunities for social participation were constrained. The picture of political participation was mixed. While the voting rate was relatively high, it was lower than in the general population; and while many respondents had some involvement in community activities, it was still the case that some were excluded from participation by reason of social isolation. It is also evident that Social Security changes and increasing pressures of long-term unemployment have placed strains on people's expectations as workers, family members, and citizens.[71]

Heath's research reveals that members of the underclass do have a significantly lower sense of efficacy and greater feelings of cynicism about the political system than other people. But they also have markedly lower educational qualifications; once survey responses are controlled for education, differences in voting turnout and sense of political efficacy are no longer statistically significant. The effect is one of education, not underclass membership; this means that the existence of a specific culture of nonparticipation remains unproven.[72]

Conclusion

The extent to which individuals and families living in persistent poverty constitute an excluded group, actually or potentially divorced from social and political participation in the community and therefore with less than full citizenship status, remains problematic. Definitions of an underclass which lies outside the class system, and its mirror-image of a dependency culture which does not share mainstream values of the work ethic and family life, are still contested. The definition of an underclass based on long-term detachment from the labour market is rejected as inadequate by those who argue that underclass membership is primarily due to inappropriate and dysfunctional behaviour. Such behaviour is reinforced by the inappropriate signals that state benefits provide, with the result that people become long-term dependants on welfare, often across generations, and form part of a 'dependency culture'.

The response to this situation has been to stress the obligations as well as the rights of citizenship, and to argue that work–welfare schemes enforce necessary obligations on those receiving state benefits. Against this has to be set the arguments that rights – the right to vote, for example – are rights *per se* and cannot be set against obligations in such a simplistic manner. Moreover, the emphasis on behaviour and obligations takes a moral and judgemental stance which views the 'undeserving' poor as a separate category. Arguments for universalism, and for minimum wage structures, are then pushed to the margins of debate. If the rights *and* responsibilities of citizens are to be addressed, then this means not only the obligations of the poor but also those of society – housing, education, jobs – to make those responsibilities possible and equitable.

Research into these issues has shown how elusive are the notions of the underclass and the dependency culture. Refining the definition of the underclass results in an ever-diminishing group, and examination of the views of long-term dependants on state benefits reveals that their attitudes do not differ significantly from those of the rest of society. Popular myth and 'common sense', however, remain concerned that inner-city areas, run-down housing estates, and the lifestyles and life chances of the poorest do reflect the existence of groups that are outside

society, and potentially a threat to its values. Two further difficulties emerge in this situation. One difficulty is that of labelling,
where the definitions serve in practice as stigmatising judgements. The second is that definitions of groups as significantly
different or apart may subject them to targeted services, so that
the poorest become residualised and marginalised, and the claim
for the universality of social citizenship is weakened.

While the debate on the underclass and dependency remains
inconclusive, the effects of long-term unemployment, and widening disparities between the top and bottom of the income scale,
pose real problems. The danger, it is argued, is that people in the
most disadvantaged groups may become a fixed and permanent
category, with their own culture. They become socially immobile,
and geographically immobile also. The ghetto poor that Wilson
portrays in American cities, however, is unlikely to emerge in the
British situation, where the scale of concentration of the most
disadvantaged is far less, as is the concentration of ethnic
poverty.

But the research reported in Smith's edited volume shows that
housing tenure (being a council tenant) was a stronger predictor
of underclass membership than social class or education. The
danger then becomes that as other tenants buy their houses, local
authority tenants become a residual group, concentrated on run-
down estates. If this happens, public housing may come to
resemble American 'welfare housing', and the underclass will
become an ecological phenomenon.[73] And the fear of deprived
neighbourhoods marked by poverty and violence as a permanent
feature of cities is growing. In *The Culture of Contentment*,
Galbraith has arged that in inner cities (including those in Britain) there is a continuing threat of underclass social disorder,
crime and conflict. In such neighbourhoods the poorest group has
become a semi-permanent rather than a generational phenomenon. The reaction of the 'community of contentment' – the con-
tented electoral majority – rejects solutions based on social or
economic planning, and reacts to the violence of the slums with
calls for more law-and-order measures.[74] The danger then is of
increasingly oppressive authority in the areas of most severe urban desolation, rather than solutions based on public services,
investment and taxation. These features will be examined in
Chapter 6 below.

Similarly, the difficulties faced by groups in extreme poverty, even where they are not defined in narrow underclass terms, pose real questions for effective citizenship and participation. The argument is that the poorest, especially lone parents on benefits, the young and the long-term unemployed, are cut off from social contacts outside the home, and that social isolation both detracts from full citizenship status and debars political participation at community level beyond the most basic act of voting. But again, the debate here remains inconclusive. The United States findings show that neighbourhood had little effect on people's political attitudes and behaviour: poor people living in poor neighbourhoods were no more cynical or likely to withdraw from the political process than poor people living in middle-class neighbourhoods.[75] In Britain, attitude survey data also reveal that there is as yet no marked distinction between the poorest and the rest. While they may be cynical about the political system, the attitudes of the poorest to political participation reflect education levels (as is the case for the rest of the population, as Chapter 3 reveals), not welfare dependency. But while attitudes may favour participation, if the poorest remain isolated because of their marginalisation, this effectively debases their citizenship.

Whether groups in society are excluded from full citizenship and effective membership of the community remains a controversial issue, but the fact that areas of cities suffer multiple deprivation and present particular policy problems has been recognised since the 1960s. A large number of successive policies, defined in both structural and sociospatial terms, have sought to address these issues. The political arena within which these policies are implemented, and the working out of citizen–community relations takes place, is that of local government. Local government itself, however, has been the subject of intense debate over the past fifteen years: about finance, functions and role. The belief that localities are the appropriate arena for self-government, expressing community aspirations as well as delivering services laid down in national legislation, developed in its modern form from the early years of the nineteenth century. The contemporary situation, it is argued, is one of increasing centralisation and debate over the 'enabling' as opposed to the 'providing' council. It is these issues that Chapter 5 addresses.

Notes

1. R. Mellor, 'Urban sociology: a trend report', *Sociology*, vol. 23, 2, May 1989, p. 251.
2. D.A. Karp, G.P. Stone and W.C. Yoels, *Being Urban: A sociology of city life*, 2nd edn (New York: Praeger, 1991), p. 72.
3. R.M. Titmuss, 'The social division of welfare', in *Essays on the Welfare State* (London: Unwin University Books, 2nd edn, 1963), pp. 34–55.
4. K. Mann, *The Making of an English 'Underclass'?* (Milton Keynes: Open University Press, 1992), p. 104.
5. R. Lawson, ' "Social citizenship", work and social solidarity: historical comparisons between Britain and Sweden', in W.J. Wilson (ed.), *Sociology and the Public Agenda* (Beverly Hills, CA: Sage, 1992), pp. 119–40.
6. Department of Social Security/Government Statistical Service, Households Below Average Income: A Statistical Analysis 1979–1990/91 (London: HMSO, 1993), tables A–G, especially table A1; D. Piachaud, 'Hopes that turned to dust', *The Guardian*, 30 September 1992, p. 21.
7. *Social Insurance and Allied Services*, Cmd 6406, Report by Sir William Beveridge (London: HMSO, 1942).
8. L.M. Mead, 'The logic of Workfare: the underclass and work policy', *The Annals of the American Academy of Political and Social Science*, vol. 501, January 1989, pp. 156–69.
9. W.J. Wilson, 'The underclass: issues, perspectives, and public policy', *The Annals of the American Academy of Political and Social Science*, vol. 501, pp. 182–92.
10. See, for example, G. Myrdal, *Challenge to Affluence* (New York: Pantheon, 1962); A. Giddens, *The Class Structure of the Advanced Societies* (London: Hutchinson, 1973); J. Rex and S. Tomlinson, *Colonial Immigrants in a British City* (London: Routledge & Kegan Paul, 1979).
11. K. Mann, *The Making of an English 'Underclass'?*, pp. 87–90.
12. K. Auletta, *The Underclass* (New York: Random House, 1982); L.M. Mead, *Beyond Entitlement: The social obligations of citizenship* (New York: The Free Press, 1986); C. Murray, *Losing Ground* (New York: Basic Books, 1984); C. Jencks and P.E. Peterson (eds), *The Urban Underclass* (Washington, DC.: The Brookings Institution, 1991).
13. J.J. DiIulio, Jr, 'The impact of inner-city crime', *The Public Interest*, no. 96, Summer 1989, pp. 28–46.
14. C. Murray, 'Underclass', *Sunday Times Magazine*, 26 November 1989, pp. 26–45; 'The underclass', in *The Emerging Underclass* (London: Institute for Economic Affairs, 1990); 'The British underclass', *Public Interest*, no. 99, Spring 1990, pp. 4–28.

15. F. Field, *Losing Out: The emergence of Britain's underclass* (Oxford: Basil Blackwell, 1989).
16. D.J. Smith (ed.), *Understanding the Underclass* (London: Policy Studies Institute, 1992), pp. 4–7.
17. M. Rוche, *Rethinking Citizenship: Welfare, ideology and change in modern society* (Cambridge: Polity Press, 1992), p. 202.
18. A. Heath, 'The attitudes of the underclass', in Smith (ed.), *Understanding the Underclass*, p. 34.
19. N. Buck, 'Labour market inactivity and polarisation', in Smith (ed.), *Understanding the Underclass*, pp. 9–31.
20. Mann, *The Making of an English 'Underclass'?*, p. 91.
21. J.M. Barbalet, *Citizenship: Rights, struggle and class inequality* (Milton Keynes: Open University Press, 1988), p. 1.
22. *ibid.*, p. 48.
23. For a discussion of 'time poverty' and the debate on working hours and family life, see P. Hewitt, *About Time: The revolution in work and family life* (London: Institute for Public Policy Research/Rivers Oram Press, 1993).
24. N. Ginsberg, 'Racial harassment policy and practice: the denial of citizenship', *Critical Social Policy*, vol. 9, 2, Autumn 1989, pp. 66–81.
25. D.S. King and J. Waldron, 'Citizenship, social citizenship and the defence of welfare provision', *British Journal of Political Science*, vol. 18, 1988, p. 440.
26. *ibid.*, p. 441–2.
27. R. Lister, *The Exclusive Society: Citizenship and the poor* (London: Child Poverty Action Group, nd [*circa* 1990]), p. 2.
28. K. McFate, *Poverty, Inequality and the Crisis of Social Policy: Summary of findings* [Project Co-Chairs R. Lawson and W.J. Wilson], (Washington, DC: Joint Center for Political and Economic Studies, September 1991).
29. *Homelessness*, Twenty-Second Report, Committee of Public Accounts, Session 1990–91, 23 May 1991, HC 477, p. v.
30. J. Baker, 'The paradox of rising incomes and increasing hardship', *Policy and Politics*, vol. 19, 1, 1991, pp. 49–60.
31. *Deep in Debt* (London: National Children's Home, 1992).
32. National Audit Office, *Department of Social Security: Support for lone parent families*, HC 328 (London: HMSO, 30 March 1990).
33. L. Burghes, *One-Parent Families: Policy options for the 1990s* (York: Joseph Rowntree Foundation, 1993). While divorce was the biggest cause of the increase in single-parent families, the fastest growing group was single, never-married mothers, who made up 30 per cent of all lone parents.
34. *Findings* (York: Family Budget Unit, Joseph Rowntree Foundation, 1992); *Families, Work and Benefit* (London: Policy Studies Institute, 1993).

35. The Audit Commission, *Remote Control: The national administration of housing benefit* (London: HMSO, 1993).
36. Department of Social Security/Government Statistical Service, *Households Below Average Income: A statistical analysis, 1979–1990/91* (London: HMSO 1993), tables F1–F3.
37. Data using both the Low Income Families statistics and the Government's own Households below Average Income statistics produce the same result; see: C. Oppenheim, *Poverty: the Facts* (London: Child Poverty Action Group, 1993).
38. D. Piachaud, *Unemployment and Poverty* (London: Campaign for Work, May 1991).
39. Department of Social Security/Government Statistical Service, *Households Below Average Income*; P. Rose (ed.), *Social Trends 23*, Central Statistical Office (London: HMSO, 1993), table 5.17 'Distribution of Household Income'.
40. Department of Social Security/Central Statistical Service *Households Below Average Income: A statistical analysis, 1979–1988/89* (London: HMSO, July 1992).
41. Piachaud, *Unemployment and Poverty*.
43. R. Berthoud, 'Welfare policy and social security', *Policy Studies*, vol. 11, 1, Spring 1990, pp. 38–45.
43. A. Bridgwood and D. Savage, and edited by E. Goddard, *General Household Survey 1991* (London: HMSO, 1993), tables 2.18, 2.23–2.30.
44. *Training in Crisis: A report on the underfunding of Training and Enterprise Councils* (London: The Labour Party, 1992); Social Security Advisory Committee, *Eighth Report, 1992* (London: HMSO, 1992).
45. Data from a Department of Environment survey on single homeless people showed that young adults under 25 were overrepresented in the survey; the great majority were unemployed, and only 11 per cent of the 16–17 year olds and 3 per cent of the 18–24 year olds were on a government training scheme: I. Anderson, P. Kemp and D. Quilgars, *Single Homeless People*, Department of the Environment (London: HMSO, 1993).
46. Local authorities have responsibility to give priority to lone parents under 21 seeking housing under the Housing (Homeless Persons) Act 1977, and an obligation under the Children's Act 1990 to house young people once they reach 18 years of age.
47. Income Support is paid fortnightly in arrears; this has led to a heavy demand on the Social Fund for crisis loans. Social Fund loans are recovered by deduction from Income Support payments, so that receiving a loan will reduce the Income Support payment an individual gets. National Audit Office, *The Social Fund* (London: HMSO, 6 February 1991); M. Huny and G. Dix, *Evaluating the Social Fund*, DSS

Research Report 8 (London: HMSO, 1992); *Annual Report, Social Fund 1991–92*, Cm 1992 (London: HMSO, 1992).

48. Social Services Committee, *Social Security: Changes implemented in April 1988*, Ninth Report Session 1988–89, vol. 1, HC 437–1.

49. D.S. Massey and M.L. Eggers, 'The ecology of inequality: minorities and the concentration of poverty, 1970–1980', *American Journal of Sociology*, vol. 95, 5, March 1990, pp. 1153–88; W.J. Wilson, 'Another look at the truly disadvantaged', *Political Science Quarterly*, vol. 106, 4, 1991–2, pp. 639–56.

50. W.J. Wilson, 'Studying inner-city social dislocations: the challenge of public agenda research', *American Sociological Review*, vol. 56, 1, February 1991, pp. 1–14. For a critique, see P.E. Peterson, 'The urban underclass and the poverty paradox', *Political Science Quarterly*, vol. 106, 4, 1991–2, pp. 617–38. Wilson's rejoinder in the same volume: 'Another look at the truly disadvantaged', pp. 639–56.

51. R. Plant, 'Citizenship, rights and welfare', in A. Coote (ed.), *The Welfare of Citizens: Developing new social rights* (London: Institute for Public Policy Research/Rivers Oram Press, 1992), pp. 15–29.

52. Murray, 'The British underclass', *Losing Ground*.

53. L.M. Mead, *Beyond Entitlement: The social obligations of citizenship*; 'The logic of workfare'.

54. Murray, 'Underclass'.

55. Mead, 'The logic of workfare', p. 164.

56. L.M. Mead, 'The new politics of the new poverty', *Public Interest*, no. 103, Spring 1991, pp. 3–20.

57. D.M. Hill, 'The American philosophy of welfare: citizenship and the "politics of conduct" ', *Social Policy and Administration*, vol. 26, 2, June 1992, pp. 117–28.

58. *ibid.*

59. National Audit Office, *Department of Social Security*.

60. S. Holtermann, *Becoming a Breadwinner* (London: Daycare Trust, 1993).

61. *From the Workhouse to the Workplace* (London: National Council for One Parent Families, 1993).

62. R. Howell, *Why Not Work? A radical solution to unemployment* (London: Adam Smith Institute, 1991).

63. R. Plant, *Social Justice, Labour and the New Right*, Fabian Pamphlet 556 (London: The Fabian Society, February 1993).

64. *A New Policy Framework for Unemployed Adults* (London: Full Employment UK, May 1991).

65. *Long-Term Unemployment: Time for a new contract* (London: Full Employment UK, January 1993).

66. J. Burton, *Would Workfare Work?* (Buckingham: Employment Research Centre, University of Buckingham, 1987), pp. 46–7.

67. For an extensive treatment of these issues, see H. Dean and P. Taylor-Gooby, *Dependency Culture: The explosion of a myth* (Hemel Hempstead: Harvester Wheatsheaf, 1992).
68. *ibid.*, pp. 27, 44.
69. *ibid.*, pp. 75–8.
70. *ibid.*, pp. 86–95.
71. *ibid.*, pp. 111–14, 123.
72. Heath, 'The attitudes of the underclass', pp. 36–7.
73. D.J. Smith, 'The future of the underclass', in Smith (ed.), *Understanding the Underclass*, p. 94.
74. J.K. Galbraith, *The Culture of Contentment* (London: Sinclair-Stevenson, 1992).
75. J.M. Berry, K.E. Portney and K. Thomson, 'The political behavior of poor people', in Jencks and Peterson (eds), *The Urban Underclass*, pp. 157–372.

CHAPTER 5

THE LOCAL ARENA

Introduction

The exercise of citizenship at the local level operates within a complex framework of public, semi-public and private bodies. As well as elected local councils there are NHS Trusts, the Training and Enterprise Councils (TECs), quasi-non-governmental organisations (quangos) such as the Urban Development Corporations, Grant Maintained (opted-out) schools, City Challenge Boards, and a wide range of voluntary bodies which provide services, and engage professional and voluntary staff. Nor is there a rigid dividing line between centre and locality; there is a complex set of relationships through professional policy networks, and links within functional policy communities. But people are related to their local authority in a different way to other bodies. The justification of local government is that it is democratic and accountable, and its decision-making is accessible and participatory. This chapter, therefore, looks at a particular aspect of the local arena, the operation of local government, and the changes which have taken place over the past fifteen years.

Local government is traditionally justified by its elected, participatory and accountable nature, a defence of local democracy that goes back to John Stuart Mill and beyond. In the 1960s this philosophical tradition was reasserted in the Herbert Report on London Government's words: 'Local government seems to us to be . . . a living thing, an organism . . . [which] seeks to give outward form to the inward unity of a living community.'[1] More recently, the Widdicombe Report of 1986 repeated the emphasis, seeing the justification of local government as its attributes of pluralism (contributing to the national political system); participation (contributing to local democracy); and responsiveness (to local needs through the delivery of services).[2] This justification incorporated a marked view of community as locality and collective interest: 'Local government is government *by* communities rather than *of* local communities. It is the means by which local communities may take decisions affecting the delivery of public services in their area.'[3] This did not mean that local government itself had to deliver all services but it was necessary that it should allow a local view to be expressed through the taking of decisions. Merely delivering services, as health authorities do, for example, was evidence not of local government but of local administration.

This long tradition does not, however, itself determine the forms and functions of local government. Local government has no special constitutional position which protects its status and role, though there is, as Elliott has put it, 'a constitutional history and tradition of local government'.[4] Local government is subject to the sovereign will of Parliament. It is subject to the law of *ultra vires*, which holds that local authorities can do only that which is permitted them by statute law, and anything else 'which is calculated to facilitate, or is conducive to or incidental to, the discharge of any of their functions'.[5] The changes of the 1980s and 1990s, therefore, have been the subject of debate not only over specific provisions – over finance, functions, structure and management – but also over the role which local government should play in the modern state. This debate has focused on the role of local authorities as 'enablers' as well as service 'providers'. Much has been made of 'empowering' people to make choices, whether as citizens through participation in and access to local government, or as consumers through the redress and influence offered by market-provided services. At the same time, controversy has surrounded the effects of the changes, with the allegation that they have weakened local autonomy and increased central control. The result is said to undermine democratic self-government at the local level, and weaken effective citizen input into decision-making.

Such charges are denied by Conservative governments, which have emphasised that the changes to local government, based on the three Es of economy, efficiency and effectiveness (formalised in the Audit Commission's *Code of Local Government Practice*[6]), have modernised the operation of local authorities. Councils are becoming more accountable, and provisions for the contracting out and opting out of services enhance consumer choice. In the 1990s the government's proposed changes to the structure of local government are based, similarly, on the assertion that unitary authorities will improve accountability to local communities.[7]

The concern with democracy and accountability has focused on the notion of the enabling council. The meaning of such a concept, however, varies between left and right. On the right, the enabling council has essentially a regulatory function, presiding over a collection of services which are largely provided by the market. On the left, the idea of the enabling council is associated with notions of 'good governance', a local authority which is responsible for the total well-being of the local community, and has a general competence to meet local needs. While this may not mean that the authority provides all services directly, it goes considerably beyond the minimalist strategic role envisaged by those on the right. But the views of left and right are not diametrically opposed in any clear-cut way. Although Graham Mather proposed a contract model for local government, and Nicholas Ridley, writing while he was Secretary of State for the Environment, argued for greater separation between purchaser and provider, Ridley's model still stressed the enabling role of the local council. By this he implied a governance role which, like that of central government, does not entail direct service provision.[8]

These concerns are the subject of this chapter: the debate on local government's role and function in the modern state; the debate on providing and enabling; the future structure and management of local government; and a general competence for local governance.

Local government: status, role and function

As we have seen, the justification of local government in representative and participatory terms, and as the locus of the exercise of citizenship, goes back to John Stuart Mill.[9] Jones and Stewart's modern restatement of the case for local government is also founded on its democratic accountability – its responsiveness and accessibility.[10] But ever since Mill's advocacy of the local arena as the setting in which individuals learn citizenship, there have been arguments about the relation between size, function and effective participation, as the seminal work of MacKenzie and Sharpe has demonstrated.[11] In the 1960s these issues formed part of the debate on local government reform. The Redcliffe–Maud and Wheatley Commissions argued for the increased size of local authorities on the grounds that while small areas might facilitate ease of access and involvement, citizen participation was an empty exercise unless local government could provide services effectively, and that meant larger authorities.[12] The government, while it did not accept the Redcliffe–Maud proposals for unitary authorities, did introduce larger units of local government in England and Wales, and in Scotland, justifying these changes on the grounds of efficiency and effectiveness.

The reforms of the 1960s, however, left the role of local government within the state unchanged. Constitutionally, all local authorities are created by statute and have no independent status or right to exist; but in practice their position is governed by constitutional convention as well as parliamentary sovereignty; a convention, Widdicombe argued, 'based on, and subject to, the contribution which local government can bring to good government'.[13] The Widdicombe Report of 1986 set out the characteristics of local authorities as bodies which were: elected; multipurpose; covering large population areas; having to act within their statutory powers rather than possessing a 'general competence'; able to raise their own revenues; and corporate bodies with powers vested corporately in councillors as a whole.[14]

The Widdicombe Committee Report went on to define the value of local government in terms of pluralism (spreading power within the state), participation, responsiveness, representation and diversity. This is the traditional normative perspective. Over the past two decades, however, this perspective has been challenged by three alternatives, based on neo-Marxist, post-Fordist and public choice approaches. The first alternative, that of Marxist-derived theories of local government, has, as Pickvance has shown, taken a very different perspective centred on the operation of the state in contemporary capitalism, based on the 'local state', 'dual politics' and 'uneven development' models.[15] Cockburn's concept of the 'local state' argues that capitalism requires for its survival certain functions (accumulation and social order) which depend on the operation of both local and central government. Local government is but one part of the total capitalist system. Saunders's 'dual state' concept sees the central and local levels of the state as possessing different functions. The central level is concerned with 'production' functions and corporatist politics, while the local level is characterised by 'consumption' functions and pluralist politics. Duncan and Goodwin's 'uneven development' theory claims that the form of local government is explained by the state's need to manage the spatial unevenness of economic development. But Pickvance rejects what he believes are the misdirected efforts of these Marxist-derived theories in favour of what he calls more prosaic structural ones by which local government is essentially a system of service-delivery ('executant') bodies characterised by the possession of both resources and discretion, such that parties and pressure groups have a significant influence on policy.[16]

A different emphasis is offered by the analysis of Stoker, Painter and others on the nature of local government in the current 'post-Fordist' era. The previous Fordist era of local government echoed postwar capitalism, with its large-scale mass production and mass consumption, and its emphasis on direct service provision and the planning and regulation of activities. The 'post-Fordist' era, by contrast, separates off service delivery from overall strategy and regulation. Stoker argues that the production of local authority services has changed in line with developments in the private sector, and is increasingly taken over by it. The Fordist approach of a standard product for a captive user is giving way to differentiated products aimed at a range of consumer groups, in local government as elsewhere. In this new era the autonomy and democracy of councils are curtailed as non-elected bodies replace or parallel local government.[17]

Public choice theory justifies the post-Fordist era of diversity and consumer choice, in contrast to the claims of the multi- or all-purpose authority of the Mill tradition. The inclusive authority of the Mill tradition provided an institutional framework within which services were planned and delivered through a democratically elected organisation. According to Alexander, this provided a co-operative and collaborative mechanism and culture, which is lost when services are provided by separate agencies.[18] But it was precisely this inclusive system which was the target for attack by Conservative governments in the 1980s. It was too bureaucratic, obsessed with power rather than accountability, and defended its own role as producer to the detriment of its consumer–citizens.

To combat these defects, the right argued, it was necessary to introduce market competition. Informing this position is a public choice theoretical perspective. Public choice theory emphasises the role of the rational individual who makes informed choices in the market-place, as opposed to a focus on people making a collective choice through their votes. The objective for those on the right is to break public sector service monopolies in favour of a market-place of competing providers from the private and not-for-profit sectors. And, within public-sector institutions, producers must be required to provide for consumer choices through provider–purchaser contracting, performance-related rewards and performance appraisal.

It can be argued, however, that these critical approaches of the neo-Marxist, post-Fordist and public choice alternative perspectives on local government give an inadequate account of the centrality of the notion of a wider public interest. Governing the locality, it is argued, must have regard to the community as a whole. To this end local government must possess a degree of autonomy over financial decisions if it is to exercise real responsibility for the management of local services to meet local circumstances. It must be accountable to a local electorate as a community of citizens, not just to consumers concerned with individual redress. From this perspective local government sets goals, is the vehicle for the expression of demands, and provides the context for economic and social development. A key part of this justification for local government has been that it delivers collectively services which cannot be purchased privately. That is, local government is the provider of public goods. Public goods (such as police and fire services) are those which are 'indivisible' – once provided, they cannot be denied to particular individuals because of the 'free-rider' problem – the service is available to everyone, regardless of whether or not the individual pays for it. The only way these services can be delivered is through public provision, paid for through taxation.

Representing this wider public interest are the body of councillors duly constituted as the corporate local council. Thus the essential feature of local government is that elected members, served by professional officers, constitute the government of the community in ways which are responsive and accountable. Just as competition assures the responsiveness of producers within markets, so elections ensure accountability. Dissatisfied voters can reject their representatives in favour of alternatives. The difficulty, however, is that these choices are bound into local party systems which are part of national politics. In this situation there may be little change at the local level over time; this in turn strengthens the call for alternative mechanisms, such as quasi-market provisions, to force accountability and responsiveness to consumers. The result has been a network of service provision, in which the providers have bilateral relations with the council and public accountability in the democratic sense, as opposed to contractual accountability, is very hard to sustain (an issue which will be considered further in Chapter 8). The result is that there is now a need, Alexander suggests, to combine constitutional accountability with the more technical contractual accountability into a new concept. Otherwise, the non-democratic and technical may come to dominate the system, and the need for local government then becomes open to question.[19]

There are additional fears that the traditional rationale of local government as accountable self-government is being eroded by the use of non-elected bodies to deliver services. Stewart has argued that there is, in effect, a 'new magistracy' – a term first used by Morris about the government of education – which is replacing elected bodies with a non-elected elite. This non-elected elite dominates an increasing range of local organisations, including Training and Enterprise Councils, hospital trusts, housing action trusts and Urban Development Corporations, and Grant Maintained schools.[20] This undermines local accountability, replacing it with a much more tenuous responsibility to government ministers and constituting, in effect, a 'democratic deficit'. By contrast with the position of elected representatives, local people rarely know who the members of the new quangos are. To be truly accountable, bodies need to make many channels of information and access, as well as elections, available to the public, and to supplement public accountability with user control and neighbourhood inputs. In practice, many of these avenues are not supplied by the unelected boards, or are supplied only weakly, for example, by meeting in public only once a year.[21]

A notable example of this trend can be seen in the aftermath of the abolition of the Greater London Council in 1986. In addition to the London Residuary Body, responsible for the disposal of the GLC's assets, and the London Regional Transport Board, which took over its public transport system, there is a range of non-governmental bodies covering a spectrum of London-wide functions. At the end of 1992 two further quangos were added: London First and London Forum, with a common Chairman drawn from the private sector. Both, argue Colenutt and Ellis, are a recasting of the Business in the Community idea into quangos that are effectively creating strategic policy for London in the absence of an overall elected body. This is true even though London Forum has two councillor members and London First has subcommittees with public-sector representatives. The two quangos are in fact entrenching a business elite claiming to be representative of London opinion and deflecting arguments for elected London government.[22] In general, the proliferation of unelected bodies throughout the country reinforces the increasingly corporatist nature of local public affairs. The new local corporatism – by which decisions are made within and between quasi-public and private bodies involving local and central public servants, sectional interests and government appointees – evades democratic accountability in any meaningful sense.

The debate on the role and status of local government has not been confined to argument between new right market consumerism and traditional left inclusive public provision.[23] As Gyford has shown, in the 1980s the Labour Party reacted against the centralising tendencies of the Thatcher governments with an emphasis on participation and decentralisation at local level. The aim of this urban socialism was to increase the involvement of tenants, women's and ethnic groups in decision-making.[24] The local right took a different perspective. As Holliday has put it, a 'New Suburban Right' with distinctive views of the local challenged those of the New Urban Left.[25] What the two had in common was a distrust of the bureaucratic paternalism developed by Labour and Conservative councils alike. But if, for the New Urban Left, the solution was a decentralised and participatory one, for the New Urban Right the commitment is to market-type provisions and a restricted local authority – the 'competitive council'.[26]

The nature of the debate on local government and its place in the state has thus altered significantly over the twenty years or so since the 1972 Local Government Act instituted the reforms of the structure, implemented in 1974. In terms of functions, local authorities have, over an even longer period, become more involved with personal rather than infrastructure services, while the public for those services has become more fragmented. In the nineteenth century and into the twentieth, local authorities were primarily responsible to the generality of ratepayer-citizens for infrastructure and utilities, that is, for roads, street lighting, water and sewerage systems, gas and electricity. As they took on more social service provision, particularly after 1945, local authorities' dominant functions became education, housing and the personal social services, while they progressively lost their infrastructure responsibilities.

The result has been a shift in the responsiveness of local authorities from a general accountability to ratepayers and electors to a more individualised responsibility to tenants, parents, families, and sectional interests. Local authorities not only establish consultation mechanisms to work with such groups, but are involved with them through grant-giving or contracts for services. In a parallel set of changes, political parties have become more actively involved in building new relationships with different groups of supporters.[27] The public has become more fragmented and more assertive. The result is, as Gyford puts it, 'an increasingly sectionalist politics which sits uneasily with the established institutions of representative democracy'.[28]

Government or agent: the changes of the 1980s and 1990s

In addition to the changes in council–citizen relationships, there have been significant shifts in the relations between localities and the centre. The role and functions of local government are contained within a complex set of central–local relations. These relations have been couched in terms of a number of models: relative autonomy; agency; partnership; reciprocal dependence (the power–dependence model); and those models subsumed under neo-Marxist, post-Fordist and public choice theories.[29] Local government and local agent are not polar opposites. Centralising forces are characteristic of modern states which provide services to national criteria and standards. The question is, rather, the extent to which the agency function remains compatible with the exercise of real political authority at the local level. The difficulty in Britain has been that in the late twentieth century, localities have been subject to a sustained period of change which they have been powerless to resist. Attempts by local authorities to claim a distinctive local mandate for their actions from their local electorate have been resisted by central governments which deny that such a separate mandate can exist in the unitary state. Although the changes evolved over the whole course of the 1980s, it is argued that cumulatively they have amounted to a coherent theory of the role of local authorities by central government, particularly from 1987 onwards. This theory is a public-choice-based one in which the local authority's role is as strategic director in a market-orientated system of local provision.

Gurr and King have described two kinds of restrictions which local government faces in trying to exercise autonomy.[30] The first kind (Type I) are those constraints that arise from local economic and social conditions. The second kind (Type II) arise from the control exercised by higher levels of government, through legal rules (for example, *ultra vires*) or guidance (government circulars), the imposition of mandatory services and standards, and above all by control over finance. Traditionally, it has been Type II constraints that have been the concern of British analysts, though comparative work has drawn attention to restrictions arising from economic and social conditions. Goldsmith and Wolman, for example, use the concept of local well-being or welfare to analyse the autonomy of cities in Britain and the United States.[31]

Over the 1970s and 1980s the change in central–local relations, observed Rhodes, shifted, from bargaining through incorporation to direction and centralisation.[32] The trend towards greater centralisation gathered momentum as governments sought to restrain local expenditure, but by the 1980s politicians of both right and left were also critical of bureaucratic structures, and their ability to deliver efficient services. Solutions differed between the two perspectives. To the right the solution was to promote the consumer in the market; to the left the need was for more decentralised and participatory structures.

Central government's moves to constrain the finances of local government, however, go back to 1976, when Peter Shore,

Labour's Minister of Local Government, announced: 'The party's over'. During the 1980s financial controls became extensive, curtailing local expenditure above prescribed central government limits by setting targets and penalties, and by laying down limits to the rates that local authorities could levy ('capping'). The Local Government Finance Act 1982 legalised targets on local spending, and introduced grant penalties. The targets were abolished in 1985, but the powers of the Secretary of State were continued by the rate-capping provisions, and the 1984 Rates Act allowed the Secretary of State to set the level of expenditure for individual local authorities; a move that was regarded as a major attack on a key area of local discretion. Limits were also set on capital expenditure, and housing budgets were ring-fenced to prevent cross-subsidisation of revenue accounts. In addition, the establishment of the Audit Commission in 1982 increased central influence over local financial practice. In spite of these strictures, current expenditure increased in real terms, and councils' share of public spending was virtually the same in 1991–2 as it had been in 1979–80. What in effect happened in the 1980s was that the governments halted what had previously seemed to be the uncontrollable growth of the 1960s and 1970s.[33]

The increased financial oversight was seen as the key factor in the changing relationship between the centre and the localities. The government made a number of attempts to control the basis of local revenue with the move in 1990 (1989 in Scotland) from a property-based local tax to a poll tax (the Community Charge) and, in 1993, back again. Although rate-capping was judged to have been largely unsuccessful, the situation was not eased by the conflict over the Community Charge. The proportion of local government spending financed by central government had risen from 48 per cent in 1980 to over 80 per cent in 1992–3; a trend reinforced by the removal, under the Local Government Finance Act 1988, of local authorities' power to set the non-domestic rate. This was replaced with a national impost, the non-domestic rate, returned to local authorities in relation to their population size.

By the beginning of the 1990s the position had been reached where all local authorities were capped at the level of their Standard Spending Assessments (SSAs); that is, at predetermined government-set levels of allowable expenditure. To observers this application of the capping regime to all local authority budgets called into question local government's claim to effective local political power, particularly in the context where only some 15 per cent of revenue is raised locally (only 11 per cent in Scotland and 8 per cent in Wales). The use of SSAs in a capped system, and heavy reliance on government grants, result in a cosmetic, not real, local accountability, since it is ministerial decisions on resources which are pre-eminent in shaping the character of services. The Audit Commission stated that the manner in which SSAs were used to limit council expenditure confused accountability for local services between central and local government. As the Commission's survey of local authorities revealed, capping limits were far more important than other factors, such as the local authority's assessment of its spending needs, in local authority budgeting behaviour.[34]

The Audit Commission suggested that to clarify accountability, the revenue-raising powers of local government could be enhanced, and referenda could be required where the local authority proposed to exceed the spending limit or to reduce spending. The alternative was to attach accountability more clearly to the centre, by central government entering into contracts with local government for the delivery of major services (though that would have significant implications for the corporate role of local authorities).[35] But to pose the issue in these terms raises the question of whether local government itself would continue to exist. True accountability, it is argued, can be achieved only through domestic rates (partially through the Council Tax, which replaced the Community Charge in 1993) and a local income tax. In this kind of financial regime, however, the issue of the amount actually raised locally still has to be addressed.[36]

Major changes in central–local relations in the 1980s were not confined to finance. Legislative changes in the 1980s promoted privatisation and contracting out, including council house sales, deregulation of municipal public transport, competitive tendering, allowing tenants to change landlords and schools to opt out of local authority control. In 1986 the Greater London Council and the Metropolitan Councils were abolished, and the 1980s also saw the establishment of additional local agencies through the Enterprise Zones, Urban Development Corporations and various economic regeneration initiatives. Nor were changes confined to finance and services. Central government also sought to reform what it saw as the politicisation of the relationship between local authority

members and officers and the one-party monopoly of key committees by (largely Labour) party groups.

Research undertaken for the Widdicombe Committee revealed
the extent to which politics drove the policy process in local authorities, and the Report itself referred to what it saw as a rising
tide of politicisation of local government. The government's response to the Widdicombe Committee, which had been set up to
examine this issue, was to require that the composition of committees and subcommittees should reflect the composition of the
council as a whole, in a proportionate manner.[37] Subsequent research by Young and Davies places the findings on 'politicisation'
in a longer-term context. They reveal that politics was becoming
increasingly intense only in those councils that were already highly
politicised; rural authorities did not follow this trend. What was
more striking was that authorities were becoming more diverse. At
the same time member–officer relations were becoming more formalised, with a clear trend to closer working relations in which
chief officers attended party group meetings, and more frequent
meetings between chief executives and council leaders. Even so,
this appeared to be a mark of an emerging convention of closer
working relations thought appropriate by both sides, rather than
increasing politicisation.[38]

The 1989 Local Government and Housing Act, however, restricted the political activity of senior officers and those with a
salary of more than £19,500, thus preventing the 'twin-tracking'
whereby a council employee of one authority could serve as a
councillor on a neighbouring authority. The relation between
councillors and officers was also altered by the Local Government
Finance Act 1988, which invested statutory powers in certain officers: the monitoring officer must report on impropriety; the head
of the service has responsibility for management arrangements;
the finance officer has a duty to report on financial matters. The
effect is to put officers in relation to those matters at arm's length
from their authority.

The centralising trends of the 1980s must be seen not only within
the debate about the need for greater localisation at sub-local authority level and the relations between members and officers, but also
in the supranational context of the European Community. The government reaffirmed in early 1993 that it would not sign the European Charter of Local Self-Government (opened for signature by

member states of the Council of Europe in October 1985), although it agreed with its broad principles. In its view the Charter would unacceptably limit Parliament's ability to determine the law concerning the finance, functions and structure of local government.[39] But the European dimension cannot be dimissed so readily; the issues of subsidiarity and the Europe of the regions remain on the agenda. To Conservative governments, subsidiarity – the devolution of decision-making from Brussels to the appropriate lowest level – has meant devolution to the national government rather than to local government, to a basic unit close to the community, as favoured by many commentators.[40] In addition, critics have argued that the extension of capping to all local authorities and the reduction in the proportion of revenue raised locally ran counter to the principles of subsidiarity.

In wider terms the European dimension, particularly the impact of the 1987 Single European Act, which provided for progressive moves to a Single Market to be completed by 31 December 1992, has important implications for local authorities' functioning. It operates alongside the central government's own oversight of local government. The opening up of public purchasing, above a certain threshold, to bids from across the European Community, the requirement that European quality and performance standards be enforced or applied, and the liberalisation of service contracts, all require revised internal procedures, and will impose an increased administrative burden. The European dimension also has implications for the ways in which local government can work jointly with the private sector to secure exemptions from competition policy restrictions, which debar state aid to schemes and projects. Again, this increases the complexity of central–local relations. The effects of the Single Market impinge on a wide range of core services: education and training, social services, planning and transportation, construction services (architects, building control, housing), libraries, financial services, fire and emergency planning, trading standards, environmental health, purchasing, personnel and economic development. To meet these challenges and opportunities, local authorities have to develop their strategic capabilities, including their internal management, relations with business and with the voluntary sector, and monitoring procedures.[41]

The rapidly changing environment of this complex network of central–local–European relations means that Sharpe's emphasis on the 'unresolved tension' in central–local relations that arises from local government's ambiguous status remains valid.[42] To this ambiguity has been added the increased complexity and fragmentation of agencies and responsibilities at the local level. The situation has become one in which the government sees local authorities essentially as the organisers of contracts for services, through their own workforces, with the private sector or with the not-for-profit and voluntary sectors. The contract model of local government, not the multipurpose and inclusive model, is in the ascendant. At the same time, however, there is continuing debate on the alternative model of community government, with broad responsibility to meet the needs of the locality. Both the contract and the community models depend on perceptions of the providing and enabling roles of local authorities, which themselves are evolving, not static, notions.

Providing and enabling

The government's approach to local government in the late 1980s and 1990s has been informed by three key elements. First, services would increasingly be provided outside the local authority through the opting-out provisions. Second, Compulsory Competititve Tendering (CCT) would mean that services were provided by contractors rather than directly employed staff. Third, services would be organised more on the lines of 'executive management' models, in effect limiting political control.

The meaning of the enabling council in practice is set out in the 1991 Department of Health paper *Community Care in the Next Decade and Beyond*, which speaks of the role of the enabling authority as being to identify needs and plan how to meet them, set overall strategies and priorities, and commission and purchase, as well as provide, services.[43] This kind of thinking has not been confined to Conservative governments. In 1993 the Labour Party, in what was seen as a reversal of its previous position, stated that local councils did not have an absolute right to be direct providers and managers of services. This version of enabling stressed that councillors should reduce the time they spent on management in favour of being advocates of their electors and communities. This in turn would mean pressing government for more powers to act in the interests of local people.[44]

The practical difficulty which arises from these developments is that services become fragmented, making it very difficult for local authorities to carry out that strategic role which governments assert will be their prime enabling function. The 1988 Local Government Act made it compulsory for local authorities to put street cleaning, refuse and some other services out to tender; opting out of schools from Local Education Authority control was introduced in the Education Reform Act 1988; and the opportunity for council tenants to transfer to other landlords was laid down in the Local Government and Housing Act 1989. But this does not mean greater autonomy, nor necessarily greater choice. Central financial control over schools and housing Trusts is likely to mirror that over the NHS Trusts. The Local Government Act 1988 also gave the Secretary of State authority to specify other services, subject to consultation, which would be introduced progressively after 1990. Following the 1992 general election, the government stressed that compulsory competitive tendering would be extended to entrench the competition and contracting-out mode of local government.

The concept of the enabling authority is used by the right to argue for the substitution of private for public provision. The left's view, by contrast, is that the local authority should have responsibility for overall local well-being, with the council at the centre of a pluralistic governance network. This governance role includes control, partnership, support, regulation and influence. The result, it is argued, is not local authorities that are less effective or influential than they were as direct providers, but a new type of authority will be called for, one that takes a holistic view of its area and its needs. The internal management of the authority will be freed from its departmental committee structure and its basis in professionalism.[45] Clarke and Stewart describe this broad view of the enabling role as 'enabling the community to meet the needs, opportunities and problems' of the area; that is, community government based on a power of general competence.[46] The aim should be not the competitive council but the co-operative council, governing, not just administering, its local area.

The warning here must be that community leadership in this form is meaningless without resources and powers. Paramount among these resources are a local revenue base over which the authority has autonomy within national guidelines, and the active support of the community conceived as groups and interests as well as voters. To this end, argue Jones and Stewart, councils must be seen to press for action on those matters which cause concern – crime, the environment, inner cities – and enter into networks and coalitions to do so.[47]

In 1988, the Audit Commission similarly viewed local authorities as facilitators which would increasingly become 'competitive councils'. People no longer accepted that the council knew best, and there was an allied questioning of the need for large-sized operations. Authorities were increasingly experimenting with locally based management, more responsive to local needs.[48] The traditional role of elected representatives would necessarily change as the competitive council assumed more of a strategic role. The most important elements of the councillor's role were policy formulation, representation, performance review, and operational management. But these tasks should involve assigning clear responsibilities and holding officers accountable for results, not day-to-day operational management through the old-style administrative committees. Contracting out made such a hands-on involvement virtually redundant.[49]

The general conclusion from all these moves is that the enabling council concept, whether of the left or the right, has called into question the former all-purpose model of local government. It has emerged from the changing relations between centre and localities that the legislation of the 1980s has brought about, with its provisions for multi-agency, public and private, local services.

Reforming local government

The changes affecting the role and functions of local government were extended in April 1991 when the Secretary of State for the Environment, Michael Heseltine, announced a review of local government structure.[50] The government appeared to favour unitary local councils and a concept of enabling authorities, which reduced the need to concentrate on size as a key determining factor. The 1992 Local Government Act established a Local Government Commission to review the structure of local government in

England, while Wales and Scotland were to move to new authorities without the use of a commission. In England the 1992 guidelines to the Commission laid down that there need not be a maximum or minimum size for a local authority, in either population or area terms. During the course of the review the Commission Chairman, Sir John Banham, reflected on the possibility of increasing the size of unitary authorities, implying that this was feasible given managerial delegation to local communities.[51] But while the report on Durham and Cleveland of May 1993 recommended a system of unitary authorities, the Commission stressed that a uniform pattern of local government was most unlikely to emerge; this was one reason why it had focused particular attention on community identity and costs. At the same time, the Commission continued to argue for the need for larger areas for the delivery of some services. This was not to ignore the government's preferred 'enabling' model of local government, but an argument for keeping joint arrangements to a minimum to ensure that local authorities were effective in their strategic management of the contract culture.[52]

A major criticism of the review process was that there had been no proper debate about the role, function and constitutional position of local government. An insight into the underlying beliefs can, however, be deduced from the supporting documentation to the review. The 1992 guidance said that there should be no presumption that each authority should deliver all its services in-house; they could be purchased from the private and voluntary sectors or obtained through joint arrangements with other authorities. The government, it stated, was committed to the concept of the enabling authority. At the same time, where a unitary authority was recommended by the Commission, the aim should be to make it responsible for all local government functions, and responsive to the needs of local people.[53] The government stated that while there was no national blueprint, substantial increases in the number of unitary authorities were anticipated.

Criticisms and uncertainties continued during the process of the review, particularly over the size and configuration of the proposed unitary authorities. There were calls for change to be limited to modification of the two-tier structure rather than major revisions. In July 1993 John Gummer, Secretary of State for the Environment, announced that the review process would be altered, but not terminated, and suggested that new councils in England, Scotland and Wales would all be in place by the spring of 1997 – a considerable shortening of the implementation period from the orginal phased timetable.[54]

In England the structure review programme was divided into five tranches, and originally implementation was to have been over a phased period. In the autumn of 1993 the timetable was accelerated to conduct all the remaining reviews simultaneously. The draft revised guidance issued in October 1993 still expected continuation of the existing two-tier system to be an exception, with a substantial increase in the number of unitary authorities in both urban and rural areas. Joint submissions among authorities would be encouraged, and the implication was that a pattern based on existing districts within their current boundaries (i.e. those serving relatively small populations) becoming unitary authorities would not be favoured. The draft revised guidance in fact encourages the merging of districts and the disaggregating of counties.[55] The result might then be that some 150 new authorities would replace the existing 296 districts and 39 counties. The government reiterated that prime consideration must be given to the four issues of identity, accessibility, responsiveness and democracy, and this had implications for very large authorities.

The government also reiterated its belief that joint arrangements between authorities for service delivery were entirely acceptable. Statutory joint authorities, it recognised, might be needed for certain services but should be kept to a minimum. An area where such a statutory joint authority might come into being is in the area of planning: this, like voluntary joint arrangements, does call into question the adequacy of accountability, in spite of the government's view that this would not prove to be a problem. The revised guidelines to the Local Government Commission also emphasised the need to take into account the scope for delegation to parish and town councils – an area of consultation the government was keen to foster and where agency agreements for service delivery should be encouraged. Similarly, there was increased emphasis on devolved management in the suggestion that councils might wish to set up 'area committees' to oversee services locally.

The government's proposals for reform of the Welsh local government system, announced in March 1993, recommended twenty-one unitary authorities, to be known as county councils, together

with the suggestion that these councils establish joint arrangements for strategic and specialist service planning. The numbers of
councillors would be considerably cut, by almost half, from 1976 to
1100.[56] There was also some indication that the new unitary authority could delegate district level functions to area committees.
The Welsh proposals offer little guidance on what the underlying
concept of local government is now to be, since it gives no defini-
tive answers on optimum size or community identity, a criticism
which has continued through the English reviews.[57]

In Scotland, the White Paper *Shaping the Future – The new councils* (July 1993) suggested that the five regional councils of Strathclyde, Lothian, Central, Tayside and Grampian would be abolished
and dismantled into smaller single-tier councils. Strathclyde, which
had nineteen district councils within it, would be split into ten units,
including a new Glasgow City Council.[58] The remaining four regional councils would remain, but the districts within them would be
abolished. The proposals would create twenty-five single-tier units
on the mainland which, together with the existing three single-tier
island councils, would bring the total to twenty-eight. Elections to
the shadow councils would take place in spring 1995, and the new
authorities would come into operation from 1 April 1996. The White
Paper recognised that councils would be expected to enter into
voluntary joint arrangements to a greater extent than in the past; as
a last resort the Secretary of State would have the power to require
two or more local authorities jointly to manage a function. These
proposals gave rise to considerable controversy, not least because
they were not based on proposals from an independent commission,
and because the new boundaries appeared to favour the Conservative Party electorally.

The Welsh review also raised the question of how joint arrangements would work in practice if different arrangements are
needed for different services. The result might then be different
boundaries for different services, which raises further questions
of overall control and accountability. A further gap in the debate
has been the absence of a regional dimension. In 1989 the Labour
Party argued in favour of around a dozen regional assemblies in
England, and there have also been suggestions for smaller functional regions of a size closer to county councils.[59] In the early
1990s, however, the regional dimension had little impact on the
reform debate.

In the reform process as a whole the Conservative government's preferred option for unitary authorities still left open the relation between size, structure and function. In particular there is the issue raised by the fragmentation of local governance between public, private and quasi-public bodies, and the increasing divergence of groups and interests within the general public. These trends in turn raise the important question of the need for a continued parish/ community level of local governance. The government, in setting up the local government review in 1991, took the view that no new powers should be given to parish or community councils. The policy guidance to the 1992 Local Government Commission, however, commented on the general arrangements for delegation from local authorities to other local authorities, and laid down that in considering the effective discharge of functions the Commission should take into account the scope for delegation to parish councils.[60]

In practice the first set of reform proposals, those for the Isle of Wight, left the decision to the proposed single (unitary) Isle of Wight authority rather than making proposals for delegation to parishes that could have acted as a general guideline. At the same time, however, the Commission's support for larger councils with relatively few councillors stressed the 'enhanced role' that parish and town councils could play in the future. This enhanced role is proposed as a counter to the effects of reform changes elsewhere; for example, the high ratio of electors to councillors, larger areas, and consequent problems of community identity with the larger authorities. The Commission appears, however, to take the view that this 'enhanced role' will largely be a consultative one, but with some devolved management for local leisure (including library) facilities. Critics fear that this role has not been properly thought through, particularly the relationship between parishes and unitary authorities. It seems probable that parishes will continue to have restricted powers and finances, and thus little real ability to empower local people.[61]

Reforming the system: electoral and management issues

The reform of local government instituted at the beginning of the 1990s paid little attention to the nature of local democracy as such.

While the review considered the frequency of council elections and the number of council members, there was little official concern with whether proportional representation would be a better method of reflecting local views, or with the relation between size and electoral participation. An earlier attempt to consider electoral systems, in Lord Blake's private peer's bill calling for proportional representation in local government, was successful in the Lords but rejected in the Commons.[62] Turnout in local elections remains low, around 40 per cent on average, and significant elements in the community, such as women and ethnic minorities, are underrepresented.

The question of improving local democracy in electoral terms is illuminated by the work of Rallings and Thrasher, which shows that electoral turnout is higher in districts than in counties, and for districts with a four-year rather than annual electoral cycle. Turnout is also higher in smaller wards, with the optimum balance between size and voting being an electorate of between 2500 and 6000. The Rallings and Thrasher findings have implications for structure: they conclude that 'it seems clear a single, identifiable and omnipotent local authority would improve both participation and accountability'.[63] At the same time, however, the issue of the representativeness of electoral systems needs to be addressed. The pattern at local level reveals wide differences in value between each party's share of the vote and its share of the seats, such that many electors are effectively disfranchised. The plurality system causes even more distortions in local than in parliamentary systems. Not only does it discriminate against third parties, it benefits Conservatives in (rural, affluent) areas where they are already strong, and Labour in their (predominantly urban) strongholds.[64] There appears to be a strong case for some form of proportional representation on these grounds, and on those of greater councillor representation for women and ethnic minorities, even though one outcome might be a greater prevalence of 'hung' councils.

At the same time as structure was being reviewed, the internal organisation of local authorities and the role of local representatives were also subjects of concern. In July 1991 the DoE published a consultation paper on internal management which stressed that local authorities' role was moving to that of setting up and overseeing contractual arrangements.[65] This was followed in 1992 by a joint DoE–local authority associations' working party which considered a number of options, including the kind of 'cabinet' system for local authority first proposed by the Maud Committee in 1967.[66] The working party did not recommend a particular management form, but suggested possible adaptations to the existing committee system and four executive models. It suggested that local authorities should be allowed to experiment with different systems, including executive models (i.e. on Westminster lines); the creation of a deliberative committee composed of members of the majority group; decentralisation of decision-making (i.e. a 'neighbourhood' level); new rights for members to scrutinise council decisions (a 'select committee' analogy); an enhanced role for members not holding executive positions which emphasised the councillor's role as representative and champion of the community. That is, the report promoted what it saw as the key elements of leadership, representation, accountability, effective decision-making and scrutiny, and responsiveness to local people. In parallel to these moves the working party recommended greater discretion in payments of allowances to council members, while recognising that there is little support for the creation of salaried council members.[67]

Critics of a two-tier system of councillors, divided into a paid executive board/cabinet and backbenchers who concern themselves with area and neighbourhood matters and draw allowances, question the practicality of such a system. Others argue that a more high-profile executive – an elected mayor, for example – could increase public interest and electoral turnout. Whether paid council membership would attract candidates, and how such members would be elected/selected – by party groups or by the electorate, for example – remain matters of concern. In particular, there are doubts over trying to set explicit frameworks for councillors' duties. There is no rigid barrier between 'cabinet' and 'ward' roles, and representatives should continue to be judged by their electorates on political, not quasi-professional, criteria.[68] But moves to 'professionalise' the work of councillors appeared to be favoured by government. It was suggested that executive and representational roles could be separated by the use of an executive and salaried 'cabinet' and 'select committees' of backbench councillors fulfilling a scrutiny role.[69]

To move further in the direction of a 'cabinet' requires consideration of how it would be responsible to the full council, and whether the council should become a legislative body with powers to agree the budget and monitor the delivery of services. Additionally, the role of committees, and the relationship between members (both those in the 'executive' and the 'backbenchers') and officers, has to be re-examined. The ward constituency role for local representatives who were not part of the 'executive' would take on increasing importance, and would require proper support and channels of communication within the authority. Councillors as caseworkers already face knowledgeable and increasingly demanding constituents and local groups, and this pressure is likely to increase. As Chapter 3 showed, pressure on councillors leads to a high rate of turnover. Studies by Barron, Crawley and Wood, and by Bloch, have shown that turnover is due in part to the time that council work demands, and the competing demands of families and jobs.[70] This reinforces the need to provide members with more support and different patterns of working. Interestingly, however, work by Game and Leach shows that councillors are also influenced in their decisions to stand down by what they see as the erosion of local government influence, and the financial and other constraints within which it has to work.[71]

Work by the Audit Commission has also emphasised the need for internal change as councils enter the age of more demanding community needs, financial constraints, and a contract and partnership environment.[72] The Commission's analysis revealed that committee work – which takes up some 60 per cent of members' time – concentrated more on operational matters than on policy (which accounted for less than a third of committee items).[73] Increasingly, however, members' role in management is that of policy, strategy and monitoring. The result is a potential division between executive and backbench roles, with more emphasis on a chief political executive (a cabinet) matching an officer chief executive with greater responsibilities.

The call for a strong chief officer executive of this kind goes back to the Audit Commission's 1988 'Competitive Council' paper, which saw this post as pivotal. As the contracting culture spreads, the committee organisation of local councils may give way to management boards of officers, under a strong chief officer, contractually responsible for services to a local authority defined in strategic terms. Right-wing writers have promulgated this 'board of directors' strategic role for some time; from this viewpoint local politicians cease to be vote-maximisers (which favours sectional interests) and become strategic minimalists.[74]

The difficulty with this analysis, however, is the assumption that policy can be sharply differentiated from implementation. This is rarely the case, and again underlines the need to look to the representative and constituency roles of councillors as well as their executive functions. Unless there are reinforced supports for constituency and neighbourhood roles, questions will continue to be raised as to whether people will be willing to serve on local councils under the new 'enabling' conditions. The public service ethos, which elected members claimed as their democratic purpose, sits uneasily alongside the demand that they give primary emphasis to their strategic role. One way in which a new role could emerge is by councillors having a watchdog function in relation to the whole range of services in their areas, including local authority, health service, water and environmental issues generally, and training. This would enable councillors to represent local people more comprehensively, and to voice local issues on a community-wide basis.

Governing the community

The changes consequent on the reform of local government will reinforce the position of local authorities as enablers and facilitators, working through teams of officers and boards of councillors and having overall strategic functions. But the debate goes beyond these changes and their underlying assumptions. The call for a general competence for local authorities is based, rather, on the belief that the authority should govern the community both by providing services directly and by working with other local service providers. A general competence would give local authorities wider opportunities, but it is important primarily because it reflects a different concept of local government whereby the authority represents the community and takes action on its behalf.

At present, local authorities' discretionary powers to provide for the general well-being of their communities are limited. Section 137 of the Local Government Act 1972 (in Scotland, Section 83 of the Local Government (Scotland) Act 1973) gave local authorities the power to incur expenditure in the interests of the area or its inhabitants. Originally limited in amount to the product of a 2 p rate, this was amended at the time of the introduction of the Community Charge, when the amount became population based. Arguments for a broader base for discretionary powers, however, go back to the 1960s.

The argument for a general competence for local authorities was put forward by both the 1967 Maud Committee on Management of Local Government and the 1969 Royal Commission (the Wheatley Commission) Report on Local Government in Scotland. The Maud Committee called for the *ultra vires* rule to be abolished, and both it and the Wheatley Commission proposed a power of general competence giving local authorities the freedom to undertake activities in the interests of their areas. These proposals were not implemented, except in the marginal provisions of Section 137 of the 1972 Act. Grant warns that a power of general competence would not mean the end to *ultra vires*, nor confer general omnipotence. In practice it might mean no more than a general spending power as recommended by the 1969 Royal Commission (the Redcliffe–Maud Commission) on Local Government in England, or Widdicombe's similar idea of extending Section 137 power to incur expenditure in the general interest of the area or its inhabitants, but without a financial limit.[75] Grant is of the view that given that local authorities underspend their Section 137 allowance, and that central government is likely to remain unwilling to allow a general competence power over local financial management, the impact of general competence would be largely symbolic. A preferable approach would be for a local authority to seek relaxation of controls affecting it, and to make a greater use of bye-laws, rather than be granted new rights to override private interests or new powers affecting individual rights.[76]

Stewart argues for wider local discretion, based on consideration of the Scandinavian free-commune idea, by which a number of local authorities are exempt from selected national laws or regulations. This was first established in Sweden; Denmark, Norway and Finland have followed suit. Stewart concludes that a free local authority experiment in Britain would enhance community self-government, release evident capacity for initiative and innovation, and thus improve the climate of central–local relations.[77] Evaluations of the Scandinavian experiments have been mixed. It has been argued that the ability of local governments to assume a more autonomous role has in fact varied, and that central governments continue to maintain a strong oversight. Rose concludes that these experiments were in fact part of a shift from direct to indirect forms of central control rather than an explicit effort to increase local autonomy.[78] The case for experiments along these lines to be tried in Britain continues to be put, however, on the grounds that it would encourage local authorities to discover how flexible a move away from the *ultra vires* rule would prove to be.

Conclusion

As this chapter has shown, the debate on local government is now dominated by the concepts of the enabling authority and the contracting council. The meaning of these concepts differs between left and right, but there are important arguments in support of the notion of community governance that cross the traditional left-liberal/conservative divide. Osborne and Gaebler's *Reinventing Government*, influential in American government circles, indicates the new thinking. Osborne and Gaebler argue that government is not the problem but the solution. Centralised bureaucracies and standard services are failing to meet needs, and governments must use a range of mechanisms to provide services, both public and private, in order to act collectively and shape their communities. Markets and communities must be balanced, and government must be exercised close to its citizens. Thus governments must move away from reliance on large bureaucracies in favour of decentralisation, citizen involvement in service management, and a mix of provisions.[79]

The public's reaction to such moves remains largely unevaluated. In Britain, the research findings of Parry, Moyser and Day showed that more people had a favourable than an unfavourable view of the operations of local government, even though they were sceptical about its capacity to tackle the major tasks, such as inner-city regeneration. A small minority considered the locality well provided for by local government, and a large majority believed that it understood local needs and problems. But Parry, Moyser and Day argue that it would be going too far to say that for most people local politics was the foundation stone of democracy:

people were not participatory-minded to that degree. Nevertheless, those people who looked for change hoped for opportunities that provided them with more say in their local affairs.[80] Research commissioned by the Widdicombe Committee reached similar conclusions. Respondents registered very strong support for the maintenance of locally elected councils, a commitment which is higher among those who are more likely to vote.[81] Respondents had a fairly high level of knowledge of local government, a high level of awareness of local government services and their location (though almost half thought hospital services were a county function), and expressed considerable support for elected local government.[82] At the beginning of the 1990s, however, views appeared to be more mixed, with MORI finding that some 40 per cent of respondents were very or fairly satisfied with county and regional (Scotland) councils, and 49 per cent had the same view of borough and district councils. Over half said that councils were too remote and impersonal.[83]

One of the few theoretical attempts to relate questions of size and democracy, that of Dahl and Tufte, lists the factors on which such debate has centred: citizen participation, security and order, unity and diversity, common interest, loyalties, emotional life, rationality and control of leaders. The ideal polity is that which satisfies at least the two criteria of citizen effectiveness and system capacity.[84] Local governments are more accessible and understandable; they nurture participation and increase the citizen's sense of effectiveness. This supports one of the traditional justifications of local government. The Dahl and Tufte study, however, suggests that to maximise participation and sense of effectiveness may require units very much smaller than is commonly assumed, and these may then not be optimal with respect to other values. Dahl and Tufte thus conclude that no single type or size of unit is optimal for achieving the twin goals of citizen effectiveness and system capacity; there is a need for both small local units below the national level and very large units above it.

In more general terms these calls for a more flexible and 'governing' approach by local authorities, whether this is based on a general competence or on variants of the 'free-commune' model, all show a move away from the local authority conceived in terms of hierarchy (comprehensive service delivery through inclusive bureaucracies) and from market models of competitive provision to what Stoker calls the network model. In the network model organisations learn to co-operate by recognising their mutual dependency, a form of co-operation that is based on trust and reciprocity rather than on hierarchy or market discipline.[85]

If the enabling council is to be the future for local authorities, then questions of how democratic accountability can be maintained will be crucial. If councillors are to control the council's contracting as well as delivery activities, a more open access must be found to encourage individuals and groups to question and hold members to account. Increasingly, councillors will be called on both to monitor the services provided by the council and by other bodies, and to act as advocates for their constituents. Whatever its form, local government remains important for the quality of democratic life, offering accessibility, involvement, and a source of identification. To do this, local government must have enough powers to be responsible and responsive to its community. This echoes the aspiration of Canon Bartlett, writing in 1893 but quoting from an earlier Cobden Club essay: 'A true municipality should completely grasp the life of the community, and in doing so should aim at expressing the communal idea, "One for all, all for one." '[86]

Local governance of this kind, directed at the well-being of the whole community, faces major problems. The health of community governance has been undermined not just by uncertainties over role and function, but has also by two fundamental threats: of unrest, and of physical and economic decay. It is these problems that will be addressed in Chapters 6 and 7.

Notes

1. Royal Commission on Local Government in Greater London, 1957–60 (the Herbert Commission), *Report*, Cmnd 1164 (London: HMSO, 1960), p. 59.
2. Committee of Inquiry into the Conduct of Local Authority Business (Chairman, David Widdicombe QC), *Report*, Cmnd 9797 (London: HMSO, 1986), para. 3.11.
3. *ibid.*, para. 3.35; original emphasis.
4. M. Elliott, 'Constitutional continuity and the position of local government', in K. Young (ed.), *National Interests and Local Government* (London: Heinemann, 1983), pp. 35–48.

5. Local Government Act 1972, S.111.
6. Audit Commission, *Code of Local Government Practice for England and Wales* (London: HMSO, 1984).
7. Department of the Environment, *Policy Guidance* to the Local Government Commission (London: Department of the Environment, 1992).
8. N. Ridley, *The Local Right: Enabling not providing*, Policy Study 92 (London: Centre for Policy Studies, 1988); G. Mather, 'Thatcherism and local government', in J. Stewart and G. Stoker (eds), *The Future of Local Government* (London: Macmillan, 1989), pp. 212–35.
9. D.M. Hill, *Democratic Theory and Local Government* (London: Allen & Unwin, 1974).
10. G.W. Jones and J. Stewart, *The Case for Local Government* (London: Allen & Unwin, 1985).
11. W.J.M. MacKenzie, *Theories of Local Government*, Greater London Papers No.2 (London: London School of Economics and Political Science), 1961; L.J. Sharpe, 'Theories and values of local government', *Political Studies*, Vol. XVIII, 2, 1970, pp. 153–74.
12. Royal Commission on Local Government in England (the Redcliffe–Maud Commission) *Report*, Cmnd 4040 (London: HMSO, 1969); Royal Commission on Local Government in Scotland (the Wheatley Commission), *Report*, Cmnd 4150 (London: HMSO, 1969).
13. Committee of Inquiry into the Conduct of Local Authority Business, *Report*, para. 3.5.
14. *ibid.*, para. 3.7.
15. C.G. Pickvance, 'Introduction: the institutional context of local economic development: central controls, spatial policies and local economic policies', in M. Harloe, C.G. Pickvance and J. Urry (eds), *Place, Policy and Politics* (London: Unwin Hyman, 1990), pp. 1–41; C. Cockburn, *The Local State* (London: Pluto Press, 1977); P. Saunders, 'Rethinking local politics', in M. Boddy and C. Fudge (eds), *Local Socialism* (London: Macmillan, 1984), pp. 22–48; S.S. Duncan and M. Goodwin, *The Local State and Uneven Development* (Cambridge: Polity Press, 1988).
16. Pickvance, 'Introduction: the institutional context of local economic development', pp. 7–11.
17. G. Stoker, 'Creating a local government for a post-Fordist society: the Thatcherite project?', in Stewart and Stoker (eds), *The Future of Local Government*, pp. 141–70; for a critique, see J. Painter, 'Regulation theory and local government', *Local Government Studies*, vol. 17, 6, November/December 1991, pp. 23–44.
18. A. Alexander, 'Managing fragmentation – democracy, accountability and the future of local government', *Local Government Studies*, vol. 17, 6, November/December 1991, p. 64.
19. *ibid.*, pp. 63–76.

20. R. Morris, *Central and Local Control of Education* (London: Longman, 1990); J. Stewart, 'The rebuilding of public accountability', in J. Stewart, N. Lewis and D. Longley, *Accountability to the Public* (London: European Policy Forum, December 1992), pp. 3–13; G. Jones and J. Stewart, 'Selected not elected', *Local Government Chronicle*, 13 November 1992, p. 15.

21. For a discussion of these issues, see G. Jones, 'The search for local accountability', in S. Leach (ed.), *Strengthening Local Government in the 1990s* (Harlow: Longman, 1992), pp. 49–78.

22. B. Colenutt and G. Ellis, 'The next quangos in London', *New Statesman and Society*, 26 March 1993, pp. 20–1; 'Boosting the Tories', *New Statesman and Society*, 30 July 1993, p. 20.

23. For an analysis of new right and new left approaches, see D.S. King, 'The new right, the new left and local government', in Stewart and Stoker (eds), *The Future of Local Government*, pp. 185–211.

24. J. Gyford, *The Politics of Local Socialism* (London: Allen & Unwin, 1988); D. Blunkett and K. Jackson, *Democracy in Crisis: The town halls respond* (London: The Hogarth Press, 1987); S. Lansley, S. Goss and C. Wolmar, *Councils in Conflict: The rise and fall of the municipal left* (London: Macmillan, 1989).

25. I. Holliday, 'The new suburban right in British local government – Conservative views of the local', *Local Government Studies*, vol. 17, 6, November/December 1991, pp. 45–62.

26. *ibid.*, p. 59.

27. G. Stoker, 'Regulation theory, local government and the transition from Fordism', in D.S. King and J. Pierre (eds), *Challenges to Local Government* (London: Sage, 1991), p. 260.

28. J. Gyford, 'Diversity, sectionalism and local democracy', Chapter 4 of Committee of Inquiry into the Conduct of Local Authority Business, Research Volume IV, *Aspects of Local Democracy*, Cmnd 9801 (London: HMSO, 1986), p. 106.

29. R.A.W. Rhodes, *Control and Power in Central–Local Government Relations* (Farnborough: Gower, 1981); R.A.W. Rhodes, 'Continuity and change in British central–local relations: the "Conservative Threat", 1979–83', *British Journal of Political Science*, vol. 14, 1984, pp. 261–83; R.A.W. Rhodes, *Beyond Westminster and Whitehall* (London: Unwin Hyman, 1988); P. Dunleavy and R.A.W. Rhodes, 'Government beyond Whitehall', in H. Drucker, P. Dunleavy, A. Gamble and G. Peele, *Development in British Government 2* (London: Macmillan, 1988), pp. 107–43.

30. T.R. Gurr and D.S. King, *The State and the City* (Chicago: The Chicago Press, 1987).

31. See, for example, M. Goldsmith and H. Wolman, *Urban Politics and Policy* (Oxford: Basil Blackwell, 1992).

32. Rhodes, 'Continuity and change in British central–local relations'.
33. T. Travers, 'So you think there's been a revolution?', *Local Government Chronicle*, 27 March 1992, pp. 16–17.
34. Audit Commission, *Passing the Bucks: The impact of Standing Spending Assessments on economy, efficiency and effectiveness* (London: HMSO, 1993), vol. 2, 'Appendices', tables A3.2–A3.7.
35. *ibid.*, vol. 1, pp. 1–2.
36. At the end of 1993 the Local and Central Government Relations Research Committee of the Joseph Rowntree Foundation began funding research on local government finance, including the search for new forms of revenue and of capital finance. See also C. Carter with P. John, *A New Accord: Promoting constructive relations between central and local government* (York: Joseph Rowntree Foundation, February 1992).
37. *The Conduct of Local Authority Business*, The Gov [sic] Response to the Report of the Widdicombe Committee of Inquiry, Cm 433 (London: HMSO, 1988).
38. K. Young and M. Davies, *The Politics of Local Government Since Widdicombe* (York: Joseph Rowntree Foundation, 1990).
39. *Local Government Chronicle*, 19 March 1993, p. 2.
40. A. Norton, *The Principle of Subsidiarity and Its Implications for Local Government* (Luton: The Local Government Management Board/ Institute of Local Government Studies, University of Birmingham, 6 April 1992).
41. For a detailed insight into these issues, see P. Roberts, K. Thomas, T. Hart and A. Campbell, *Local Authorities and 1992* (Manchester: The Centre for Local Economic Strategies [CLES], 1990).
42. L.J. Sharpe (ed.), *The Local Fiscal Crisis in Western Europe: Myths and realities* (London: Sage, 1981), p. 5.
43. Department of Health, *Community Care in the Next Decade and Beyond* (London: HMSO, 1991).
44. *The Future of Local Government: What should it look like?* (London: Labour Party Local Government Unit, 1993).
45. R. Brooke, 'The enabling authority: practical consequences', *Local Government Studies*, vol. 15, 5, September/October 1989, pp. 55–63; *Managing the Enabling Authority* (London: Longman/Local Government Training [now Management] Board, 1989).
46. M. Clarke and J. Stewart, *Challenging Old Assumptions: The enabling council takes shape* (Luton: Local Government Training [now Management] Board, 1989), p. 1.
47. G. Jones and J. Stewart, 'Support strategy', *Local Government Chronicle*, 19 June 1992, p. 15.
48. Audit Commission, *The Competitive Council*, Management Paper No. 1 (London: HMSO, March 1988).

49. *ibid.*, p. 9. See also *More Equal Than Others: The chief executive in local government*, Management Paper No. 2 (London: HMSO, January 1989).

50. *The Structure of Local Government* (London: Department of the Environment, 23 April 1991).

51. 'Districts lose in Durham and gain in Cleveland', *Local Government Chronicle*, 14 May 1993, p. 3.

52. *The Future Local Government of Cleveland and Durham: A report to local people* (London: The Local Government Commission for England, May 1993).

53. Department of the Evironment, *Policy Guidance to the Local Government Commission*, paras. 10, 11; and Annex B: 'Local Government Functions: Considerations Relevant To Structural Change'.

54. J. Arnold-Foster, 'Review rolls on but change of direction promised', *Local Government Chronicle*, 16 July 1993, p. 5; 'Reorganisation to be complete by 1996', *Local Government Chronicle*, 10 September 1993, p. 1.

55. G. Jones and J. Stewart, 'Rush to the border', *Local Government Chronicle*, 12 November 1993, p. 10.

56. N. Willmore, 'Welsh districts fight alone against cuts in members', *Local Government Chronicle*, 3 September 1993, p. 4. The Welsh Office's proposals were based on one council member to 2,000 electors, compared with the existing one county member for each 4,400 electors and one district member for each 1,500 electors. See N. Willmore, 'Counties plan new option for Wales', *Local Government Chronicle*, 23 July 1993, p. 7.

57. *Local Government in Wales: A charter for the future* (London/Cardiff: DoE/Welsh Office, March 1993).

58. Scottish Office, *Shaping the Future – The new councils*, Cm 2267 (Edinburgh: HMSO, July 1993).

59. *Towards Regional Government and Local Government Reform* (London: The Labour Party, 1989); J. Simmie, 'A single-tier solution', *Town and Country Planning*, vol. 60, 4, April 1991, pp. 108–9.

60. Department of the Environment, *Policy Guidance to the Local Government Commission*, para. 18; Consultation Paper, 'The role of parish and town councils in England' (London: Department of the Environment, 1992).

61. 'New unitary authorities: a model for the future?', *LGIU Briefing No. 71*, July 1993, p. 4.

62. The Local Government (Choice of Electoral Systems) Bill 1985.

63. C. Rallings and M. Thrasher, 'Democracy needs a health audit', *Local Government Chronicle*, 13 March 1992, pp. 20–1.

64. V. Bogdanor, 'Electoral systems in local government', *The Future Role and Organisation of Local Government Study Paper No. 4* (Birmingham: Institute of Local Government Studies, August 1986).

65. Local Government Review, *The Internal Management of Local Authorities in England. A consultation paper* (London: Department of the Environment, July 1991).

66. Committee on the Management of Local Government (the Maud Committee), *Management of Local Government*, vol. 1, Report of the Committee (London: HMSO, 1967).

67. *Community Leadership and Representation: Unlocking the potential*, Report of the Working Party on the Internal Management of Local Authorities in England, July 1993 (London: HMSO, 1993).

68. For a discussion of this issue, see J. Benington and M. Taylor, 'The renewal of quality in the political process', in I. Sanderson (ed.), *Management of Quality in Local Government* (Harlow: Longman, 1992), pp. 164–86.

69. P. Wintour, 'Trial to tempt higher calibre councillors', *The Guardian*, 10 April 1993.

70. J. Barron, G. Crawley and T. Wood, *Councillors in Crisis: The public and private worlds of local councillors* (London: Macmillan, 1991); A. Bloch, *The Turnover of Local Councillors* (York: Joseph Rowntree Foundation, 1992).

71. C. Game and S. Leach, 'The recruitment, retention and turnover of elected members', (Birmingham: INLOGOV/Local Government Management Board, mimeo, nd [1993]).

72. Audit Commission *The Competitive Council*; *We Can't Go On Meeting Like This: The changing role of local authority members*, Management Paper No. 8, 1990 (London: HMSO, 1990).

73. Audit Commission, *We Can't Go On Meeting Like This*, pp. 6–7.

74. G. Mather, 'Thatcherism and local government: an evaluation', in Stewart and Stoker (eds), *The Future of Local Government*, pp. 212–35; *Wiser Counsels* (London: Adam Smith Institute, 1989).

75. M. Grant, 'The case for diversity in local government', in C. Crawford and C. Grace (eds), *'Conducive Or Incidental To . . .'? Local authority discretionary powers in the modern era* (Birmingham: Institute of Local Government Studies/Faculty of Law, University of Birmingham, June 1992), pp. 36–48.

76. *ibid.*

77. J. Stewart, *An Experiment in Freedom: The case for free local authorities in Britain*, Constitution Paper No. 2 (London: Institute for Public Policy Research, 1991).

78. L.E. Rose, 'Nordic free-commune experiments: increased local autonomy or continued central control?', in King and Pierre (eds), *Challenges to Local Government*, pp. 212–33.

79. D. Osborne and T. Gaebler, *Reinventing Government: How the entrepreneurial spirit is transforming the public sector* (Reading, Mass.: Addison-Wesley, 1992).

80. G. Parry, G. Moyser and N. Day, *Political Participation and Democracy in Britain* (Cambridge: Cambridge University Press, 1990), pp. 410–11.
81. K. Young, 'Attitudes to local government', Chapter 5 of Committee of Inquiry into the Conduct of Local Authority Business (the Widdicombe Committee), Research Volume III, *The Local Government Elector*, Cmnd 9800, tables 5.6–5.8, pp. 64–7.
82. *ibid.*, pp. 99–100.
83. C. Maclure, 'Behind British Rail in the popularity polls', *Local Government Chronicle*, 16 August 1991, p. 5.
84. R.A. Dahl and E.R. Tufte, *Size and Democracy* (Stanford, CA: Stanford University Press/London: Oxford University Press, 1974), p. 20.
85. G. Stoker, *The Politics of Local Government*, 2nd edn (London: Macmillan, 1991), pp. 265–6.
85. Canon Bartlett, 'The ideal city', in H.E. Meller (ed.), *The Ideal City* (Leicester: Leicester University Press, 1979), p. 65.

CHAPTER 6

DISORDER AND UNREST: THE UNCIVIL CITY

Introduction

Dislocations in civic society are the obverse of the praised values of community and citizenship. Twice in the 1980s disorder erupted into major urban riots, with further unrest in the early 1990s. The violence in 'inner cities' has become a major element in urban policy responses, in law-and-order mechanisms, and in relations between sections of the city and between races. Analysts of the right and the left, however, disagree on the causes and outcomes of urban disorder. To those on the right, explanations lie in individual behaviour and moral values,[1] and remedies must be sought in appropriate law-and-order policy. To those on the left, unrest and riot arise in the context of multiple deprivation, and unrest is evidence of policy failure. Solutions must both combat crime and remove the underlying causes of alienation and inequality.

Two further elements have been central to the debate. The first is that of race relations and the extent to which disorder and crime are concentrated both spatially and in terms of specific ethnic groups. The question then arises of the extent to which Britain is approaching the 'ghettoisation' of crime, including that associated with drugs, evident in the United States. The American literature on crime and the underclass illustrates how dramatically certain neighbourhoods are set aside by their levels of crime and drug activity. Explanations of these phenomena centre on violent and disruptive behaviour, and on social dislocation caused by the absence of middle-class institutions, role models and networks.[2] The result is a pathology not only of social life but of individual behaviour, putting individuals and areas outside mainstream society values.

The second central element in the debate is the policing of civic unrest, the relations between the police, local authorities and local neighbourhoods, and the allied questions of police responsibility and accountability. Underlying these questions, argues Lord Scarman, is the need to recognise that the core of the problem is injustice: 'in any society where there is a substantial minority of fellow citizens labouring under a sense of injustice you will get urban unrest – and you may get much more'.[3] This injustice has an important racial dimension. Policy must tackle the crisis of the inner cities not because of the fear of conflict but because of the need to affirm justice.[4] The concern here is that the disaffected do not identify with a society which appears to reject them, and that policy responses may degenerate into containment rather than real change. Fears grow, says Ravetz, that sections of the city 'seem to be slipping out of control, dominated by unemployment, violence and fear of crime, and ignored by the good citizens who drive through them, just as godly men of property once ignored the Victorian poor'.[5]

These issues are examined in this chapter: the history of the disorders of the 1980s; crime and the inner cities; issues of ethnicity; police–community relations; accountability; and law-and-order mechanisms.

The disorders of the 1980s

The 1980s witnessed major riots in London, Liverpool, Bristol, Birmingham and other cities. The unrest was the subject of major inquiries (the 1981 Scarman Inquiry in Brixton; the 1985 Silverman Inquiry in Handsworth/Lozells; and the 1986 unofficial Gifford Inquiry into the Broadwater Farm Estate) and a series of 'inner-city' policy initiatives. If the unrest was inexplicable to some, others pointed to the long history of violence in British cities going back to the beginnings of the Industrial Revolution, seeing it as the weapon of the excluded and the powerless. The obverse of this violence was the picture of the police forced into twin policies of containment and community involvement: trying to control escalating situations with a combination of riot units and new hardware in an arguably paramilitary response on the one hand, and to institute community policing on the other.

A common theme in the analysis of the riots was that whatever the context – deprived areas, economically and racially disadvantaged individuals, crime levels – a major triggering factor was the police handling of what they regarded as standard and routine operations such as searches and arrests, and what those affected believed was harassment. What was evident was a significant deterioration in police–community relations prior to the riots. Essentially, argue Waddington, Jones and Critcher, this deterioration arose out of situations over who had the right to be on the streets, on what terms and under whose conditions.[6] A parallel can be drawn with the findings of the Kerner Commission into the causes of the major riots in the United States which erupted in the summer of 1967. The 1968 Kerner Report pointed to situations where increasing tension over community–police relations spilled over into violent confrontation, often as a result of a single police incident.[7]

The events and responses of the 1980s began with the unrest in the St Paul's district of Bristol in April 1980, followed by the violent disturbances in Brixton, in the London Borough of Lambeth, in April 1981. This was followed in July and August of that year by disturbances in Southall, Liverpool (Toxteth), Manchester (Moss Side), Birmingham (Handsworth), and other urban centres. Four years later violence resurfaced. In September 1985 the riot in the Lozells Road area of Handsworth in Birmingham resulted in the death of two Asian shopkeepers, and there were disturbances in other cities, one of which was again in the St Paul's area of Bristol. Violence erupted again in Brixton (following the search of the house of Mrs Cherry Groce, in which she was accidentally shot and permanently injured), Toxteth and, in October 1985, on the Broadwater Farm Estate in Tottenham, following the collapse and death of Mrs Cynthia Jarrett from natural causes during a police search of her house. In the Broadwater Farm riot Police Constable Keith Blakelock was stabbed to death. Further disturbances continued throughout the remainder of the 1980s (though with considerably reduced media interest). When violence again broke out in 1991 and 1992, on peripheral estates as well as inner areas, it was marked, as on the Hartcliffe estate of Bristol in July 1992, by confrontation between police and young people (predominantly white) on run-down estates and, on at least two occasions, following deaths after police car chases or other joyriding incidents and car crime.

The government's response to the disorders of the 1980s was that it was criminality, not deprivation or disaffection, which was the cause of the riots. In 1985 a Home Office Minister said that contributing factors were 'hostility to the police, criminal opportunism, and a general alienation from authority in areas with special social problems'.[8] This stance was reiterated following the Meadow Well riots in Tyneside in September 1991, which the government blamed on criminal elements and the breakdown of parental authority. It dismissed suggestions that poverty was to blame (while at the same time the new Archbishop of Canterbury, Dr George Carey, was blaming social deprivation, poor housing and illiteracy), though there was some moderation of this view following the publication of Home Office data in 1993.

Other perspectives in the 1980s focused particularly on the issue of youth and crime. It was argued that unemployment and school dropout led to a situation where unoccupied youths were just hanging around on the streets, leading to friction with the police. Calls for the police to combat crime then exacerbated this situation into further friction. This kind of situation was evident even where, as in the Lozells area of Birmingham, the scene of rioting in 1985, massive efforts had been invested in a community policing project.[9] This pattern was repeated elsewhere. In London the post-Scarman emphasis on community policing did not avert the 1985 riots.

Underlining the tension between communities and the police were the arguably conflicting roles of the police as liaising and consulting with local people while being essentially agents of the state. In many areas the police found themselves in a difficult position. Community policing cannot be sustained when drug trafficking becomes obtrusive, and demands from the general public that the police combat the drugs trade can lead to confrontation with local communities over searches, arrests and raids, and over what drugs activity should be targeted (for example, over the 'ganga culture' of Rastafarians versus cocaine trafficking). The Scarman Report, for example, adjudged the history of the relations between the police and the residents of Brixton a failure. Although there were faults on both sides, police attitudes and tactics had aggravated the situation. The recommended solutions included tightening police discipline in relation to racially prejudiced or discriminatory behaviour, increasing consultation, increasing accountability through lay vistors to police stations, more independent investigation of serious complaints, and narrowing the scope of highly discretionary powers.[10]

Gifford argued, by contrast, that the assertion that there were two opposing concepts of policing based on notions of a police force or a police service was false.[11] People in deprived communities want effective police action against serious crime. The independent inquiry conducted by Lord Gifford into the Broadwater Farm disturbances stated that the causes were related to the failed initiatives in police–community relations, with the immediate precipitating cause being the sequence of events which started with the arrest of Floyd Jarrett and the search of his mother's house, during which Mrs Jarrett collapsed and died.[12]

Assertions by those on the left that deprivation was the prime cause of the disorders of the 1980s was as simplistic a response as the right's belief that individual criminality and moral turpitude were to blame. Nor were 'community' analyses unambiguous. Broadwater Farm, for example, had been regarded before the 1985 riots as a model estate administered by neighbourhood offices rather than by a remote town hall (the Priority Estates Project of the Department of the Environment). At the same time, however, it was castigated as a design disaster, with flats that were difficult to let and problems of unemployment, single-parent families and a high crime rate. More sustainable explanations of the riots were that while, as Scarman himself had argued, the immediate problem was young black people's outburst of anger against the police, this had taken place within conditions of unemployment, deprivation, racial disadvantage and political exclusion.

Benyon, Solomos, Taylor and others have suggested that there are three distinct perspectives on the riots of the 1980s: the conservative, the liberal and the radical.[13] The conservative perspective stresses that individual action, not social and political structures, is to blame. Disorder is an unjustified aberration atributable to criminal elements, and to loss of discipline and respect for authority. This perspective stresses that society already provides adequate political mechanisms for all groups, and rioting is therefore irrational. The liberal approach focuses on the conditions of disadvantage and discrimination, and on a political system which does not represent all demands adequately or fairly. The radical view is that violence is a rational protest for those who are politically excluded, with no other avenues of redress against injustice. Radicals thus believe that only a fundamental transformation of economic, social and political structures will remove the root causes of violence.

All three perspectives were used to try to explain the unrest of the 1980s, with the conservative view predominating among the police and parts of the media, the Scarman Report tending to the liberal view, and the radical explanation by some left-wing and community leaders.[14] In the 1990s there were additional explanations based on 'fashion' or 'association' – for example, those that looked at rising youth crime in the form of increased joyriding incidents in several areas of urban unrest stretching from Oxford (the Blackbird Leys estate) to Tyneside (the Meadow Well estate). Another sociological approach, which appeared to be endorsed by sections of both right and left, argued that there were clear links between family breakdown and social disorder. This view was put forward by Dennis and Erdos, who argued that it was family breakdown, not poverty and unemployment, that underlay the Meadow Well rioting of 1991.[15]

The analysis of the causes of urban violence by Benyon and Solomos, by contrast, stresses predisposing conditions: racial disadvantage and discrimination; high youth unemployment; deprivation; political exclusion; hostility to the police. But in addition there are crucial characteristics which help to translate these predisposing conditions into violence. These include ineffective government programmes for the inner cities, particularly where these have raised expectations which are then unfulfilled; a subcultural identity which runs counter to prevailing values; low opportunities for participation; a declining perception of the legitimacy of the political system, and – the central theme – social injustice.[16] What have to be set aside are media distortions that criminal opportunists – extremists coming in from other areas – were a major element. Similarly, over a third of those arrested in the aftermath of the 1981 Toxteth riots were not unemployed. It appeared that individual experience of unemployment was not itself a causal factor; rather, the sense of grievance which unemployment as a whole gave to the riot community was the key.[17]

Other research has shown that explanations of disorder based on police–ethnic community confrontation of the kind that emerged after the Toxteth and Brixton riots must be treated with caution. Benyon points out that data for the July riots of 1981 suggest that large majority of rioters were white.[18] In Liverpool, white and minority groups participated in the riot in proportion to their representation in the population as a whole; it was a Toxteth riot, not an ethnic one. Conflicts between ethnic groups, rather than between these groups and the police, have been a notable element of only a minority of disturbances; for example, in the confrontation between local Asians and white skinheads in Southall in July 1981, and that between rioters and Asian shopkeepers on the Meadow Well estate, North Shields, in September 1991. In the latter case this had followed the original incident in which two 'joyriders' had died during a police chase some three days earlier.

The sources of unrest

Policy responses to the riots of the 1980s were a mix of programmes aimed at urban regeneration and the strengthening of police powers and consultative procedures. But while governments in the 1980s argued that riots were an aberration without justification, critics argued that tension was endemic, fostered by economic, ethnic and social divisions. These tensions were particularly evident in run-down areas of cities, within the urban core and on peripheral estates.

By the 1980s the defects of the public housing estates built in the 1960s, and their settings as areas of deprivation and crime, had been acknowledged. As Robins observes, life in the large-scale estates has been far removed from the ideals promoted when the housing was built. Moreover, the estates are not homogeneous communities but are divided by religion, race, generation, and sometimes language. High rates of unemployment among the young, and poor transport and facilities, have led to a high level of incivility, marked by harassment of other residents by young people, crime, and long-running friction with the police. The divisions within such communities produce both purposive involvement and a criminal subculture, a mixture of street life and participation, self-help and militancy.[19]

To conservatives on both sides of the Atlantic the underclass threatened to become, if it was not synonymous with, the dangerous class. As such it was not only socially and economically marginalised, but unconstrained by the moral values of society. This idea has a long history, re-emerging in the postwar literature with Edward Banfield's *The Unheavenly City*, which argued that the culture of poverty in the urban ghetto was marked by crime among irresponsible young males and a general lack of mainstream values of work, family life and education.[20] Neoconservatives, while they disagreed with Banfield and other traditional conservatives that nothing could be done, held the common conservative belief that the underclass was a product of behavioural and attitudinal problems rather than, as liberals argued, socioeconomic structural ones (see above, Chapter 4). An alternative perspective on ghetto crime has rejected the neoconservative emphasis on behaviour and attitudes of the most disadvantaged in favour of the role that criminals play in perpetuating the underclass problem. DiIulio maintains that underclass neighbourhoods are disadvantaged because of the large number of street criminals in their midst. These criminals both victimise their neighbours directly and worsen the social and economic ills of the ghetto.[21]

The causes of crime remain problematic. Criminological explanations reject a causal relation between urban decay and delinquency, while recognising a strong correlation between them. Nor are the extreme conditions of the American ghetto, its racial concentrations, physical decay, or social deprivation, to be found in Britain. But in the British situation there are concerns that there is a persistent problem of deprivation, criminality and potential unrest; these concerns have in turn led to debate on policies of containment and amelioration. Although there are no simple causal explanations, violent crime is correlated with other indicators of urban decay and poverty associated with the inner city, including unemployment, family breakdown, poor educational attainment, deteriorated housing, and ethnic concentration.

British research reveals the association between crime and area. The British Crime Survey, using the ACORN classification which assigns every home in the country to one of eleven groups according to the demographic, employment and housing characteristics of its immediate location, reveals the degree of risk of crime associated with different urban areas. Residents of the poorest council estates face a risk of burglary that is 2.8 times the average. Poor council estates, mixed inner metropolitan areas (and high-status non-family areas) were also high-risk areas for autocrime and robbery/theft from the person.[22] Of households in the highest risk ACORN neighbourhoods, 50 per cent live in inner-city locations.[23] These figures, which are based on survey data and cover crimes which go unreported to the police, must be distinguished from recorded crime data. In 1993 reported crime rates appeared to be rising faster in rural shire counties than in inner-city areas, and explanations became a matter of dispute between those who argued that the effects of unemployment and relative disadvantage were spreading, and those who favoured opportunity factors such as proximity to motorway networks and adjacent metropolitan areas.

Analysis of crime based on spatial factors has revealed mixed outcomes. While city centres may be revitalised, they often adjoin areas where deprivation and crime have increased. The spatial problems become exacerbated as crime and the fear of crime isolate deprived areas still further. Those who can leave the area do so, and neighbourhoods and estates suffer from 'labelling'. The problem then becomes circular. Not only is there a self-selection process as people move away, but the worst-affected estates become the repository for the 'problem' families.[24] Nevertheless, it remains difficult to demonstrate the sequence of cause and effect linking urban decay to changes in crime levels because of the multiple factors involved. Hope and Foster's work on how design and management factors affected crime levels in a 'problem' housing estate shows the important effect of the social mix of an area.[25] Important variations in estate culture between different groups, notably between the longer-established and 'respectable' tenants and the more vulnerable and 'problem' families, particularly those composed of young single occupants of flats, had a marked effect on incivility. Concentrating large numbers of vulnerable people in an already stressed environment led to further concentrations of criminality. The internal culture of the estate mediated the causal influences on crime (deprivation, vulnerable groups, urban decay) such that changes to environmental design, management and social mix encouraged both informal social control and criminality.

Part of the crime debate addresses the relation between deprivation and delinquency among young people. Work done in Scotland disputes the charge that there is a delinquent underclass of young people, concentrated in inner-city ghettos and associated with a dependency culture. While the rate of offending was marginally higher in the most deprived areas of Edinburgh, where the research was conducted, the pattern was effectively constant across social class. Two of the often-accepted indicators of dependency culture, welfare dependency and housing tenure, were not strongly correlated with offending. The picture became more complex, however, when family structure was considered. While children from two-parent homes were less likely to offend, the rate of offending in both single- and two-parent families rose where any adult was in full-time employment, with children of working single mothers most likely to commit offences.[26] The association – even if the government has denied that a causal link exists – between poverty, unemployment and family breakdown and crime remains a major concern of research. There does appear to be a link between rising crime and the state of the economy, and research commissioned by the Association of Chief Officers of Probation revealed that young offenders were invariably poor, had low educational attainment, and were likely to leave home at an early age, and be unemployed.[27]

The issues of crime, locality and race are made more complex by incidents involving firearms and drugs. These problems were highlighted by the shooting of 14-year-old John 'Benji' Stanley in the Moss Side estate, Manchester, on 2 January 1993. Moss Side is an area of high unemployment (40 per cent in early 1993, with a rate of 80 per cent among young Afro-Caribbeans). It is also the centre of Manchester's drugs trade, with police conducting major raids and arrests, and recovering hand guns, shotguns and other weapons. Guns are increasingly being used by petty as well as major offenders, and are frequently associated with drugs crimes. In major urban areas the drugs problem has been associated with deprivation, high unemployment, particularly among youth, and multi-problem mass housing estates. The police have combined major national and international efforts to combat drugs misuse with low-level enforcement strategies, with policing at neighbourhood level being seen as part of drugs prevention strategies as well as part of crime control. In recent years the move to smaller Basic Command Units in the police force and the stress on working more closely with the community have reinforced this strategy, but it is the difficulty of drugs-related crime, rather than drugs misuse prevention, which has received most emphasis.

Dealing and drugs use in deprived neighbourhoods creates a violent and fearful environment in which local people are preyed upon by dealers and criminals. It is local people who suffer most from these activities. As the areas deteriorate further, those who can leave do so. While closer collaboration between the police and other agencies might contribute to preventive and rehabilitative strategies, the emphasis is still on the need for the police to target drugs-related crime to protect the general well-being of the community and control the potentially escalating violence associated with drugs. If this is to succeed, support from the community is needed. Where community support breaks down, drugs raids can lead to conflict between the police and local residents, accusations of heavy-handed police tactics and potentially serious disorder.

The urban environment is also a place of potential high risk for women. Work carried out by the Home Office Safer Cities Project has shown how the fear of attack has affected women's access to town centres, public transport, and leisure facilities. The response to these problems has come from local initiatives, particularly in London, where the former Greater London Council set up women's committees and tried to address transport and other problems, and from the government's Safer Cities programme. The object of both local and central policy responses to the problem of the crime risk to women was to improve safety as part of the improvement of the quality of community life, and to protect the economic vigour of central locations. The policy responses included improving public transport, better public lighting of car parks and other public spaces, enhanced surveillance of residential environments, and planning design improvements derived from Newman's 'defensible space' proposals.[28] One outcome of these proposals has been the liaison between some police forces and local authorities over crime prevention schemes at the planning stage. As a result, crime preventional design guidelines have been produced in a number of authorities, and these guidelines can become desiderata in the granting of planning permission.[29]

A policy response aimed specifically at problems of particular groups and the inner cities has been the Safer Cities programme, established as part of the Action for Cities Project of 1988. By 1992 there were twenty Safer Cities Project areas, including a number of London boroughs. The projects were part of a local–central partnership, with each project area guided by a steering group with members from the local authority, police, probation, voluntary organisations, ethnic minorities, business, and representatives of Task Forces and City Action Teams where appropriate. The three main aims of the Safer Cities initiative were to reduce crime, to lessen the fear of crime, and 'to create safer cities where economic enterprise and community life can flourish'.[30] In January 1993, twenty new Safer Cities projects were announced. The guaranteed Home Office funding for sixteen of the twenty earlier projects will end in 1994, but the hope is that they will continue with local backing. These developments also reflect the continued advocacy of the multi-agency approach to crime control, though this itself has not been without difficulty. The different agencies involved have differing methods of organisation and various professional perspectives. These differences, and the potential police dominance of the agenda, can create conflict even where there is implicit consensus over the need to co-operate in local initiatives.

Malaise and the multi-ethnic city

Problems of unrest, and of relations between the police and different areas and groups, have a potent spatial dimension. The relation between race, community and neighbourhood has been a powerful symbol of the nature of spatial differentiation in the city. Historically, the London and West Midlands conurbations have been areas of high concentration of ethnic minorities. Within major urban centres minorities have been further concentrated in inner areas. There is a high degree of geographical clustering of ethnic minority households, but it is still the case that the majority of such households live in enumeration districts with predominantly white populations.[31] These patterns arose as the result of employment factors, and were reinforced by local authority housing policies as well as the mutually supportive environments sought by many of the first immigrants.[32]

Over time, movement out of these initially settled areas, and upward movement within the housing market, made the patterns of concentration more complex, and more varied as between the Caribbean and Asian groups. While Afro-Caribbeans have moved into the council housing sector, Asians have been concentrated at the bottom end of the owner-occupier market. This has resulted in high racial segration, which Henderson and Karn believe has become entrenched.[33] Disadvantage and harassment are also spatially concentrated, with over a quarter of racially motivated incidents reported to the police taking place on local authority housing estates. In addition, Asians have a disproportionate likelihood of being victims of crimes such as vandalism and victimisation by groups of strangers.[34] Both Afro-Caribbeans and Asians are more at risk from crime than whites. This is largely explained by social and demographic factors, and the areas in which they live. For their part, Afro-Caribbeans, and particularly Asians, see many offences against them as being racially motivated.[35]

The difficulties arising from minority concentration have been reinforced by the changes in employment and access to it. Industrial changes and the declining demand for unskilled and semi-skilled labour, together with the movement of business and industry out of the inner areas, have affected minority employment particularly severely. The issue of minority disadvantage in employment is a combination of several factors, including racism, education and skill levels, the state of the labour market, and geographical mobility. These factors are combined with class differences to reinforce discrimination outcomes.

While equal opportunity legislation and practices may widen access for the few to professional and business positions (and to those in politics and the arts), the majority remain trapped in areas with poor housing, and with severely depressed labour markets for unskilled and semi-skilled industrial work. This remains so even though a significant proportion of young Afro-Caribbeans and Asians aspire to skilled jobs. It is not necessarily true that school leavers from these groups have poorer qualifications than whites. They are in fact more likely than inner-city whites to possess modest qualifications and to be moderately ambitious – but hence the greater gap between their aspirations and the opportunities available. The frustrations of all young people in high-unemployment areas are thus particularly strong among ethnic minorities, as research into urban unrest and unemployment has stressed.[36]

As a result of these configurations, inter-areal and intergroup relations have frequently been cast in interracial terms. From the 1950s onwards, when postwar immigration, particularly from the new commonwealth, began to have an impact in the major industrial cities, questions of race relations became a major part of local as well as national policy. At local level, three main issues dominated debate: the access of different groups to public services, particularly housing; employment practices; the establishment of consultative and advisory mechanisms either of a multiracial kind or directed at specific minority groups. In the area of differential access to public services, local policies led to the concentration of minorities in declining areas or on the least desirable housing estates.[37] In employment, however, discrimination against minority workers eventually resulted in statutory equal opportunities legislation.

In the 1980s, local authorities became actively engaged in equal opportunities work as a response to Section 71 of the Race Relations Act 1976, which required local authorities to carry out their duties with regard to the need to eliminate unlawful racial discrimination and to promote equality of opportunity and good relations between members of different racial groups. In the area of consultation and advice, policies have been much more contentious. In the 1970s it was argued that the initiatives which local authorities had built up – special officers to deal with immigrants' problems, the use of the Section 11 (Local Government Act 1966) and Urban Programme projects (the 1969 Local Government Grants (Special Need) Act), the establishment of voluntary Community Relations Councils – were no longer adequate. They served to demonstrate, it was alleged, the marginality of such issues within the local political system. Additionally, such measures were arguably part of the stereotyping of minorities as 'a problem'.

The 1980s also saw much more assertive and confrontational approaches by minority groups and by black political leaders, particularly in London and other major cities. For their part, some local authorities, notably the former Greater London Council, became more active in supporting minority groups and in emphasising a decentralised and more participatory local political culture.

Such situations were given a high profile in the media, and led to partisan political conflict over the action of 'left' Labour councils in combating racism. While some solid gains were made in hiring practices within local authorities and in promoting equality of access to and benefits from services, the financial constraints of the later 1980s and early 1990s, and the changing 'enabling' culture of the competitive council, have cast doubt on the extent of these gains. So too has the issue of multiculturalism in education and the wider, but rather different, debate on the wish of some groups to remain apart from dominant cultural values, for example, the establishment of separate schools by Muslim communities and the arguments about 'integration' which this has raised.

The issue of the areal component of social problems is made more complex by the divisions and segmentation within neighbourhoods. Different sectional interests within an area make claims to represent all or part of the neighbourhood, and separate associations may emerge to represent different groups, divided on class and/or race lines. 'Communities' can become ethnically defensive, resenting incomers who are regarded as 'other'. Alternatively, within areas, divisions between disadvantaged groups can become as marked as those between deprived areas and the rest of the city. The 1985 riots in Handsworth, for example, revealed tension between moderate Asian leaders and moderate Afro-Caribbeans following destruction of commercial properties by ethnic minority and white youths.[38] These divisions may result in conflict over resources, access to services, and political representation. One result has been the reluctance of minority groups to become too closely associated with local public bodies, and a questioning of their claims to speak for minorities. This delegitimation is reinforced by the alleged tokenism of the small numbers of minority members holding posts or elected office on local councils, at senior levels of the local bureaucracy, or in the police force. Conflict may also arise within a minority community on a generational basis, for example, between organisations representing traditional social concerns and unattached youth.

The concentration of unrest and disorder in spatial terms has been associated with urban decay and deprived neighbourhoods, but the incidence of violence involving aspects of race is made more complex by issues of stereotyping, racial attacks and harassment. There is a perception that delinquency and disorder are concentrated among young males from minority groups. This perception goes back to the late 1960s and was reinforced by the urban disorders of the 1980s, particularly in popular media images.[39] But the view went beyond certain sections of the media. For example, as Solomos notes, the Scarman Report 'used the image of the rootless black youngster as a visible symbol of the despair and injustice suffered in areas such as Brixton'.[40]

In practice, minority groups are themselves the target of attacks. Home Office data show that the number of racial attacks in Britain grew from 4383 in 1988 to 7780 in 1991. Many incidents go unreported, and the real figure is thought to be far higher.[41] Although it is Asian communities which have commonly been subject to racial harassment,[42] other groups have also been affected and the problem itself is not new to the 1980s. The government has stressed the need for the police to respond effectively to racial incidents and to co-operate with other bodies in a multi-agency approach to combat racial attacks and harassment.[43] Assumptions that views of crime vary between different ethnic groups must also be treated with care. *The Second Islington Crime Survey* found that the differences between black and white views on the police and about crime were less significant than those between men and women and young and old.[44]

Police–community relations

Spatial and ethnic aspects of urban unrest have focused debate on two dimensions of police–community relations. On the one hand there is the stress on community policing as a means of implementing policing by consent – concepts which are themselves contested, in that police work takes place largely in an adversarial context. On the other hand there is the issue of the relations between the police and sections of local society, particularly ethnic groups and young people.

Community policing became a high-profile concept in the 1980s, but disagreement over its meaning had emerged a decade earlier around assertions that it implied special treatment of minorities. The Scarman Report defined community policing as 'policing with the active consent and support of the community', and also stressed that it was accountability which was the constitutional mechanism that rendered the police answerable for their actions.[45] There is a question, however, over whether 'active consent and support' implies, as Boateng argues, that the ideal police service is one which has its roots in the community from which it recruits its members, and is responsive to the needs of the area in which it works. This cannot be divorced from the related issue that community policing can be a solution only when it is linked to structures of control over the police through police authorities which are elected, not appointed.[46]

Concern over the concept of community policing arises because it is unclear whether this concept refers to decentralised policing in which responsibility is shared between police and community, to a contrast to rapid-response methods, or to a method of improved communications. John Alderson, the former Chief Constable of Devon who was a major proponent of the idea, saw community policing as a way by which communities regulated themselves once they were stimulated by appropriate police leadership.[47] Results, however, have been adjudged mixed or, at best, piecemeal.[48] Lord Gifford, in the context of the Broadwater Farm disturbances, rejected the cliché of 'community policing' for 'co-operative policing': 'a policing strategy by which the police at all levels co-operate (on a basis of mutual respect and equality) with those various agencies which represent the community, in order to deter and detect those crimes which the community believe to be priority evils'.[49] The emphasis is on the community's perspective, and a multi-agency approach. For co-operation to succeed, the community, not the police, had to determine who its representatives were to be.

But what is the community that is being addressed in this perspective? The belief that crime has sociospatial as well as individual roots is not new.[50] Nor is the idea that crime results from a failure of community life, of those institutions of socialisation and informal control which act to prevent or contain criminality. But the focus on community as neighbourhood, as in 'Neighbourhood Watch' schemes, for example, obscures divisions within an area. Neighbourhood Watch can reinforce class distinctions between middle-class residents who will co-operate with the police, and people in working-class areas who may be much less willing to do so. Community policing, for its part, has often in practice been used as an approach to minority groups, again with the danger that these groups are labelled as 'problems'.[51] Alongside this issue of which groups or areas are being addressed is the question of the nature of policing as it becomes more specialised and reliant on technology. In the wake of the miners' strike in 1984 there were also allegations that a virtual national force was emerging, and that the police were becoming remote from the public, using methods that did not have community support. This debate continued in the 1990s with the suggestions for major changes to the composition of the police authorities and the financing of police forces.

The second aspect of police–community relations which continues to give rise to controversy involves ethnic minorities. Pearson *et al.* see the parameters of the debate as: how the police enforce the law (overpolicing); police response to racial attacks and harassment (underpolicing); how the police deal with racism inside the service (police racism); and problems of group representation within the 'community relations' approach to policing (white racism).[52] In practice, research into relations between the police and the public reveals that there are tensions with the young, the unemployed, and with minorities, particularly where these categories overlap. Being young, unemployed, disadvantaged and from an ethnic minority is associated with a high probability of being subject to search and arrest by the police, and ethnic youth sees itself as being harassed by overpolicing.[53] In part these differential arrest rates are the result of discrimination and police stereotyping, but they are also due to differential rates of offending attributable to age and deprivation factors.[54] While racial prejudice within the police force exists, it is often argued that this reflects attitudes within society generally, and that prejudicial attitudes are not necessarily translated into police behaviour.[55] Reiner argues persuasively that ensuring accountability of the police to the community is dependent not on particular mechanisms but, rather, on the spirit which pervades the political system as a whole.[56]

The Scarman Report commented on the remoteness of the police from the community, and advocated the establishment of consultative committees to promote better relations. The Police and Criminal Evidence Act 1984 requires that arrangements have to be made for obtaining the views of the public on the policing of their area. Although this did not mean that consultative committees were compulsory, Home Office guidelines indicated that the 1984

Act's requirements were interpreted to mean the setting up of police community consultative committees in police subdivisions.[57] Morgan's research on the effectiveness of these consultative committees concludes that they are of limited practical use to neighbourhoods.[58] The subdivisions themselves do not coincide with local authority areas, and the claim to represent communities is thus a weak one. While they serve to ventilate local opinion, their ability to influence policing resources or tactics is limited. Committees and members who are content with police services ask few questions; those who do ask may be regarded with suspicion.

The claim of consultative committees to represent community groups and views is also weak. Divisions within the community and between generations lead to assertions that the consultative committees are ineffective and, since they are not accountable to the community, lack legitimacy. Sections of the community may then refuse to be involved in the committees' work. The consultative committees may be seen as a classic top–down form of public participation, promoted by governments who can then claim that there is real meaning to policing by consent. The committees do involve councillors and community leaders, but initially they had little success in involving ethnic minority representatives and young people. Nevertheless, they are a permanent and evolving part of police–community relations; they have important consumer education and viewpoint roles, but their contribution to crime prevention and conflict resolution is more problematic.[59] As Clarke suggests, the outcome offered by community control of crime is not so much a reduction in crime as a sense of security deriving from a belief that informal and formal collective resources are being used to combat the conduct which is held to be most offensive.[60]

The debate on accountability

The nature of police–community relations in the 1980s and 1990s is part of the debate on accountability. The structure of police accountability in England and Wales consists of three elements: a police force under a Chief Constable acting for certain areas of policy independently of local and central government; a police authority, made up of two-thirds county councillors and one-third magistrates; and the Home Secretary. Reform of this structure was under consideration in 1993 (see below). Continued doubts have been expressed about the nature of police accountability, despite moves since the Police and Criminal Evidence Act 1984 to establish Consultative Committees, lay visitors to police stations, and multi-agency work involving police and other public services which have gone some way to increase a more localised and community approach.

Problems of accountability, however, which have resonated since the 1964 Police Act, remain. The operational independence of Chief Constables, supported by the Home Office, has made it very difficult for police authorities to claim to be democratically responsible and accountable to their areas. Policing by consent then becomes an illusion. For Margaret Simey, who became Chair of the Merseyside Police Authority in 1981, the prime issue in accountability was the professional's claim to autonomy by virtue of that professionalism. The impact of the Liverpool riots in 1981 was to turn the Police Authority from a consensual position to a questioning one, beset by local demands that explanations be found for the breakdown of law and order, and fresh solutions sought. What was at issue was the accountability of the Chief Constable, not his legal duty to enforce the law.[61] The responsibility of the Police Authority is to ensure that an effective service is provided, and to strike a balance between public control and professional autonomy. In practice the reporting and other mechanisms have posed questions over the effectiveness of local accountability.

Even this degree of local responsibility, however, is set to change, according to the terms of the White Paper *Police Reform: A police service for the twenty-first century*, published in June 1993. Future police authorities are to be free-standing corporate bodies with greater independence from local authorities. They will have their own Standard Spending Assessments and be subject to individual capping, with Chief Constables able to decide spending priorities within their cash-limited budget. The police authority will receive its share of cash-limited specific grant directly from the combination of Home Office funds, revenue support grant and non-domestic rates, and will precept on its constituent local authorities for that 49 per cent of its budget which will be met by the

Council Tax. National performance indicators will also be introduced, and national league tables published. Police authorities will be expected to set local performance targets within each of the areas of the national indicators.

Under the terms of the White Paper proposals the new police authorities will be composed of sixteen members: three magistrates, eight councillors, and five members from the locality appointed by the Home Secretary. That is, the proportion of local councillors on police authorities falls from two-thirds to half. The Home Secretary will also appoint the police authority's salaried Chairman from among the overall membership.[62] The police authority will have autonomous status and power to run their own affairs, including the setting of the budget, and will have to ensure that there are regular and systematic consultations with local people. The provisions for the Home Secretary's appointment of the five local members and of the Chairman[63] represent a significant increase in centralisation: a further trend towards government by the appointed. In essence what is proposed reinforces both centralisation and decentralisation: to the Home Secretary on the one hand, and to basic command units at areal level on the other. In between is a free-standing agency in the form of a quango. These proposals have been criticised as counterproductive and undemocratic, since they would diminish rather than enhance channels of accountability, erode that public support which was the lifeblood of policing, and exclude the elected principle.[64] Fears have been expressed that the proposals point in the direction of a national police force and threaten the independence of the chief constable. The White Paper also outlined the government's longer-term suggestions for the reduction in the number of police forces, though there was no immediate programme of compulsory amalgamations. The Police and Magistrates' Courts Bill, announced in the Queen's Speech of 18 November 1993, will pave the way for a reduction of police forces from forty-three to around thirty. In any event, problems over size will emerge with the reformed structure of local government and the move to unitary authorities. This is likely to lead to the need for joint arrangements for the police service, again reducing accountability.[65]

As well as the proposed changes in police structures, the government has also been anxious to improve internal management accountability. The use of performance indicators in policing followed the Audit Commission Report recommendations of 1992, and within police forces appraisal schemes and other measures are being set up to strengthen internal accountability. McLaughlin has argued that discussion about accountability has in fact narrowed to questions of fiscal and managerial accountability and customer service, with demands for greater democratic oversight being judged an irrelevancy.[66] Advocates of this approach see local councillor involvement not as essential democratic accountability but as political interference in police autonomy. Real police accountability, the government argues, is to local people as customers and community residents. In this model of accountability customers are also active citizens in a self-help policing sense (as in Neighbourhood Watch), assisting the police within a more decentralised structure in which local police commanders have managerial and operational control over their area (the Basic Command Units) and are matched by Consultative Committees. The questions of how this is to be sustained in areas of urban decay, with their multiple problems of poverty and discrimination, and where consumer police–public relations face much more assertive policing methods, continue to raise real issues of democracy and citizenship.[67]

Conclusion: policy responses

The response to the riots of the 1980s was to address the outcomes of violence rather than its roots. Crime and disorder were seen by the government as law-and-order issues which called for public order legislation, improved police effectiveness (including, where necessary, new control techniques and equipment) matched by improved community–police relations, and greater personal and parental responsibility for behaviour. The vigour with which the violence was labelled as criminal and irrational meant that, as Solomos asserts, 'the language of liberal reform has found itself pushed into a corner'.[68]

In the 1990s the government continued to deny that disadvantage was the root cause of violent crime and vandalism in inner cities. In February 1993 Prime Minister John Major, in a speech to the Carlton Club, highlighted the inner cities as places where the state and socialist policies had effectively destroyed communities. As a result businesses had fled, vandalism was rife, and there was fear of violent crime. These factors, and the disappearance of respect for other people, were responsible for crime, not problems of unemployment.[69]

This narrow focus occurred at the same time as public expenditure on those programmes which had been directed at conditions in the inner cities was being curtailed. Also disquieting were the cutbacks to the youth service, which those involved saw as crucial to combating alienation and potential criminality among the most vulnerable age groups. Instead of reductions, the aim should be to increase participation by young people to combat the danger of a drift into crime.[70] An additional issue in this area was the cuts in benefits to 16- and 17-year-olds. Originally introduced to persuade them to remain within the family, where parents would be responsible for their maintenance, this failed when recessionary conditions meant that these young people had no training and no work. Many left home, and the number of young homeless increased markedly. As the Chief Probation Officers' survey revealed, many young offenders were unemployed, homeless and in poverty.[71]

Responses based on a different aspect of areal deprivation and delinquency were those derived from the concept of defensible space, originally promoted by Oscar Newman in the United States and taken up by Coleman and others in Britain, and the allied concern with protecting women, who were felt to be particularly vulnerable in threatening urban environments.[72] Newman argued that vandalism and crime in general could be deterred by architectural design which encouraged greater contact between people and increased community co-operation. Criticism of the original thesis as 'architectural determinism' has not detracted from continued attempts to manage space to produce a less crime-prone environment, including local authority work with women's groups and the Safer Cities Project.[73] Local authorities are also experimenting with a variety of initiatives such as remote surveillance television systems in town centres and shopping malls.

Against these positive responses, whatever their impact in practice, must be set the negative consequences of policy, particularly in the area of housing provision. Page's 1993 study of six new housing association estates revealed that the extent of social deprivation was greater than that existing on the Broadwater Farm estate in Haringey at the time of the 1985 riots. The estates were large, and all suffered from very high unemployment: 75 per cent compared with Broadwater Farm's 38 per cent. On some estates there was extensive vandalism, while others had such high child density levels that the danger of juvenile criminality was very real. The situation has arisen from the 1988 Housing Act provisions, which transferred the prime housing role from local authorities to housing associations. These associations, under governmental financial pressure, are building very large estates which are in danger of ghettoisation. Government guidelines require that at least half of the houses be allocated to the homeless, while the reduced funding regime has raised rents beyond the level of many low-income families, so that only those on housing benefit could afford to become housing association tenants. The pattern of disadvantage is evident across the whole public housing sector. Social housing now accommodates a very high proportion of the poor, the unemployed and the disadvantaged, and this proportion is increasing.[74]

Policy responses to unrest, violent crime and incivility have as their background the continued debate on widening disparities in economic and social conditions between inner cities and other areas, and the problems of racism and discrimination. The violence of the early 1980s reawakened interest in the 1969 Urban Programme as a vehicle for social projects in multiracial areas. The number of 'ethnic' projects funded under the Urban Programme increased, and black community organisations figured more and more prominently as sponsored applicants. But if, in the early and mid-1980s, there was a consensus that something had to be done, by the end of the decade there was less certainty, and even conflict, over equality of outcomes, anti-racism policies and the debate on multiculturalism.[75]

Ambiguity remains, however, over the part ethnic considerations should play in determining policy choices. Essentially, area objectives have continued to be preferred to group objectives. Traditionally, policy norms in Britain have emphasised universalistic programmes of benefit, with discretionary judgements fitted to the circumstances of particular cases. In the case of race issues, however, policies have been aimed at areas, not at ethnic minorities as such. The targeting of areas, not groups, is part of a wider ambivalence in British policy about the proper role of ethnicity in provision. The emphasis on areal solutions was strengthened as inner-city policies increasingly focused on economic regeneration.

By the early 1990s, however, it was judged that the many attempts at urban regeneration had achieved little. In practice the process had drastically reduced the level of house-building, and the poverty gap had widened.[76] Changes to programmes aimed at disadvanged areas and particular groups, including the use of Section 11 of the Local Government (Special Need) Act 1966 for programmes for minority needs, were also judged to be of limited effect. While they were widened in scope, these projects were reduced in impact by increased funding constraints.

During the course of the 1980s the Urban Programme changed its focus from broadly social to economic objectives. As a result, minority groups working for a greater emphasis on social and community projects were increasingly marginalised. By the early 1990s government policy was effectively proposing to phase out the Programme. In 1993–4 the government grant was cut from 75 to 57 per cent, and is scheduled to be cut to 50 per cent in 1995–6. At the same time, City Challenge, which finances regeneration in areas where large numbers of ethnic minorities live, was to be suspended.

The relations between urban decay, disorder and criminality have constituted a subtheme to the whole range of policy, from urban regeneration and housing to social services and relations between the police and local communities. Major problems remain, particularly over the concentration of deprivation, over persistent outbreaks of disorder, and in the area of race relations. The cumulative effect has been to reinforce the picture of fragmented urban policy. Efforts at co-ordination have been at the localised level, involving a variety of multi-agency approaches and central–local partnerships. Local authorities' ability to act as initiators of policies and co-ordinators of action has weakened, rather than increased. These problems are part of the wider debate on how cities might be reclaimed from this depredation. It is this issue of regeneration which will be addressed in the next chapter.

Notes

1. In April 1992 the new Secretary of State for Education, John Patten, asserted that dwindling belief in redemption and damnation had led to

a loss of fear of the eternal consequences of goodness and badness. This had a profound effect on personal morality, and especially on criminality. See W. Bennett, 'John Patten links Hell and the rise of crime', *The Independent*, 17 April 1993.

2. See, for example, the analysis developed in A.V. Harrell and G.E. Peterson (eds), *Drugs, Crime and Social Isolation* (Washington, DC: The Urban Institute Press, 1992).

3. Lord Scarman, 'The quest for social justice', in J. Benyon and J. Solomos (eds), *The Roots of Urban Unrest* (Oxford: Pergamon Press, 1987), p. 127.

4. Lord Scarman, 'Injustice in the cities', *New Society*, 14 February 1986, pp. 286–7.

5. A. Ravetz, 'The lost promise of the healthy city', *Town and Country Planning*, vol. 60, 11/12, December 1991, p. 323.

6. D. Waddington, K. Jones and C. Critcher, *Flashpoint: Studies in public disorder* (London: Routledge, 1989).

7. *Report of the National Commission on Civil Disorders* (the Kerner Report), (New York: Bantam Books, 1968).

8. Giles Shaw, Home Office Minister; written reply to parliamentary question, *House of Commons Debates*, vol. 84, 1985, cols 557, 558.

9. G. Cumberbatch, 'Black and blue in Handsworth', *New Society*, 20 September 1985, pp. 425–6.

10. *The Brixton Disorders 10–12 April 1981: Report of an Inquiry by the Rt. Hon. the Lord Scarman, OBE*, Cmnd 8427 (London: HMSO, November 1981).

11. *The Broadwater Farm Inquiry*, Introduction by Lord Gifford QC, *Report* of the Independent Inquiry into disturbances of October 1985 at the Broadwater Farm Estate, Tottenham, Chaired by Lord Gifford, QC (London: Karia Press, 1986), p. 196. The inquiry was instigated by Haringey council after the government refused to order a formal investigation. The Metropolitan Police declined to give evidence to the inquiry.

12. *The Broadwater Farm Inquiry*, p. 190.

13. J. Benyon and J. Solomos, 'The simmering cities: urban unrest during the Thatcher years', *Parliamentary Affairs*, vol. 41, 3, July 1988, pp. 402–22; S. Taylor, 'The Scarman Report and explanations of riots', in J. Benyon (ed.), with an epilogue by Lord Scarman, *Scarman and After: Essays reflecting on Lord Scarman's report, the riots and their aftermath* (Oxford: Pergamon Press, 1984).

14. Benyon and Solomos, 'The simmering cities', pp. 407–8.

15. N. Dennis and G. Erdos, *Families without Fatherhood* (London: Institute for Economic Affairs, September 1992).

16. Benyon and Solomos, 'The simmering cities'.

17. P. Cooper, 'Competing explanations of the Merseyside riots of 1981', *British Journal of Criminology*, vol. 25, 1, January 1985, pp. 60–9.

18. J. Benyon, 'The riots: perceptions and distortions', in Benyon (ed.), *Scarman and After*, p. 41.

19. D. Robins, *Tarnished Vision: Crime and conflict in the inner city* (Oxford: Oxford University Press, 1992). Incivility is the term used to describe street behaviour such as noisy neighbours, unruly youths hanging about, and drunks in the street: T. Hope and M. Shaw, 'Community approaches to reducing crime', in T. Hope and M. Shaw (eds), *Communities and Crime Reduction*, Home Office Research and Planning Unit (London: HMSO, 1988), p. 15.

20. E. Banfield, *The Unheavenly City: The nature and future of our urban crisis* (Boston, Mass.: Little, Brown, 1968).

21. J.J. DiIulio, Jr, 'The impact of inner-city crime', *The Public Interest*, no. 96, Summer 1989, pp. 28–46.

22. P. Mayhew and N. Aye Maung, 'Surveying crime: findings from the 1992 British Crime Survey', *Research Findings No. 2* (Home Office: Home Office Research and Statistics Department, October 1992), pp. 4–5.

23. P. Mayhew, N.A. Maung and C.M. Black, *The 1992 British Crime Survey*, Home Office Research Study No. 132 (London: HMSO, 1993), table 4.2 and pp. 45–8.

24. D.J. Walmsley, *Urban Living: The individual in the city* (London: Longman, 1988), p. 145.

25. T. Hope and J. Foster, 'Conflicting forces: changing the dynamics of crime and community on a "problem" estate', *British Journal of Criminology*, vol. 32, 4, Autumn 1992, pp. 488–504.

26. R. Kinsey, 'Innocent underclass', *New Statesman and Society*, 5 March 1993, pp. 16–17.

27. S. Field, *Trends in Crime and Their Interpretation: A study of recorded crime in postwar England and Wales*, Home Office Research Study No. 119, Home Office Research and Planning Unit Report (London: HMSO, 1990); B. Loveday, 'Right agendas: law and order in England and Wales', *International Journal of the Sociology of Law*, vol. 20, 1992, pp. 297–319; *Social Circumstances of Younger Offenders Under Supervision* (London: Association of Chief Probation Officers, 1993).

28. S. Trench, T. Oc and S. Tiesdall, 'Safer cities for women', *Town Planning Review*, vol. 63, 3, 1992, pp. 279–96.

29. *ibid.*, p. 293.

30. N. Tilley, 'Crime prevention and the safer cities story', *The Howard Journal*, vol. 32, 1, February 1993, pp. 40–57.

31. C. Brown, *Black and White Britain: The third PSI Survey* (London, Policy Studies Institute, 1984) pp. 309–10; S. Saggar, *Race and Politics in Britain* (Hemel Hempstead: Harvester Wheatsheaf, 1992), Chapter 3, 'The Social Demography of Multiracial Britain'.

32. J. Henderson and V. Karn, *Race, Class and State Housing: Inequality and the allocation of public housing in Britain* (Aldershot: Gower, 1987).

33. *ibid.*, pp. 4, 270–73. See also J. Solomos and G. Singh, 'Racial equality, housing and the local state', in W. Ball and J. Solomos (eds), *Race and Local Politics* (London: Macmillan, 1990), pp. 95–114.

34. *Racial Attacks and Harassment*, First Report from the Home Affairs Committee Session 1989–90, HC/17, Cm 1058, April 1990, p. vi.

35. P. Mayhew, D. Elliott and L. Dowds, *The 1988 British Crime Survey*, Home Office Research Study No. 111, A Home Office Research and Planning Unit Report (London: HMSO, 1989), Chapter 5, 'Ethnic minority risks', pp. 41–50.

36. K. Roberts, 'Youth unemployment and urban unrest', in Benyon (ed.) *Scarman and After*, pp. 179–80.

37. For a discussion, see B.D. Jacobs, *Black Politics and the Urban Crisis in Britain* (Cambridge: Cambridge University Press, 1986).

38. *ibid.*

39. J. Solomos, *Race and Racism in Contemporary Britain* (London: Macmillan, 1989), Chapter 6, 'Policing, Law and Order and Urban Unrest'.

40. *ibid.*, p. 116.

41. M. Braid, 'One in ten non-white families suffer racial harassment', *The Independent*, 11 March 1993.

42. *Racial Attacks: A survey in eight areas of Britain* (London: Commission for Racial Equality, July 1987); A. Sampson and C. Phillips, *Multiple Victimisation: Racial attacks on an East London estate*, Crime Prevention Unit Paper 36 (London: The Home Office, 1992).

43. *Racial Attacks and Harassment*, 22 November 1989; *Racial Attacks and Harassment*. The Gov [*sic*] Reply to the First Report from the Home Affairs Committee Session 1989–90, HC 17, Cm 1058, April 1990.

44. A. Crawford, T. Jones, T. Woodhouse and J. Young, *The Second Islington Crime Survey* (London: Middlesex Polytechnic, 1990).

45. *The Brixton Disorders 10–12 April 1981*, paras 5.46, 5.58.

46. P. Boateng, 'The police, the community and accountability', in Benyon (ed.), *Scarman and After*, p. 152, 158.

47. J. Alderson, *Policing Freedom* (Plymouth: Macdonald & Evans, 1979).

48. N. Fielding, C. Kemp and C. Norris, 'Constraints on the practice of community policing', in R. Morgan and D.J. Smith (eds), *Coming to Terms with Policing* (London: Routledge, 1989).

49. *The Broadwater Farm Inquiry Report*, p. 194.

50. Hope and Shaw (eds), *Communities and Crime Reduction*; *Crime Prevention on Council Estates*, Safe Neighbourhoods Unit, Department of the Environment (London: HMSO, 1993).

51. For critical analyses of Neighbourhood Watch schemes and community policing, see contributions to Hope and Shaw (eds), *Communities and Crime Reduction*.

52. G. Pearson, A. Sampson, H. Blagg, P. Stubbs and D. Smith, 'Policing racism', in Morgan and Smith (eds), *Coming to Terms with Policing*, pp. 120–1, 131.
53. J. Bright, 'Community safety, crime prevention and the local authority', in P. Wilmott (ed.), *Policing and the Community* (London: Policy Studies Institute, 1987).
54. R. Reiner, *The Politics of the Police* (Brighton: Wheatsheaf, 1985), pp. 81, 128–33.
55. C. Norris, N. Fielding, C. Kemp and J. Fielding, 'Black and blue: an analysis of the influence of race on being stopped by the police', *British Journal of Sociology*, vol. 43, 2, June 1992, pp. 207–24.
56. Reiner, *The Politics of the Police*, p. 203.
57. R. Morgan, 'Police accountability: developing the local infrastructure', *British Journal of Criminology*, vol. 27, 1, Winter 1987, pp. 87–96.
58. R. Morgan, 'The local determinants of policing policy', in Willmott (ed.), *Policing and the Community*, pp. 29–44.
59. R. Morgan, ' "Policing by consent": Legitimating the doctrine', in Morgan and Smith (eds), *Coming to Terms with Policing*, pp. 217–34.
60. M.J. Clarke, 'Citizenship, community, and the management of crime', *British Journal of Criminology*, vol. 27, 4, Autumn 1987, pp. 384–400.
61. M. Simey, *Government by Consent* (London: Bedford Square Press, 1985), p. 11.
62. *Police Reform: A police service for the twenty-first century*, Cm 2281 (London: HMSO, 1993).
63. The provisions for the Home Secretary to appoint the Chair of the Police Authority created widespread disquiet, including reservations among police officers. Following outspoken opposition in the House of Lords, including that of Lord Whitelaw and other former Home Secretaries, Michael Howard announced on 2 February 1994 that the Police and Magistrates Courts Bill would be amended such that the Chair of a Police Authority would continue to be elected by the Police Authority from among its membership. Further concessions were announced in the House of Lords on 1 March 1994 when the Home Office Minister, Earl Ferrers, announced that the minimum size of police authorities would be increased from sixteen to seventeen, with nine councillor members, giving that group a majority of one over the five Home Office nominees and the three magistrates.
64. R. Reiner and S. Spencer (eds), *Acountable Policing: Effectiveness, empowerment and equity* (London: Institute for Public Policy Research, July 1993).
65. For a discussion of this problem, see B. Loveday, 'The local accountability of police in England and Wales: future prospects', in *ibid.*, pp. 55–80.
66. E. McLaughlin, 'The democratic deficit: European union and the accountability of the British police', *British Journal of Criminology*, vol. 32, 4, Autumn 1992, pp. 473–87.

67. *ibid.*, p. 485.
68. Solomos, *Race and Racism in Contemporary Britain*, p. 183.
69. A. Bevins, 'PM blames socialism for crime', *The Independent*, 4 February 1993.
70. J. Graham and D. Smith, *Diversion from Offending, The role of the youth service* (London: Crime Concern, 1993).
71. *Social Circumstances of Younger Offenders Under Supervision.*
72. O. Newman, *Defensible Space – Crime prevention through urban design* (New York: Collier, 1972); A. Coleman, S. Brown, L. Cottle, P. Marshall, C. Redknapp and R. Sex, *Utopia on Trial: Vision and reality in planned housing* (London: Hilary Shipman, 1985); B. Poyner, *Design Against Crime: Beyond defensible space* (London: Butterworths, 1984).
73. Walmsley, *Urban Living*, p. 148; Trench, Oc and Tiesdell, 'Safer cities for women'.
74. D. Page, *Building for Communities* (York: Joseph Rowntree Foundation, April 1993).
75. K. Young, 'Approaches to policy development in the field of equal opportunities', in Ball and Solomos (eds), *Race and Local Politics*, pp. 22–42.
76. P. Willmott and R. Hutchison (eds), *Urban Trends 1* (London: Policy Studies Institute, 1992).

CHAPTER 7

REGENERATING THE CITY

Introduction

The malaise in contemporary cities is manifested not just in crime and unrest but in physical decay and economic decline. To talk of the regeneration of cities implies at least three different perspectives on the nature of the urban experience: the need to encourage community and citizen participation; the strengthening of the innovation and dynamism associated with city life and culture; the halt to physical and economic decline. Regeneration is not concerned just with limited areas within cities but with the well-being of the city as a whole, including issues of the environment, transport, and energy consumption. What has dominated both social science discourse and government policy over the past twenty years, however, has been a focus on 'inner cities' as the locus of economic and social problems. Immediately, however, issues of definition and appropriateness arise.

The emphasis on the inner city in analysis and policy response is essentially a concern not with location but with marginality: of parts of the urban economy, of multifaceted social problems, of families and individuals allegedly detached from mainstream values and lifestyles. It is an 'imaginary space' in which the down side of the deregulation and free-market strategies of governments on both sides of the Atlantic in the 1980s and 1990s has been manifested. 'Inner city' is not just, however, a synonym for economic and social marginality. It also implies a threat to the values of civic culture and civic pride, those virtues by which citizenship could fully express itself.

In Britain governments have, over a long period, been accused of failing to provide a long-term and coherent policy for cities. The Audit Commission report of 1989 criticised government urban support programmes as a 'patchwork quilt of complexity and idiosyncrasy'.[1] The Policy Studies Institute's 1992 analysis, *Urban Trends 1*, reports that 'surprisingly little has been achieved' in addressing the problems of deprived urban areas.[2] Over time, policy has evolved from state-led social projects to market-led economic programmes. In the late 1960s policy was grounded in welfare initiatives to address poverty. By the early 1980s the emphasis had shifted to economic growth led by the private sector. Associated with this trend has been the increasing role played by information technology, and the shifting balance between old industries and both high-status professional, and low-skill, service industries. The outcome has been that both economic decline and the changing patterns of economic growth have produced endemic poverty. These structural changes, as much as cyclical economic problems, call for a more sustained government policy. Governments have continued, however, to press market-led solutions; and urban policy approaches have increasingly stressed the role of agencies outside existing local government, and the need for a mix of private, not-for-profit and voluntary inputs.

Regeneration has become as contentious a notion as that of the 'inner city'. From one perspective, regeneration is the pragmatic application of land-use planning, deregulation, and financial incentives, to revive the urban economy. From an alternative viewpoint the term is a euphemism for the process which has been occurring in the economy as a result of the restructuring of international capitalism. From the latter perspective, state and local policies ameliorate, rather than radically alter, the impact of this capitalist restructuring. A version of this perspective focuses on cultural renewal – museums, theatres, festivals, refurbishing of urban space – which is meant to sustain the viability of city centres. But from an alternative viewpoint regeneration is a positive public-sector input, promoting inward investment, skills training, public–private partnerships, and the provision of residential as well as business and commercial development. Allied to this approach is the need for public policies to address social issues, including crime, poor housing, low educational attainment, family breakdown, and racial disadvantage.

This chapter addresses four elements in the regeneration debate. The first element is the question of what should be the focus of renewal policies. That is to say, what is 'the problem'? In this context the contention is that the inner city is a metaphor for multifaceted problems of concentrations of poor people. The second element in the analysis of regeneration is the evolution of urban policy since the late 1960s, and particularly since 1977. The third is the role of local authorities: elected local councils have become one actor among many, and have arguably lost the leading role to a series of non-elected bodies in a complex pattern of local programmes. The final element in the regeneration debate sums up the experience of the last two decades by asking whether the goal is policies for places or policies for people.

The inner city as metaphor

The inner city, it can be argued represents politics as symbolic action. It is more important to be seen to be taking action than to examine the agenda itself. Policy, that is, is palliative; part of that tradition, as Keith and Rogers put it, 'of the symbolically rich, effectively marginal, policy palliatives that were offered to the urban crises from the 1960s onwards'.[3] From a different perspective, the inner city is an ideological concept, associated with new right thinking in the United States and Britain.[4] In the 1980s this ideological concept was used to alter the policy agenda radically, reducing public services in favour of private and voluntary action, restructuring the labour market and using social policy in much more controlling and punitive ways. The inner city thus became a microcosm for growth strategies based on financial services and property development, on deregulation and on polarised labour markets characterised by divergent skills and growing social inequality.[5]

The phrase inner city calls up a negative image of decay and deprivation at the heart of major urban areas. This is misleading; city centres themselves are generally business, commercial and retail districts, with the areas of most deprivation in adjacent areas and on outer council housing estates. And to recognise the relative concentration of deprivation in spatial terms does not mean that poverty cannot be found in other areas, both urban and rural.

In practice, since 1945 anti-poverty measures have been addressed in both universalistic and spatial terms. In the immediate postwar period there appeared to be a consensus on the appropriate universal policies to address social and physical issues. The programmes of the welfare state, in health, education, housing and social security, together with a policy of full employment, were promoted to resolve major social problems. The town planning legislation, from the Town and Country Planning Act of 1947 onwards, was established to rebuild the physical infrastructure, promote housing development in urban, suburban and New Town projects, and facilitate industrial and business sites through its zoning provisions.

In this postwar policy scenario, the inner city was not the prime focus. The emphasis was on universal programmes, national standards, and economic growth. Within this overall welfare state framework, there was a growing recognition of the need to address the 'depressed areas'; that is, those regions in the North, North-East, North-West, the central Scotland belt and South Wales which had been at the heart of the interwar depression. Concern with specific areas within cities, however, was at this stage seen as the need to rebuild war-damaged housing and industry, and to clear and replace slums, largely through the town planning apparatus.

By the late 1960s this consensus had begun to erode, over both the nature of the problem and how it might be addressed. At this time the inner city became a metaphor in two primary senses: for the concentration of poverty, and for the issue of racial injustice. The rediscovery of poverty in the United States and the conflict over civil rights and the incidence of urban riots was paralleled in Britain by a concern with social problems and controversy over immigration. The result was a series of initiatives in Britain with a distinctively urban remit, concentrating largely on locality, rather than the individual or group, as the object of policy.

A major part of this renewed focus on the inner city as a metaphor for poverty and race was the couching of programmes in terms of community. Community, like inner city, was a complex of ideas. Community had a place reference, an area with boundaries and characteristics. Community was also an assumed cohesion, founded on neighbourliness, mutuality of interests, and shared institutions. Communities of this kind were often seen as part of an heroic golden age, where poverty had itself created mutual support in the face of need. The dislocations of decay, slum clearance and large-scale public housing had eroded community; the aim was to sustain it where it still existed, and help to recreate it where it did not. Community was also used within the programmes of the late 1960s to refer to the common experience and interest of sections of society, particularly ethnic groups (see Chapter 3 above). Specific services could be provided for these groups, together with structures to encourage participation and consultation, such as community relations councils. The community of groups and the community of area frequently coincided (or were judged so to do), and the label of the inner city acted as a shorthand for both the problems and the policies directed at them. By the end of the 1960s, then, poverty had become urban poverty, and urban policy had shifted from universalism to a concentration on particular areas.

The period of urban programmes based on welfare initiatives and with a community remit became overlaid in the 1970s with concerns over unemployment. The 1977 Labour Government White Paper *Policy for the Inner Cities* marked the change of emphasis, recognising for the first time that inner cities were a cohesive problem, and calling for the regeneration of business and industry, as well as positive state action on public services.[6] Urban policy as it had developed from the late 1960s concentrated on the inner city – arguably, the two terms had become interchangeable – but with a shift to economic rather than social projects. This emphasis was reinforced when one of the main urban programmes, the Community Development Project, ended in acrimony. The stress on economic approaches continued after 1979, but within a different context. The incoming Conservative government's policy was that of overall economic growth through the promotion of the free market. Within this framework, the existing urban programmes were continued (after initial speculation that they would be abandoned), and with little change of direction. Essentially they were subsidiary to the supply-side emphasis on economic growth as the driving force of policy. It was the urban riots of 1981 which brought about a re-evaluation of this approach.

The riots provided a new metaphor of the inner city as delinquent. The inner city was not only the place of the poor and the minorities, but the source of criminality and violence. The inner city as delinquent embodied a powerful message: that the problems were in part self-induced and self-perpetuating. Correct behaviour and attitudes were as essential to improvement as public programmes. The best projects would be those which encouraged enterprise and the means to participate in mainstream economic life – while exercising firm control over crime and disorder, and discouraging dependency. Social policies were aimed at restructuring and replacing the welfare state and welfare dependency, such that the inner city became both the arena for these policies and the symbol of the new philosophy of welfare. Critics of this perspective pointed to a harsher metaphor, that of the inner city as the exemplification of the growing divisions brought about by Thatcherism. Part of this criticism was a challenge to the morality of government policies and the 'excessive individualism', in the words of the Archbishop of Canterbury's Commission report, *Faith in the City*, of public and private life. The poverty evident in inner cities was 'deeply disturbing', calling for a more just and compassionate social order. The controversy over the report indicated the right's hostility to its implied moral judgement about capitalism. The right favoured, rather, the critique offered by Lord Jakobovits's *From Doom to Hope*, which argued that the main attack on poverty must come through self-help, the work ethic and voluntary action.[7]

In practice Conservative governments, from 1981–2 onwards, augmented existing programmes with a range of projects whose emphasis was on the leverage of private investment, the relaxation of planning controls and regulation (as in the Enterprise Zones), and the import of central government officials and business leaders into new quasi-governmental agencies at local level. The town planning regime, which had been a noted feature of British local government action, was rejected by the Conservative governments of the 1980s and 1990s. Land-use planning and the public sector were seen as obstacles, not as solutions. The government was determined to promote private-sector-led redevelopment, and to set aside planning controls. In spite of these changes, the inner city remains a metaphor for the social, economic, racial and delinquency aspects of urban dislocation. It is a label for social problems, defined in spatial terms, however ambiguous 'inner city' is in defining what 'the problem' essentially consists in.

Like the term 'inner city', 'regeneration' is also ambivalent about its target and its coverage. Part of this ambiguity arises from the benefits that renewal brings. Where capital is attracted into urban areas, creating major business, leisure and residential projects that attract upper-income groups, those central areas cease to be 'inner cities'. Such changes both underline and create the growing disparities between areas, social groupings and labour-market skills. The result is that economic regeneration can increase spatial and social segregation and exacerbate, rather than reduce, inequality. This has been little affected by urban policy: in general, the gap between deprived and other areas remains as wide as it was in 1977, when the government's White Paper sought to reduce it.[8]

As well as fomenting ambiguity over objectives, regeneration has also failed to provide a coherent policy response because of the difficulties of fragmentation between agencies and programmes at national and local levels. Not only has the policy response been fragmented, it has also raised questions of accountability: to the community, to residents, to citizens. Local authorities both provide mainstream services and have a part in the targeted urban renewal projects, but their role has changed significantly since the Urban Programme was established in the late 1960s. The local authority has become one actor among many in urban regeneration rather than the overall agent of public provision. Critics would go further, arguing that local authorities have not merely lost their leading role, but have become marginalised. This has occurred in spite of, or perhaps because of, the evolutionary nature of urban policy in Britain.

The development of urban policy

Urban policy in the late 1940s and 1950s had its base in physical land-use planning, public-sector housing, and slum clearance. This approach to urban policy was framed within a welfare state consensus of universal benefits and nationally derived standards. The 'rediscovery' of poverty in the 1960s, together with attempts to combat racial injustice, redirected urban policy towards a series of area-based social policies. The traditional Urban Programme was developed by the Home Office in 1968 to provide additional grants for schemes to meet special social needs. It was formalised in 1969 in the Local Government Grants (Social Need) Act. The Home Office-based Community Development Project of the same year established twelve Inner Area projects, each with an action and a research team. In 1978 the Inner Urban Areas Act introduced the 'enhanced' Urban Programme, which covered economic and environmental as well as social projects.

The period between 1969 and 1979 has been extensively documented; its main feature was the concern with social deprivation and what were essentially welfare responses, but limited by modest funding. Poverty was labelled as urban or inner-city deprivation, a spatial determinism which was contested by those involved in the Community Development Project (CDP). No official final report was produced, but CDP's own summary, published in 1977 as *Gilding the Ghetto,*[9] was critical of government policy. It argued that poverty was not confined to urban neighourhoods marked by a pathology of families caught in a 'cycle of deprivation'; it was a structural social and economic problem of major proportions.

The publication by the Labour government of the White Paper *Policy for the Inner Cities* in 1977, and the 1978 Inner Urban Areas Act, officially recognised the policy shift from a broadly welfare to an economic emphasis. It also represented a move away from mainly public-sector provision to a more mixed approach. The emphasis was on partnership between central and local government; and although the involvement of business was sought, local councils were still to be the leading authorities. The 1978 Act reformulated the 1969 Urban Programme to direct additional funding to support partnership areas in major cities and other designated 'programme areas' of local authorities. Partnership and programme authorities became eligible to receive 75 per cent government grant for regeneration projects, with local authorities meeting the remaining 25 per cent.

Over the 1980s the balance of Urban Programme spending shifted to reflect the increasing emphasis on economic regeneration. The partnership arrangements brought together representatives from local and central government, health authorities, the police and voluntary agencies. The difficulty was again restricted funding, especially for the 'programme authorities', which had a secondary status to the full partnership authorities. A major, and continuing, criticism of this approach to urban policy is that the projects could as readily have been carried out through existing local authority programmes had central governments so chosen, but in practice mainstream funding was reduced. Under the Urban Programme projects are, in any event, time-limited. When revenue projects have been operating for three or four years they are said to have become 'time-expired', and to revert to local authorities' own programmes.[10]

The move to an emphasis on economic factors was continued after 1979 by the incoming Conservative government. The government's urban policy, restated in Ministerial Guidelines in 1985, was to improve employment prospects in the inner cities; to reduce the amount of derelict land and buildings; to strengthen the social fabric and encourage self-help; and to reduce the number of people in acute housing stress.[11] To this end the government introduced a series of financial measures, beginning in 1981 with the Urban Development Grant (UDG), modelled on the Urban Development Action Grant introduced by President Jimmy Carter in the United States in 1977. The Urban Development Grant aimed to encourage private-sector investment by means of development grants administered through local authorities.

Although it was adjudged a success in attracting private investment into some inner areas, the number of jobs created under UDG, while substantial, were in part displaced employment.[12] In addition the UDG programme, heavily dependent on projects initiated by local authorities, was criticised for the length of time applications took to be processed, both locally and nationally. In 1987 the UDG was reformulated into the Urban Regeneration Grant, which went directly from central government to the private sector for larger projects. In 1988 it was relaunched as City Grant, which further reduced the role of local authorities, which had previously helped developers with their applications, in favour of direct DoE administration. A Derelict Land Grant was introduced in 1982 to encourage public and private bodies to bring derelict land back into use. Common to all these measures was the spatial targeting of financial incentives on specific urban areas and projects, rather than the provision of funding for local authority services as such, and an emphasis on inputs from developers and other private business leaders.

Policy reformulation in the direction of greater private-sector involvement was not confined to finance. A number of new structures were set up to encourage investment in decayed urban areas. In 1981 eleven Enterprise Zones, created under the provisions of the 1980 Local Government, Planning and Land Act, were established with modified planning requirements and financial incentives, including dispensation from local rates. Twenty-seven Enterprise Zones in all were created. By 1992 a number had seen out their ten-year period of tax advantages, leaving seventeen in England, four in Scotland and two in Wales. Judgements on their success were mixed. While redevelopment schemes had been brought forward and employment created, there was evidence that much of the business had relocated from elsewhere. While more than half the Enterprise Zone jobs were in manufacturing, much of this investment was by firms moving from within the local area, and it is generally accepted that the employment they created was an expensive means of regenerating decayed areas.[13] The Housing and Planning Act 1986 modified the idea further by introducing simplified planning zones, which repeated the reduced planning benefits of the Enterprise Zones, but without providing the financial incentives.

The 1980 Local Government, Planning and Land Act also enabled the Secretary of State for the Environment to establish Urban Development Corporations (UDCs). In 1981 the first two were set up in Liverpool and London Docklands; by 1992 the number had grown to twelve. UDCs had powers of land assembly and planning consent, outside the control of local authorities. But as the Public Accounts Committee pointed out, the Department of the Environment had failed to define the 'regeneration' that the UDCs were supposed to achieve.[14]

The pragmatic and *ad hoc* approach was continued when eight City Action Teams (CATs) were set up in 1985, together with Task Forces in 1986 (sixteen by 1991). Both CATs and Task Forces were interdepartmental teams. The former were comprised of regional Directors of the Departments of the Environment, Employment and Trade and Industry, while the latter were made up of small groups of secondees from the civil service, local government, and the public and voluntary sectors. While the CATs coordinated the programmes of different government departments at local level, the job of the Task Forces was to promote enterprise, helping the development of small businesses by providing loans and advice. The Task Forces were small-scale, temporary organisations set up to deal with limited areas with special problems.

Further processes were added in 1991, when local public–private partnerships were created under City Challenge. City Challenge was a further attempt at coordinating programmes, together with a bidding system for allocating funds to local authority projects (eleven were awarded in the first round of the national competition). Doubts were cast over its future, however, when the government announced in November 1992 that the third round of the competition, for 1994–5, would not take place. In 1993 the Leasehold Reform, Housing and Urban Development Act established the Urban Regeneration Agency (URA) in England. Named English Partnerships, the URA was launched in November 1993. Funded from the existing Derelict Land Grant, City Grant and English Estates, its remit was to upgrade derelict land for redevelopment in partnership with local councils and the private sector.[15] The Agency had powers to override local authority planning restrictions – a continuation of the property-led, top–down approach, though guidance to the URA also emphasised local involvement and the need to work with local people and groups. The Urban Regeneration Agency was also the source of controversy over its coordinating role in urban renewal when the government announced in November 1993 that the management of regeneration would be under the control of one senior regional director in each of ten regional offices. These senior civil servants would coordinate regeneration policies across the Departments of Environment, Employment, Trade and Industry, Education and, to a certain degree, Transport. A single regeneration budget will bring together, from April 1994, twenty existing programmes. Existing funding for inner-city programmes, including that for the URA, would thus be brought into a single budget, and the regional offices of Whitehall departments would be integrated.[16] While coordination was welcomed, critics argued that instead of elected regional bodies the government had increased central administrative powers along the lines of the French prefecture system.

The theme running through these changes was the harnessing of private-sector inputs in new structures in which civil servants played a major coordinating role. Changes of policy location were also introduced at central level. In summer 1987 the Department of Trade and Industry became a major agency for urban policy when the Inner Cities Unit was transferred to it from the Department of Employment. The Department of the Environment's 'traditional urban programme', which had supported specific projects by 150 local authorities, was discontinued, and resources were concentrated on the fifty-seven Urban Programme authorities, now termed 'priority areas', managing Inner Area Programmes (IAPs). Nine of the fifty-seven authorities are covered by special partnership arrangements, with formal committee structures and the participation of ministers. The Department of the Environment's responsibilities, however, continued to grow. In August 1989 the Action for Cities Unit transferred from the Cabinet Office to become the Action for Cities Co-ordination Unit, and a parallel Inner Cities Policy Unit was created. The Department of the Environment was also given responsibility, in December 1989, for the CATs, transferred from the Department of Trade and Industry. The DoE gathered together its urban responsibilities into an 'urban group' for more coherent management. In spite of these changes, there were criticisms that there was no concerted urban policy. Concerns over the lack of a central 'master plan' to promote and oversee the various programmes were rejected by the government. The analysis by parliamentary committees, the Audit Commission and private consultants has largely supported this view, while still calling for better central coordination; it remains to be seen if this can be effected through the new regional controllers.

The impact of these initiatives has varied considerably from place to place. While one city might be an Urban Programme partnership area and have a local CAT, Task Force or UDC, another might be an Urban Programme authority with no other projects involving central departments. The Department of the Environment denied that this created problems of overlap and duplication. In practice the various agencies worked in different ways: CATs subregionally and at city-wide level; Task Forces at neighbourhood level; Urban Programme authorities usually dealt with one or two local authorities; and the UDCs were single-purpose agencies. The result, in the view of the Public Accounts Committee, was that doubts remained over coordination.[17] Another continuing weakness has been the shift in responsibilities from one central department to the other, with the Inner Cities Unit being placed in the Department of Trade and Industry and the Department of the Environment taking the lead over major programmes.

In 1988 there was a refocusing of these initiatives in the Action for Cities programme, set up following Margaret Thatcher's June 1987

election night speech: 'We have a big job to do in those inner cities
. . . because we want them too next time'. The programme consisted
of a range of initiatives, and was an attempt to coordinate the
various programmes run by government departments. Launched in
March 1988 as a glossy brochure rather than the planned White
Paper, Action for Cities was in effect a reordering of existing programmes, together with an extension of Urban Development Corporations and City Action Teams to additional cities. The stated aims
were to facilitate economic revival by promoting private investment,
and improving infrastructure and the environment; to encourage
new business and provide better education and training; and to
reduce crime, improve health care and develop better arts and leisure facilities.[18] No single department had overall responsibility for
the inner cities under the Action for Cities initiative, although a
minister at the Department of the Environment had a coordinating
role. The £3billion programme targeted existing commitments on
those areas seen as the most deprived.

The policy was designed, however, not to increase government
expenditure but to promote private enterprise, through a partnership between central departments and business which bypassed
local government. The policy was distinctive in that it proposed a
set of transforming values – the enterprise culture – which would
have not only material outcomes but moral ones as well.[19] These
new right ideas saw the moral thrust of the enterprise culture as
revitalising cities through the revival of personal worth and initiative, and thus the defeat of dependency. The strategy was to promote the private sector, limit central government expenditure, and
curtail the role of Labour-led local councils. The government
stressed that a key theme was the promotion of civic pride; not
merely as a reflection of nineteenth-century civic virtue but as a
pragmatic element in the refurbishment of cities to attract business
and high-quality residential development.

The effect of this changing set of urban initiatives was that local
authorities, which in the 1960s and early 1970s had major responsibilities for urban social and economic problems, became during
the 1980s part of a complex network of provision through public,
private, and voluntary agencies. The result was decreased accountability to local citizens and an urban policy which was criticised for
its piecemeal nature. The 'patchwork quilt' to which the Audit
Commission referred implied that the programmes were varied in

their coverage and their impact. By the early 1990s the concentration on small areas and disadvantaged groups had become even more accentuated. There was some attempt to rehabilitate local authorities, and the City Challenge initiative recognised that local authorities must take a leading role in the collaborative partnerships. Nevertheless, the Audit Commission concluded, fragmentation continued.[20]

There is a further dimension to the uneven development of regeneration and the fragmenting role of local authorities for the well-being of their cities: the wider employment context and the programmes of training and job placement which governments have promoted. During the 1980s the government changed its employment and training provisions from a quasi-autonomous national agency, the Manpower Services Commission and its successor the Training Commission, to the Department of Employment's Training Agency, and thence to eighty-two area-based Training and Enterprise Councils (TECs) (in Scotland, twenty-one Local Enterprise Companies). All these measures made special provision for the long-term unemployed, and for ethnic minorities. The TECs, an idea borrowed from the American Private Industry Councils (PICs), were proposed in the 1988 White Paper *Employment for the 1990s* (Cm 540). Introduced progressively from March 1989, TECs took over responsibility for the Youth Training Scheme (which in 1990 became Youth Training [YT]) and Employment Training schemes, and for the Training Agency's programmes to promote small businesses.

The TECs differ radically from previous agencies not only in their area remit but in that control is vested in a board composed of two-thirds senior business executives (serving in their personal capacity, not representing their employer) and one-third local authority and other members. These arrangements superseded the area office structure of the Training Agency (which became the Training, Enterprise and Education Directorate [TEED]) and the Area Manpower Boards, which had been in suspension since the abolition of the Training Commission in September 1988. The aim of these changes was to encourage employers' commitment to training by giving them control of the larger part of training funding. TECs did not organise programmes directly but subcontracted them to local providers in the same way as the Training Agency area offices had done.

The mandate of the TECs was to meet skill needs more quickly and flexibly. But the TECs, based primarily on travel-to-work areas rather than administrative boundaries, cover areas larger than that of local authorities (eighty-two TECs covering some three hundred shire districts in England and Wales; some counties have two TECs operating within their boundaries). And although each TEC publishes a business plan and holds public meetings to discuss it, its accountability operates through the contract with the Secretary of State, and the local community as such has very little influence. The TECs' remit was subsequently widened to cover training credits, Compacts, the Careers Service and the further education sector. Compacts are school–industry links, taken from United States examples. They were introduced into Britain by the London Enterprise Agency and the Inner London Education Authority, and adopted by the government as part of the Action for Cities initiative. The objective of the Compacts was to agree a set of goals between pupils and employers in which pupils agree a high level of school attendance, and employers offer work experience and a guarantee of jobs for those students who achieve their Compact targets. While Compacts have had a useful inner-city role, their impact is relatively marginal to the wider unemployment problems of 16–17 year olds.

Criticisms of this series of training provisions point to the dropout rate from ET, the programme for long-term unemployed, and the slow provision of places on its replacement, Employment Action. There have also been cutbacks in resources and difficulties in meeting the Youth Training guarantee for unemployed school leavers. The replacement of ET with Employment Action caused particular concern, since it was primarily a temporary work programme without a mandatory training element, similar to the Community Programme which ET had replaced, and providing places for far fewer people. The overall judgement must be that training is characterised by those semi-autonomous, public–private features that mark urban policy as a whole in the 1990s.

Reviving the cities: leveraging the private sector

The history of urban policy in the 1980s and early 1990s is thus marked by three characteristics: a continued spatial targeting; an emphasis on the private sector and a reduced role for local authorities; and the time limits envisaged for the programmes. Urban policy concentrates on specific projects and areas, as the nomenclature running through the programmes clearly indicates. The participation of the private sector has been a prime objective. This has been underpinned by planning deregulation, tax and other financial incentives, and the direct involvement of business leaders in policy development and implementation. The majority of programmes have a limited, initiating or specific task-orientated remit. Thus as some Task Forces came into being, others closed, and Urban Development Corporations were expected to have a ten-to-fifteen-year life span, and to finish their work in the mid-1990s. Overall, the government's 1992 Autumn Statement revealed plans to wind down the Urban Programme and City Challenge, and to replace them with smaller-scale capital partnership projects.

Thus the major policy assumption from 1979 onwards was that urban redevelopment should be private-sector-led. Public funds should lever investment from the business and financial institutions, on the premise that this revitalisation would be more permanent and more effective than public funding alone. Public funding, it was argued, crowds out private investment. Britain should follow the example of the United States, where large-scale refurbishment of decayed areas of major cities – Boston, Baltimore, San Francisco, Atlanta, Pittsburgh – had shown a dramatic reversal of urban decline. There are a number of difficulties with this approach. A key problem of regeneration in American cities has been the intense competition between cities for inward investment, which meant they were compelled to offer financial incentives and the relaxation of planning and other regulations. Among these inducements were large injections of public funds, which it was often very difficult for local governments to recoup. Far from cities leveraging funds from the private sector, it was the availability of public funds over long periods (and the input of monies from defence-related expenditure) which sustained growth.[21] A further difficulty has been that while renewal took place at the centre or in other prime sites – the inner harbour area in Baltimore, for example – dereliction continued or increased in adjacent areas. The benefits of regeneration were shared very unequally. Even where redevelopment did not displace the poor on the scale of the urban renewal of the 1950s and 1960s, it put great pressure on housing throughout the city.

In the British case, difficulties in leveraging private investment have stemmed to a considerable degree from the concentration of finance capital, and corporate headquarters, in London, while the regions and localities have little private capital. In addition it can be argued that large projects have not leveraged money from the private sector so much as enjoyed substantial state investment – in the case of London Docklands, £1049.01 million in the decade 1981–2 to 1991–2.[22] Leverage, that is, is a synonym for subsidy. Once it is recognised that subsidies may be essential, the issue then becomes the nature of the investment, especially in job-creation and skills training, and how susceptible the development is to local, as opposed to central, control and influence.

Within the British experience the comparison with the re-development of the East End of Glasgow over the decade from 1976, and other urban initiatives, is instructive. Unlike that of England, Scotland's urban redevelopment has been closely bound up with a regional development body, the Scottish Development Agency (SDA), set up in 1975. SDA built on the Scottish tradition of state intervention, and although it was originally reluctant to become involved in urban problems, by the late 1970s it was making area policy a central part of its work. SDA directed the Glasgow Eastern Area Renewal (GEAR) project, which had a comprehensive approach to urban renewal but gradually moved from a welfare orientation to one based on economic policy with substantial public funding.[23] Notably, GEAR involved public–public cooperation, between SDA, Strathclyde Region and Glasgow District authorities, and other public bodies. SDA also had a promoting and coordinating role in other urban projects, moving during the 1980s to a position where it encouraged public–private initiatives, locally devised and controlled. In 1987 the GEAR project was completed, and in 1991 the SDA was replaced by six local agencies, one of which was the Glasgow Development Agency.

GEAR's achievements were in physical renewal: only housing and environmental conditions showed significant improvement, while economic aspects of the project were disappointing. For Glasgow as a whole, however, the collaboration between SDA and local authorities, and the business investment that was attracted, resulted in major leisure and cultural attractions as well as city-centre redevelopment. These were substantial achievements, but as with redevelopment in England and Wales, critics pointed to the partial nature of the outcomes which benefited the few rather than the many, the city centre rather than the peripheral estates, commercial projects rather than residential areas. Nor could the renewal policies counteract the fundamental shifts in employment which, in the case of Glasgow, had turned the city from a major manufacturing centre to one with a preponderance of service jobs and a high level of unemployment. In essence, urban policy diverged: between local economic policy led by business opportunities, and social projects for deprived peripheral areas – though both promoted a philosophy of self-help and private-sector leadership. As a result, argues Boyle, urban development becomes diluted into business development, and the goals of business are presented as the goals of the community.[24]

Thus the Scottish experience, in spite of the cohesion offered by a regional agency, the Scottish Development Agency, ultimately leads to similar conclusions to the experience in England and Wales: the goals of business come to dominate, with social problems falling as a residual category to local authorities. Wales has had similar initiatives, including two Enterprise Zones, the Urban Development Corporation in Cardiff Bay, and the Valleys Programme in the South Wales area. The Welsh Valleys Initiative, instituted by the Welsh Secretary, Peter Walker, in 1988, was aimed at regenerating the area hardest hit by mine closures. As elsewhere, it was a market-led approach and, as with other regeneration projects of these years, criticised for alleged inadequacies in its training provisions, and for the paucity of programmes for the unemployed and the working poor. In addition, it was argued that it eroded the role of local authorities, since the Welsh Development Agency, rather than the councils, decided on most of the large projects, though a more decentralised and local strategy was promised by the Welsh Secretary David Hunt in April 1993.[25]

Urban regeneration policy has provided positive but limited benefits. In halting physical decline and refurbishing infrastructure, it has had some notable successes: assembling land, coordinating public–private projects, and improving the environment. There have been criticisms of the piecemeal and *ad hoc* nature of the programmes, and doubts about their efficiency. The National Audit Office's examination of Urban Regeneration

Grant projects, for example, noted that the majority of projects would not have proceeded without grant aid, but queried whether public-sector contributions were in fact necessary in several prestige projects which would probably have gone ahead anyway.[26] And as a contribution to job creation, the history of the past fifteen years has been much less successful. Social problems have also proved intractable, and the disadvantaged have seen only marginal improvements. Levels of poverty have remained higher in deprived areas than in England as a whole, and the gap between deprived areas and other areas has widened rather than narrowed, while housing conditions have deteriorated since 1977.[27] Socioeconomic inequalities have not diminished, nor has regeneration had a major impact on racial disadvantage.

In terms of this last dimension, the ambiguity over whether urban policy should have an explicit focus on race continues.[28] Despite the history of limited specific funding for ethnic minorities since the 1966 Act, in the 1980s race effectively became marginalised as policy stressed general assumptions about the benefits of 'trickle-down' regeneration for all residents. Moreover, involvement by ethnic groups underwent overall decline as regeneration projects increasingly emphasised economic objectives. This meant that the Urban Programme, which had been promoted as the major source of funding for schemes designed to redress racial disadvantage, increasingly, if unintentionally, excluded black organisations from funding as capital spending on economic projects rose and social expenditure fell.[29]

In addition, a Department of the Environment study published at the end of 1992 showed that local authorities view the needs of ethnic minorities 'as at best subsets of broader economic development strategies' rather than as the result of detailed study of specific needs both of the ethnic community and of different groups within it. There is also the danger that stressing response through the voluntary sector could have the effect of removing important ethnic minority issues from mainstream Urban Programme activity. What is needed, rather, is to make mainstream Urban Programme delivery more sensitive to ethnic minority needs.[30] The DoE report went on to recommend ways of remedying this situation, including the use of the Urban Programme to improve both economic opportunities and the administration of service delivery to promote a much more openly proactive approach.

Overall, however, leveraging the private sector as the leading element in urban revitalisation has meant that the social aspects of renewal have remained the responsibility of hard-pressed local authority mainstream programmes. As a result, social projects to address the problems of the poor and of minority groups are largely marginal to the regeneration effort.

Local authorities, urban policy and regeneration

For much of the postwar period local authorities were the main providers of services concerned with the physical and social well-being of cities. There were criticisms of the relationship between centre and locality over resources, and between local authorities and developers over commercial and business redevelopment and over mass-housing schemes, but local authorities were nevertheless regarded as having an initiating and proactive role in urban policy and its implementation. The financial crisis of the mid-1970s marked a change in central–local relations, with Environment Secretary Peter Shore's 'The party's over' reference to local expenditure, and a re-examination of the direction of urban policy. As we have seen, the emphasis moved from welfare approaches to economic issues and, progressively, to a series of targeted projects involving both central government and the private sector, rather than a general enhancement of local authority services. These changes gave rise to controversy: the responses to urban problems were fragmented; local authorities had become marginalised; and regeneration was dominated by business goals to the detriment of a balanced approach.

A key element in these criticisms has been the part played in regeneration by the structures set up after 1981: Enterprise Zones, Urban Development Corporations, CATs, and Task Forces. The Urban Development Corporations (UDCs) were at the forefront of urban policy in the 1980s, representing a fundamental shift away from local authorities towards the private sector and specialised quasi-government agencies (quangos). The first two UDCs, the London Docklands Development Corporation (LDDC) and Merseyside Development Corporation (MDC), designated under the Local Government Planning and Land Act 1980, were launched in

1981 in the aftermath of the urban riots of that year. Following the 1987 general election, further UDCs were established in the Black Country, Trafford Park, Teesside, Tyne and Wear, Cardiff, Bristol, Leeds, central Manchester and, in 1988, Sheffield.

The UDCs were accountable to Parliament through the Secretary of State for the Environment, not to local authorities, and they had their own planning powers. The use of this form of urban intervention, argued the Employment Select Committee:

> arose from the frustration of the administration at the apparent inability of the local authorities, in many cases after repeated attempts, to achieve the nationally important task of solving the problems of these difficult areas, which the new bodies were expected to take by the scruff of the neck.[31]

That is, they were seen as bypassing the bureaucratic inflexibility of local councils by promoting a more entrepreneurial spirit. Ministers had direct control of the UDCs in that they appointed their boards, which were normally made up of local business leaders, one nominee from each council in the Corporation area, and the Corporation's Chief Officer. The Birmingham Heartlands UDC, established in 1992, was the first to have equal government and council representation.

The first UDCs, in response to the call for a new approach, concentrated on physical redevelopment. There was no precise definition of regeneration, and no specific requirement of job creation was laid upon them. The government, for its part, rejected the Employment Select Committee's call for a more precise definition of 'regeneration' to include employment objectives and community benefits.[32] Nevertheless, UDCs were criticised for their market-led philosophy to the exclusion of social infrastructure and skills training. It was argued that the UDCs, and London Docklands in particular, suffered from inadequate consultation with their local authorities and local communities, and that local people were at a disadvantage in that only a minority of the new employment went to local residents.[33] Nor was the majority of this employment genuinely new; in London Docklands more than three-quarters of the jobs 'new' to the area were simply transfers from outside.[34]

By the beginning of the 1990s, however, UDCs were concerned to present themselves as working with and for their local communities, including the introduction of some social programmes. In

London, for example, the LDDC had set up a Community Services Department. This was not, however, a major change of direction but, Oc and Tiesdell suggest, 'a means to more purposefully direct the trickle-down of benefits'.[35] Some UDCs attempted wider commitments. The extended Merseyside Development Corporation, for example, adopted a co-operative rather than confrontational stance, and entered into informal local plans, the Area Strategies, which involved local authorities, residents and the private sector.[36] The recession of the early 1990s and the decline in the commercial property market also meant that UDCs and developers were looking to provide affordable housing for sale and rent, in small-scale community developments. Local residents and community groups, however, continued to express frustration about consultation and information, and cynicism about community benefits, even if the opposition (and in the case of LDDC, conflict between the Corporation and organised local groups) of earlier years had largely subsided.

There were wide variations between the UDCs in terms of the private–public investment ratio, the nature of the community (there were few residents in the Trafford Park or central Manchester UDCs), and their expected time span (ten to fifteen years for the first and second generation, but five to seven years for the third generation of smaller UDCs). Judging the success or failure of the UDCs, however, depends crucially on how urban regeneration is defined: narrowly as property development or more broadly in terms of social outputs. This in turns affects relations between UDCs and surrounding local authorities, and in particular the way in which the planning system has been effectively marginalised. As non-elected quangos UDCs are determinedly deregulated bodies serving primarily private-sector interests, and their planning powers are unaccountable to local citizens. Judging the success of the UDCs has also been difficult given their time-limited nature, and as the reduction in their funding in 1992–3 became the latest in a series of cuts in inner-city spending.

In the 1980s the movement of resources from the Urban Programme to the UDCs appeared to make them the flagship of urban policy.[37] Over the 1980s, however, the government continued to use the Urban Programme, in order to exert specific influence over local authorities and move them further in the direction of co-ordinated projects that involved other bodies. In 1986–7 the Urban

Programme was reviewed in order to bring the number of qualifying local authorities to fifty-seven, and to require them to prepare annual Inner Area Programmes (IAPs) to secure funding. Again the aim was to promote greater co-ordination between the public, private and voluntary sectors.

The 1980s were in fact a decade of conflict between the centre and localities over urban strategy, underpinned by philosophical disagreement over local government's role and purpose. As Moore has put it, urban renewal is a key issue in the shaping of local communities, and in policy terms this has meant 'competing conceptions between different levels of the State of what renewal means and how to achieve it'.[38] By the end of the 1980s there was general agreement, the Audit Commission controversially suggested, that private-sector-led growth was the main long-term answer to urban deprivation. Even those local authorities which had tried to pursue their own 'planned economy' strategies had come to recognise the need to encourage private initiatives.[39] Local authorities, however, already had a substantial history of support for economic development, and many complained that central government policy marginalised, rather than reinforced, their role. In practice, regeneration has been an arena of both partnership and conflict between centre and locality.

Local authorities have also argued that their actions to regenerate the inner cities have been severely constrained by the overall downturn of resources and the way these are applied. As central government directed funds to specific projects, so funding for mainstream programmes fell short of what local authorities believed was necessary to reflect need. The impact of these cutbacks varied. While there was a general loss of government grant to local authorities throughout the 1980s, deprived urban authorities lost less grant than other authorities. Additionally, spending on the 'mainstream' Urban Programme also declined in real terms in England in the 1980s.[40]

In the case of capital resources, local authorities had long complained of the shortcomings of the capital control system.[41] In the 1992 Autumn Statement the government announced the establishment of the Capital Partnership programme, under which councils would bid for a share of the Urban Partnership Fund, which replaced the Urban Programme. These monies would lever private-sector funds, which would provide the bulk of the finance for the projects. Like City Challenge, Urban Partnership funding was based on competitive bids, not on evidence of need in a generic sense, but with the additional criterion that the local authority provide part of the finance out of its capital receipts from the sale of council housing and other assets. For councils these capital constraints have been affected only marginally by the help available from the European Community. The European Social Fund supports the promotion of job opportunities. Almost all the European Regional Development Fund (ERDF) allocations are for capital projects. The problem has always been the additionality issue: the extent to which the capital approvals used to match EC money were deducted from councils' total capital spending. In spring 1993 some £500 million in European aid was unavailable because of the government's failure to implement the additionality agreement of February 1992.

Local authorities' own promotion of urban renewal takes place both through their mainstream programmes of education, housing, planning, highways and transportation, and through specifically targeted projects. Specific development initiatives include land assembly and processing, providing sites and industrial units, working with private developers, providing infrastructure services such as highways and transportation, and sponsoring Enterprise Boards, agencies, companies that provide advisory services, and joint companies for specific projects. A major factor contributing to successful policy at local level has been local authorities' ability to integrate urban regeneration objectives into those of their main programmes, and to work with a whole range of local agencies. Business, for its part, has advocated partnership with a wide range of bodies and, in particular, local authorities. Results of all these initiatives have been mixed, but are generally adjudged a success, particularly in the mid-1980s period of national economic growth.[42]

Local authorities have set up a variety of committees to oversee these economic initiatives and to manage what the Audit Commission has termed the 'spider's web' of relationships which must be maintained among local bodies involved in regeneration.[43] In collaborating with the private sector, local authorities have often sought to incorporate social objectives, particularly jobs for local people, and the associated education and training inputs this objective requires. Local authorities are legally forbidden, however, from inserting contract compliance clauses into agreements whereby developers are required to provide a certain proportion of jobs for local people or for particularly disadvantaged groups: the long-term unemployed, women, ethnic minorities and the disabled. Local authorities have, nevertheless, been able to enter into understandings with business that these objectives will be pursued.

Local authorities' powers to participate in urban renewal and regeneration have depended on a series of general and, in some areas, local Acts. A prime source was Section 137 of the Local Government Act 1972, which gave local authorities the power to spend up to the product of a 2p rate in the interests of their area. In the former GLC and other metropolitan areas, this amounted to considerable sums. It was not until 1989, however, under the Local Government and Housing Act of that year, that local authorities had a general power to promote economic development, following the Widdicombe Committee's recommendation that local government involvement in economic development should be reviewed, including its powers to use Section 137 money (Section 83 under the 1973 Scottish Local Government Act) and to set up companies.[44] The 1989 provisions alter the funding provisions from the produce of a 2p rate under the 1972 Act to a system based on the adult population of the area, and require local authorities to develop a published strategy. Section 35 of the Act requires local authorities to produce an annual document setting out their proposals, including the objectives and financial strategy involved. The progress of a more proactive economic development strategy along these lines is still dependent on local authorities' ability to involve outside local organisations to a more significant degree than they have hitherto achieved.[45]

Since 1989 there has also been a positive attempt, at both central and local level, to improve coordination and consultation. In particular, the government's 1990 *People in Cities*, the second follow-up to the 1988 *Action for Cities* strategy, placed less emphasis on regeneration of the physical environment and more on partnership, and on the role of people living in the inner cities. A positive element has been the generally close cooperation between the local Task Forces, set up to stimulate small business in defined inner areas, and local authorities. Business, for its part, has sought, following the CBI's 1988 report *Initiatives Beyond Charity*, to work more closely with local councils, through Local Business Leadership Teams, which normally also involve Chambers of Commerce.[46] Additionally, Business in the Community (BIC), an association of major UK businesses, is committed to promote corporate social responsibility and revitalise economic life in local communities. BIC has nine regional offices in England and one in Wales. It works with a wide range of local bodies, including local enterprise agencies and neighbourhood partnerships, and joins in collaborative efforts with other bodies, including the CBI.[47] Community enterprises, an emerging grass-roots movement embracing development trusts, community companies, cooperatives and other voluntary organisations, is another example of an alternative approach which seeks local business and voluntary inputs into 'people-centred development'.[48] Within the constraints of investment and funding, these collaborative efforts, and the extension of public–private not-for-profit networks, have been adjudged a success.

Local authority leadership and revitalisation networks

In 1991 there appeared to be a further move towards a greater emphasis on local authorities' leading role within local networks with the establishment of the City Challenge programme, by which English Urban Programme authorities submitted competitive bids for funding. This was reflected in the fact that the composition of the City Challenge boards was left largely to the discretion of the local authorities and the bodies they work with, though it was expected that there would be strong business and community involvement. City Challenge was seen as a practical example of what a positive approach to the 'enabling' role of local authorities could achieve. Some of the City Challenge local authorities engage in wide-scale public consultation; others have worked with local community councils or tenants' groups, and with voluntary groups. The initiative, however, involved no new money: the funds were 'top-sliced' from the DoE's existing Urban Block funding. City Challenge, while it enhanced the role of local councils, continued and accentuated the theme of urban policy since the early 1980s: a concentration on small areas and on disadvantaged groups. And it proved similarly short-lived, giving way to the Urban Regeneration Agency, launched barely a year after City Challenge, which was seen as providing the main administration of inner-city initiatives formerly provided by the Department of the Environment. At local level, smaller-scale capital partnership schemes replaced City Challenge and the phased-out Urban Programme.

Urban policy thus continues to have as its focus not the citizen within the total community, able to hold a representative body, the council, accountable for the whole range of renewal, but spatial targeting with a limited role for particular sections of the community, and residents and groups within it. Against this must be set the government's professed intention to set limits to the existence of the various agencies, returning planning powers and such management as remains to local authorities. But by then the physical regeneration will be in place, together with the parameters of industrial and business development. The local authority, too, will have been recast, both in terms of structure following the local government reforms of 1993–6, and in its role and functions – the 'enabling' rather than the 'providing' authority.

Within these complex local networks local authorities have sought to work with the voluntary and not-for-profit sectors as well as business and government agencies.[49] A range of initiatives were developed in the 1980s, both in relation to job creation and community work with specific groups, and through education and training projects. Since the Department of Employment's Community Programme, which had links with the urban programme, was replaced by Employment Training in 1988, workers employed by voluntary bodies have been lost, and projects have had to close. In addition a wide range of social and environmental projects supported by voluntary bodies was put at risk, including projects for the disabled, the elderly, and children.[50] The TECs tended towards mainstream providers of training rather than the voluntary sector. Employment Training did not fill the gap left by the Community Programme, and disadvantaged groups and the disabled were particularly adversely affected.

The result of these employment, training and regeneration changes has been to place additional burdens on the voluntary sector. There has, however, been some growth within the sector. For example, by 1992 the Urban Fund programme of the Church of England's Faith in the City project, set up following the report of 1985, had become the country's tenth largest charity. Another successful example is the community development trusts. The trusts, originally established in the 1960s and 1970s, have provided a model of sustainable, community-based regeneration. By 1992 there were some hundred locally based, not-for-profit development trusts or similar bodies concerned with local improvement, and involving partnerships between voluntary, private and public sectors. Although in the recession of the early 1990s the trusts experienced problems of insecure funding from the public sector, a number have proved their abilities to attract funding from Task Forces and City Grant, and under the City Challenge programme.[51] These kinds of linkages between voluntary groups and agencies such as UDCs and Task Forces reflect the multiplicity of alliances that are now possible in the local arena. This does not necessarily mean that the local council is automatically central. As Stoker and Wilson note, groups are now in a position to establish complex alliances which bypass the local authority.[52]

The initiatives that local authorities have taken over the past two decades have thus involved a complex set of interventions, promoted through a network of relationships. The difficulty has been that local authorities are constrained both by the funding available to mainstream and to targeted projects, and by the nature of the partnerships involved. Some commentators have argued that local government has been caught up in partnerships that are dominated by business, through the non-elected bodies set up by successive governments since 1979; the result is reflected in the shift from a 'welfare state' to an 'enterprise state' at local level.[53] The pattern of non-elected collaborative partnerships has involved centrally devised agencies and civil servants, and a wide range of local public and private bodies. The resulting complexity has raised two difficulties: how local people are consulted and involved; and, relatedly, how accountability is maintained. On both dimensions, urban policy has fallen a long way from the democratic ideal of accountability to local citizens exercised through representative public bodies. The issues of accountability and consultation which have been raised by the redefining of urban policy as spatially targeted regeneration reveal a central dilemma: is policy for people or for places?

Conclusion: policy for people or for places?

'Inner city' and 'regeneration' remain powerful concepts because they offer a perfect combination of disease and cure, both spatially determined.[54] In this approach urban policy departs radically from the postwar consensus. Now, the assumption is that economic revival is the key to urban change, and that this must be led by the private sector. To this end the public sector has a facilitative, not a providing, role. Urban policy directed at inner cities also enjoys the advantages of symbolic politics of being relatively low-cost, while enabling governments to be seen to be responding positively to problems. It also allows governments to experiment, and to set time limits to particular initiatives, rather than promoting a comprehensive, long-term strategy. It has been easier for ministers to set up new initiatives than to persuade the Treasury to provide real growth in existing programmes. At the same time, regeneration for the inner cities cannot be regarded as a purely localised phenomenon, of little interest to the wider community: on the contrary, it is vital to the common good, to the well-being of the city as a whole. And if local authorities are to take up a more proactive enabling role, they will need effective mechanisms of coordinating inputs from a diverse set of local bodies.

The programmes that make up urban policy, while they have had successes, have been criticised for their *ad hoc* nature, their high cost and their limited impact. By 1992 it was calculated that there were thirty-four different urban policy initiatives covering five government departments. Local authorities have found themselves competing for a leading role which, arguably, is theirs by right by virtue of their representation of the whole community and their concern for the common good. In practice, local authorities have found themselves responding to the consequences of economic activity as much as trying to promote greater private enterprise.[55] At the same time, privatism and centralisation have increased. The urban programmes run in partnership with local authorities have been reduced in real terms, and resources switched to programmes such as City Grant, administered directly by central government, and to unelected quangos such as Urban Development Corporations, City Action Teams and Task Forces. Although there will be a return of planning powers and some management overview to local councils as these time-limited agencies come to an end, local authorities themselves will be far from the proactive and providing bodies they were before 1979.

During the lifetime of the quango agencies, the problems of accountability and consultation have not been resolved. If, at the end of their administrative life, powers over regeneration revert to local authorities, that will still be within an arena of public–private partnerships, contracting out and privatism. Issues of accountability and consultation will persist. At the same time, local authorities operate increasingly within an international economic environment. The demands of this global capital restructuring, with a declining manufacturing sector in Britain and the loss of skilled and semi-skilled jobs, have consequences for labour markets which make providing a stable local economic environment very difficult.[56] The local 'branch' economy becomes vulnerable to regional and international movements of investment, and also to the counter-urbanisation that inward investment fosters (the demand for suburban and green-field sites, for example).

In this climate, balancing proactive urban initiatives between a multiplicity of local actors with the demands of community responsibility and responsiveness is a major task. So, too, is balancing social with economic objectives. The enabling authority in this situation needs to be concerned with the good governance of the community in a proactive way, seeking means of including local citizens and focusing on a bottom–up, not a top–down, approach to urban renewal. Local people have to feel that they are stakeholders in the process, and that they have something to contribute as well as receive. This is particularly pressing, given that individuals and groups have become more demanding in their relations with both public- and private-sector bodies.

High on the current agenda is the environment of urban life. Central to the environmental debate are problems of pollution and transport, waste management, energy consumption, and a renewed concern with land use. This reflects, at local level, national and international concerns with sustainability and environmental protection.[57] Blowers, as Chairman of the Town and Country Planning Association Working Group on planning for sustainable development, put forward five fundamental goals: conservation, balanced development, environmental quality, social equality, and political participation at all levels.[58] In practice, by the 1990s local authorities were taking steps to develop environmental strategies.[59] 'Think global, act local' refers to the international dimension and local activism of the environmental movement, as endorsed by the UK statement to the 1992 United Nations Conference on Environment and Development in Rio de Janeiro.[60] The Rio summit encouraged all local authorities, under *Agenda 21*, to prepare plans for sustainable development by 1996. The UK local government follow-up was to launch Local Agenda 21 in November 1992 to assist local authorities to prepare strategies. Subsequently, a Central and Local Government Environment Forum was established; in 1993 this Forum published an Environment Charter and guidance to local authorities on environmental management. The Local Authorities Associations also published a Declaration on Sustainable Development as part of the Local Agenda 21 Campaign, reaffirming the role of local government in achieving its objectives.

Quality-of-life questions stemming from these developments are likely to become an increasing part of community governance as local authorities adopt environmental plans to coordinate their efforts in this area. In part these documents reflect the wider debate about the role of local government in a reformed structure. They are also part of the reaching out by local authorities to the EC on environmental matters, as an ally and a source of funds.[61] These 'green' issues will add to the dynamism of local affairs. The different agendas and demands of the various lobbies mean that regeneration will continue to be an arena of conflict: over growth, costs, continued urbanisation and suburban sprawl, waste incineration versus recycling, leisure demands, and job creation. Governing the community calls for the management of this conflict in an open and accountable manner.

Local authorities, however, find themselves pursuing the ends of good government in a vacuum of national policy. There is no coherent urban policy. The Audit Commission's 'patchwork quilt' persists, and this, together with increasing centralisation, have severely constrained the role of local authorities. The government's position on coherent urban strategy over the past decade has been to place the needs of the private sector at the forefront of policy. As a result of these centralising and privatising forces, the social and economic divisiveness of regeneration has been more obvious than its service to the common good. This is where the local authority has an obvious leadership part to play. The need to be concerned with issues of equity is as pressing as the need for efficiency, economy and effectiveness. The focus on the inner city has perpetuated the spatial determination of regeneration which emphasises places, not people. What is required is a better mix of social and economic objectives, and a better balance between measures designed as alleviations of targeted problems and questions of justice.

The ability of local authorities to fulfil a leadership role in community well-being, for both people and places, has been called into question, however, by the debate in the 1990s over the part the consumer, rather than the citizen, plays in local affairs. The concept of the enabling authority is matched by the idea of accountability of services to those who use them, as parents, tenants, and customers. Chapter 8 will consider these issues.

Notes

1. Audit Commission, *Urban Regeneration and Economic Development: The local government dimension* (London: HMSO, 1989).
2. P. Willmott and R. Hutchison, *Urban Trends 1* (London: Policy Studies Institute, 1992), p. 82.
3. M. Keith and A. Rogers, 'Hollow promises? Policy, theory and practice in the inner city', in M. Keith and A. Rogers (eds), *Hollow Promises? Rhetoric and reality in the inner city* (London: Mansell, 1991), p. 22.
4. S. MacGregor, 'The inner-city battlefield: politics, ideology and social relations', in S. MacGregor and B. Pimlott (eds), *Tackling the Inner Cities* (Oxford: The Clarendon Press), p. 64.
5. D. Massey, 'Local economic strategies', in MacGregor and Pimlott (eds), *Tackling the Inner Cities*, pp. 251–69.
6. *Policy for the Inner Cities*, Cmnd 6845 (London: DoE, 1977).
7. Archbishop of Canterbury's Commission on Urban Priority Areas Report, *Faith in the City* (London: Church House Publishing, 1985). In 1986 the Church's Board for Social Responsibility argued against the new right philosophy of individual freedom based on the theories of Nozick and Hayek, calling instead for interdependence, and justice for the poor: *Not Just for the Poor: Christian perspectives on the welfare state* (London: Church House Publishing, 1986); Sir [now Lord] Immanuel Jakobovits, *From Doom to Hope* (London: Office of the Chief Rabbi, 1986).
8. Willmott and Hutchison, *Urban Trends 1*.

9. CDP, *Gilding the Ghetto: The state and the poverty experiments* (London: CDP Inter-Project Editorial Team, Mary Ward House, 5 Tavistock Place, 1977).

10. National Audit Office, *Regenerating the Inner Cities*, HC 169 (London: HMSO, 24 January 1990), pp. 35–6.

11. House of Commons Tenth Report from the Committee of Public Accounts, Session 1985–86, *The Urban Programme*, Department of the Environment, HC 81 (London: HMSO, January 1986); National Audit Office, *Regenerating the Inner Cities*.

12. Department of the Environment Inner Cities Directorate, *An Evaluation of the Urban Development Grant Programme*, Report prepared by the Public Sector Management Research Unit, Aston University (London: HMSO, 1988).

13. House of Commons, Committee of Public Accounts, Thirty-Third Report Session 1989–90, *Regenerating the Inner Cities*, HC 216 (London: HMSO, 11 July 1990).

14. House of Commons, Committee of Public Accounts, Twentieth Report Session 1988–89, *Urban Development Corporations*, HC 385 (London: HMSO, 1989).

15. *The Urban Regeneration Agency: A consultation paper* (London: Department of the Environment, July 1992).

16. J. Arnold-Foster, 'Ten regions to split regeneration aid', Local Government Chronicle, 12 November 1993. Environment Secretary John Gummer also asked London, Birmingham and Manchester to take part in a new urban initiative called City Pride, though no new money was involved. The urban regeneration budget is the responsibility of John Gummer, guided by a new cabinet sub-committee (EDR), chaired by Lord Privy Seal Tony Newton.

17. House of Commons, Committee of Public Accounts, Thirty-Third Report Session 1989–90, *Regenerating the Inner Cities*, pp. vii, ix.

18. National Audit Office, *Regenerating the Inner Cities*, p. 7.

19. J. Edwards and N. Deakin, 'Privatism and partnership in urban regeneration', *Public Administration*, vol. 70, Autumn 1992, p. 360.

20. Audit Commission, *The Urban Regeneration Experience – observations from local value for money audits*, Occasional Paper No. 17 (London: HMSO, October 1991), p. 4.

21. M. Parkinson, B. Foley and D. Judd (eds), *Regenerating the Cities: The U.K. crisis and the U.S. experience* (Manchester: Manchester University Press, 1988).

22. Willmott and Hutchison, *Urban Trends 1*, table 6.8, 'Government grants to Urban Development Corporations: England', p. 74.

23. R. Boyle, 'Private sector urban regeneration: the Scottish experience', in Parkinson, Foley and Judd (eds), *Regenerating the Cities*, p. 78.

24. Boyle, 'Private sector urban regeneration', p. 89.

25. C. Gasson, 'Extended valleys initiative meets Welsh cynicism', *Local Government Chronicle*, 8 April 1993, p. 4.
26. National Audit Office, *Regenerating the Inner Cities*, pp. 21–2.
27. Willmott and Hutchison, *Urban Trends 1*, pp. 40, 64.
28. G. Ben-Tovim, 'Race, politics and urban regeneration: lessons from Liverpool', in Parkinson, Foley and Judd (eds), *Regenerating the Cities*, pp. 141–55.
29. I. Munt, 'Race, urban policy and urban problems: a critique on current UK practice', *Urban Studies*, vol. 28, 2, 1991, pp. 183–203.
30. Department of the Environment, Inner Cities Research Programme (Victor Hausner and Associates), *Economic Revitalisation of Inner Cities: The Urban Programme and ethnic minorities* (London: HMSO, December 1992), pp. 6–7.
31. Third Report of the Employment Committee Session 1987–88, vol. 1, *The Employment Effects of Urban Development Corporations*, HC 327–1 (London: HMSO, 28 July 1988), p. vii.
32. *Observations by the Government on the Third Report of the Employment Committee*, Session 1987–8 (London: HMSO, 1988).
33. House of Commons, Committee of Public Accounts, Twentieth Report, Session 1988–89, *Urban Development Corporations* HC 385 (London: HMSO, 17 May 1989).
34. S. Potter, 'Britain's Development Corporations', *Town and Country Planning*, vol. 59, 11, November 1990, table 3, 'Employment growth in Urban Development Corporations', p. 295.
35. T. Oc and S. Tiesdell, 'The London Docklands Development Corporation (LDDC), 1981–1991', *Town Planning Review*, vol. 62, 3, 1991, p. 322.
36. J. Dawson and M. Parkinson, 'Merseyside Development Corporation 1981–1989', in Keith and Rogers (eds), *Hollow Promises?*, p. 52.
37. National Audit Office, *Regenerating the Inner Cities*, Figure 5, p. 15.
38. C. Moore, 'Reflections on the new local political economy: resignation, resistance and reform', *Policy and Politics*, vol. 19, 2, April 1991, p. 75.
39. The Audit Commission, *Urban Regeneration and Economic Development*, p. 1; for an opposing view, see R. Hambleton, 'The regeneration of U.S. and British cities', *Local Government Studies*, vol. 17, 5, September/October 1990, pp. 60–61.
40. Willmott and Hutchison, *Urban Trends 1*, p. 79.
41. Audit Commission, *Urban Regeneration and Economic Development*, pp. 43–4.
42. For an account of the local authority Enterprise Boards in London and elsewhere, see A. Clarke and A. Cochrane, 'Investing in the private sector: the Enterprise Board experience', in A. Cochrane (ed.), *Developing Local Economic Strategies* (Milton Keynes: Open University Press, 1987), pp. 4–22.
43. Audit Commission, *Urban Regeneration and Economic Development*, para. 132, p. 39.

44. Committee of Inquiry into the Conduct of Local Authority Business, *Report*, Cmnd 9797 (London: HMSO, 1986).
45. Audit Commission, *The Urban Regeneration Experience*, paras. 31–6.
46. Confederation of British Industry, *Initiatives Beyond Charity: Report of the CBI Task Force on Business and Urban Regeneration* (London: CBI, 1988).
47. For the range of work carried out by Business in the Community, see B.D. Jacobs, *Fractured Cities: Capitalism, community and empowerment in Britain and America* (London: Routledge, 1992), chapters 9, 10.
48. J. Pearce, *At the Heart of the Community Economy* (London: Calouste Gulbenkian Foundation, 1993).
49. For an analysis of the non-profit sector, see B.D. Jacobs, 'Charities and community development in Britain', in A. Ware (ed.), *Charities and Government* (Manchester: Manchester University Press, 1989), pp. 82–112; Jacobs, *Fractured Cities*.
50. House of Commons Committee of Public Accounts, *Regenerating the Inner Cities*, para. 15; National Audit Office, *Regenerating the Inner Cities*, para. 5.26.
51. N. Bailey, 'Riding the recession?', *Town and Country Planning*, June 1992, p. 169.
52. G. Stoker and D. Wilson, 'The lost world of British local pressure groups', *Public Policy and Administration*, vol. 6, 2, Summer 1991, p. 32.
53. S. Duncan and M. Goodwin, *The Local State and Uneven Development* (Cambridge: Polity Press, 1987); Stoker and Wilson, 'The lost world of British local pressure groups', p. 29.
54. Keith and Rogers, 'Hollow promises?', p. 20.
55. D.S. King, 'The state, capital and urban change in Britain', in M.P. Smith and J.R. Feagin (eds), *The Capitalist City: Global restructuring and community politics* (Oxford: Basil Blackwell, 1987), p. 225.
56. For a discussion of the international setting and the urban crisis, see Jacobs, *Fractured Cities*.
57. *Our Common Future* (The Brundtland Report), World Commission on Environment and Development (Oxford: Oxford University Press, 1987); *This Common Inheritance*, Cm 1200 (London: HMSO, 1990).
58. A. Blowers, 'Planning a sustainable future: problems, principles and prospects', *Town and Country Planning*, vol. 61, 5, May 1992, pp. 132–5.
59. *Environmental Practice in Local Government*, 2nd edn (Luton: Local Government Management Board, Association of County Councils, Association of District Councils, Association of Metropolitan Authorities, 1992).
60. *A Statement on Behalf of United Kingdom Local Government to the United Nations Conference on Environment and Development* (Luton: Local Government Management Board, 1992).
61. S. Ward, *Thinking Global, Acting Local? Local authorities and their environmental plans*, UWE Papers in Politics No. 2 (Bristol: University of the West of England, March 1993).

CHAPTER 8

CITIZENS OR CONSUMERS? THE SOVEREIGNTY OF CHOICE?

Introduction

As the previous three chapters have shown, the problems of deprivation, unrest and regeneration have been addressed through a series of *ad hoc* policies targeted at areas and groups. This approach has been criticised as inadequate, lacking the purpose of a coherent urban policy. Such criticism, however, overlooks, the two main developments of the 1980s. The first, as we have seen, is the recasting of local government from all-purpose authorities to strategic, enabling ones. The second is the emphasis on the individual in the marketplace, exercising choice in the use of services. Together these form, it can be argued, a purposive urban policy of multi-agency provision and consumer choice.

Between 1945 and 1948 the common themes running through the legislation that established the welfare state were universality and citizenship. The theme of the legislation of the 1980s and 1990s is the consumer in the market, exercising individual choice. Exercising choice, it is argued, provides a more realistic and immediate form of accountability than that of local government, given the low turnout and infrequent local elections. The move to quality in public services enables this kind of choice to be realised. The emphasis is on improving service to the customer by providing more information and better access, establishing complaints procedures and monitoring standards. Although both right and left are increasingly concerned with the quality of services and their responsiveness to user demands and needs, critics argue that the danger is that citizenship rights are being equated with consumer rights, and active involvement in overall policy is being discouraged.

The 1980s legislation on contracting out local authority services, the local management and opting out of schools, and tenants' choice of landlords, emphasise accountability to customer, parent, tenant. This theme also underlies the Citizen's Charter, presenting a picture of the individual as customer, not as citizen–elector. But what is the nature of the choice which is being exercised, and who is the customer being addressed? Two aspects are relevant. Choice for the individual may, in fact, be limited. The parent may choose the school, but has little control over the curriculum, which is established by central government. Contracting out provides a choice by surrogate; the customer has no power over who the provider will be, and few alternative sources of supply. In Hirschman's terms of exit and voice, the customer has no effective exit (to an alternative service) but must seek redress through mechanisms of protest, that is, by exercising 'voice' within the system.[1] The second question on the nature of choice concerns who is to count as the customer: the parent? The child? The community as a whole? The quality, nature and range of education, for example, constitute a matter of the common good which goes beyond the individual user, and restricting choice to individuals who are parents at a given time constrains the community's interest.

Balancing these different interests calls for a public body that is answerable to the whole community. The legitimation of the local authority is its democratic accountability to citizens who have rights, not merely to consumers who have demands. In the 1990s the constitutional position of the local authority as having a legitimate role to represent the community and mediate interests has been called into question in two ways. The first is in centrally determined limits to local spending and standards of service. The quality of services delivered is not merely a matter of due powers (the *ultra vires* rule), nor of centrally determined services. The existence of Standard Spending Assessments, the amount government lays down that each council should spend to produce a standard level of service, replaces local accountability with national norms. When it is tied to a capping system (which, in effect, means that councils are self-capping in keeping expenditure down to government-set spending levels), the result is to undermine the local authority's ability to make judgements; that is, to exercise accountable responsibility.

A second and related consideration is that local authorities have regulatory as well as service-delivery functions. It is thus questionable whether the customer or contractual relationship is appropriate for the whole range of local activity. Local authorities have regulatory and control functions – in planning and certain aspects of social services, for example – which render the language of consumerism inappropriate. There is also the difficulty, evident in the language of social services, where the concepts of client, claimant or 'case' suggest that the individual, far from being a consumer, is being submitted to a form of social control.

The language of consumerism was promoted by the Citizen's Charter of 1991.[2] The language of the Citizen's Charter is that of the user of services, and its advocacy of redress is that pertaining to consumer rights. Interestingly, it contrasts with the language of participation in the 1960s and 1970s. That debate advocated individual and group involvement in services in terms of citizen participation. Calls for greater participation in social policy focused on clients or users, and on the mechanisms for introducing them into the making of public policy.[3] In that context such participation was seen as crucial to protect people from arbitrary decisions and those of entrenched professionals. The concern was with the citizen's involvement in the taking of decisions, not with improving the individual's redress in markets or quasi-markets.

The legislation of the 1980s and 1990s, however, appeared to undermine local authorities' ability to exercise responsible accountability; that is, to make judgements about the balance of interests within its legitimate domain. An essential element of this exercise of responsibility is the concern with equity: between and within groups and areas, over time, and applied to processes as well as resources. The concern with equity as well as standards is a central theme of the public service orientation. This set of ideas can be traced to the emphasis on the responsiveness of organisations to customers set out in Peters and Waterman influential work *In Search of Excellence*.[4] As developed by Stewart and Clarke, the public service orientation emphasises that public authorities are responsible and responsive to individuals as customers and as citizens. Customers are entitled to a good service, citizens are entitled to be treated as such; services are provided *for*, not merely *to*, customers; and authorities are accountable to citizens.[5] Stewart and Clarke recognise that the customer of public services is not just the immediate user but all those who have an interest in the quality of services in their area. In this sense what Stewart and Clarke refer to as 'customer' should be more properly be recognised as the citizen, since what is being argued is the relationship of obligation and accountability, not an economic transaction in a market. The consumer is an economic actor, while the citizen is a political one.

In certain circumstances, of course, individuals are customers of local authority services; for example, when they are paying for the use of leisure facilities. Most of the time they are not customers in this direct sense, but users or consumers of a publicly provided service for which there is no alternative. And even where a market alternative does exist, the user – for example, the resident of a home or a tenant in public housing – may not be able, for financial or other reasons, to exercise that choice. What is being conflated in these approaches is the public choice and public service orienta-tion frameworks. In public choice theory service provision is best achieved through the market, since the defect of public providers is that they are self-interested producers organised in inflexible bureaucracies which are insufficiently responsive to demands. Where individuals cannot purchase goods and services in a market, then the best provision of services will be through incorporating as much of a market mechanism or market surrogate as possible. Public choice theory, then, places the customer within an economic transaction. Public service orientation emphasises not an economic but a political transaction: the provision of services by public bodies that owe a duty of accountability to the user as citizen as well as consumer. The public service orientation must have regard to equity and due process for all citizens, as well as good standards, information, access and redress for actual consumers.

Alongside the analytical development of the public service ori-entation has gone internal change in local authorities themselves. Walsh has described these changes as the 'new management'. The new management, in contrast to the rigidity and paternalism of traditional bureaucracies, is characterised by responsiveness and diversity. It favours smaller units and decentralisation, and co-operative working with public and private organisations. It is consumer-controlled (in the sense of seeking views and promoting influence), and concerned with process as much as with structure.[6]

The public service orientation and the new managerialism can be contrasted with the new right approach to public services. The new right promotes the enabling and empowering theme from a very different philosophical base. While local authorities take strategic decisions, award contracts and monitor performance, powers over services are devolved to individuals and the community.

The change to an enabling role for local authorities, whether in the liberal democratic or new right formulations, in turn implies changes for council members. In operating a contract market and a provider–purchaser split, councillors will be setting standards and monitoring performance. In so doing they have the opportunity to take on the role of consumer advocate for their constituents. This advocacy role could extend to the whole range of services provided in the locality, not just those for which the council has direct responsibility – covering, for example, the Training and Education Councils, health authorities, boards of governors, and quangos such as Urban Development Corporations.[7] If the reformed system of local government encourages some form of 'cabinet' management system within local councils, then the consumer advocacy role will be attractive to many of the 'backbenchers' as an extension of their existing constituency work. Moving in this direction will create opportunities to re-examine committee structures, including decentralisation to neighbourhood bodies which will allow a more 'bottom–up' approach to service delivery – an issue to which we return below.

The confusion over customer and consumer, and the interest in markets, surrogate markets, public service orientation and new management approaches by both staff and councillors, runs throughout the contracting-out, opting-out and Citizen's Charter provisions. The protagonists in the debate talk of consumer when they mean user, customer or citizen; this chapter, therefore, while emphasising these distinctions, will continue to refer to consumer where this is the usage of the legislative provisions themselves.

This chapter addresses these issues of service delivery in the local context: the mixture of consumer choice, regulation, and local democracy. It argues that democratic politics must be re-affirmed as the legitimate base for choices if equity as well as service standards is to be realised. The question of choice, and the outcomes of formulating that choice in segmented and individual terms, is explored through the example of three major legislative changes of the late 1980s and 1990s: education, housing and community care.

The exercise of choice: education, housing and community care

Three major areas of legislation in the late 1980s and early 1990s significantly altered the delivery of services and the traditional understanding of local authorities' role and function: the Education Reform Act 1988 and the Education Act 1993, the Housing and Local Government Act 1989, and the National Health Service and Community Care Act 1990 (which came into force on 1 April 1993).

The major themes of all three areas of legislation were consumer choice and empowerment on the one hand, and the local council as the enabling authority on the other. The most widely debated area was education. The provisions for devolved powers introduced by the 1988 Act were extended in the Education Act 1993, which accelerated the pace towards the opting out of schools from local authority control to Grant Maintained status.

Education

The 1988 Education Reform Act removed powers from local authorities in two directions: through greater centralisation to Whitehall over curriculum and assessment, and through decentralisation from the local authority to boards of governors, head teachers and parents. The Act also abolished the Inner London Education Authority, transferring its education responsibilities to the twelve inner London boroughs and the City of London. The curriculum and assessment functions became the responsibility of new national quangos (the National Curriculum Council [NCC] in England, the Curriculum Council for Wales [CCW] and the Schools Examinations and Assessment Council [SEAC]), with members appointed by the Secretary of State, who was also responsible for funding for maintained (opted-out) schools. Local authorities lost powers over the curriculum, and acquired duties to implement testing assessments. Powers over the curriculum had already been eroded by the Technical and Vocational Education Initiative (TVEI), aimed at 14–18 year olds, which was introduced by the Department of Employment as a pilot exercise in 1983 and extended nationally in 1987. Operated under the Manpower Services

Commission and later the Training Agency, it was the first centrally managed national curriculum development project funded and administered by central government.[8]

The 1988 Education Reform Act extended the role of parents on governing bodies first introduced in the Education (No. 2) Act 1980 and expanded by the Education (No. 2) Act 1986. Under the 1988 legislation, boards of governors were established composed of parents, members of business and other groups, but with no teacher governors. Governors became responsible for appointments and managing the staffing complement of the school. Local authorities lost control over further education colleges, including tertiary and sixth form colleges, under the Further and Higher Education Act 1992; they were transferred out of LEA control on 1 April 1993, having seen the (then) polytechnics pass to independent corporate status when the Education Reform Act created a separate Polytechnics and Colleges Funding Council (PCFC).

The role of Local Education Authorities under the 1988 Act was to set budgets for schools within centrally determined formulae, and manage the resources of those schools without devolved budgets (primary schools with fewer than two hundred pupils). These powers were circumscribed by the requirement that 75 per cent of delegated budgets to schools were determined by pupil numbers, with the remaining 25 per cent being calculated on the assessment of need rather than on the basis of historic spending. The 1988 Education Reform Act provided for the Local Management of Schools (LMS), which devolved financial control from the local authority to the school. But schools were funded on the basis of average, not actual, salary costs, with a resulting incentive to employ fewer, or cheaper and less experienced, staff. Class size was also set to rise under this funding system. Similar provisions were introduced in Scotland, though at a slower pace than those in England and Wales.

The 1988 legislation, while it still placed local authorities in a strategic role with responsibilities for the number of school places, in practice allowed opted-out schools to perform this function. That is, the viability of maintained schools would, through formula funding and open enrolment, be controlled by the market-place (at least in theory; some of the schools which opted out did so in order to preserve small establishments which were otherwise threatened under strategies to close places as pupil numbers fell).

The thrust of the Education Act 1993 was to make it easier for schools to opt for Grant Maintained status. There were doubts, however, over whether this would accelerate the pace of change. Despite the financial inducements (each opted-out school was given an extra 15 per cent annually on its budget to cover the central costs which were previously the responsibility of the local authority, and additional capital grants), the expected flood of applications following the 1992 general election did not materialise. By late 1993 opted-out schools accounted for only 1 per cent of all schools and less than one in six of secondary schools. In part this was due to the success of LEAs in devolving budgets to schools. The 1993 legislation also affects local authorities' ability to provide financial, administrative and advisory services to Grant Maintained schools, in that it assumes the existence of a private sector of suppliers which will encourage schools to abandon the local authority services. In the interim, the legislation extends the powers of LEAs to provide advisory and other services to schools, but only for up to two years, until private-sector alternatives are available.

As well as the opting-out provisions, the 1993 Act also created a new funding quango, the Funding Agency for Schools (FAS), (in Wales, the Schools Funding Council), with the power to take decisions affecting all schools, within both the local authority and the Grant Maintained sector. The provisions of the legislation envisage a progressive erosion of Local Education Authority powers. The FAS shares responsibility for school places with Local Education Authorities when 10 per cent of local pupils are in Grant Maintained schools. When the figure reaches 75 per cent, then the FAS takes over all responsibility. That then leaves the LEA with only a statutory responsibility for pupils excluded from schools, special education needs and school transport. But the powers of the FAS go further. It can propose closures, extensions and the creation of new schools, including proposals from religious groups and independent providers (parents, voluntary groups).

The 1993 legislation also furthered the provision of alternative schools through the expansion of the City Technology Colleges (CTCs). The idea of the CTCs was originally launched in 1986; the 1988 Education Reform Act established CTCs outside local authority control. The original target was twenty CTCs, with an emphasis on science and technology (and directed at inner cities in the initial proposition), with funding from the private sector, which would provide all or a substantial part of the capital. In the event, three-quarters of the capital of the fifteen CTCs approved by 1993 was provided by government. The 1993 Education Act no longer requires that CTCs be purpose-built; new Technology Colleges[9] will be allowed to evolve out of existing schools. Such Colleges will be required to devote 60 per cent of their curriculum to science and technology, and to raise business sponsorship (and sponsors are to be given up to four seats on a College's governing body). In September 1993 Education Secretary John Patten announced that the New Technology initiative, replacing the Technology Schools initiative, would extend the Technology Colleges programme. This development again envisaged a move away from local authorities: schools had to become Grant Maintained before they could benefit from the new status; thus local authority schools were excluded from applying. At their inception the CTCs were seen as pioneering a new approach to technical skills, and as introducing a much-needed specialisation into an overly uniform state school system. To others they were seen initially as socially divisive. As they stand, however, they are marginal to the main issue of scientific and vocational education in secondary schools as a whole.[10]

Local authorities also lost responsibility for schools inspection. In September 1991 Secretary of State for Education Kenneth Clarke launched the Parent's Charter, which provided for a new system under which school governors would contract with private companies for a four-yearly cycle of inspection. In September 1992 the Office for Standards in Education (Ofsted), was established under the Schools Act 1992 to organise school inspections. Under this legislation private contractors were set to replace local authority inspectors, and Her Majesty's Inspectorate was reduced in size.[11] The 1993 legislation provides for the replacement of HM Inspectorate by Ofsted.[12] Ofsted, not the local authority, will also judge the 'failure' of schools, and will have the power to set up an Educational Association (EA) to run the school. The EA will have extensive powers to dismiss staff and reallocate budgets. When the EA has completed its work, the school will either be closed or become Grant Maintained.

As with the previous education legislation, the effects of these provisions is to make it virtually impossible for Local Education Authorities to close small schools or rationalise provision, since threatened schools will seek Grant Maintained status. Alternatively, the powers of closure and rationalisation will lie with the FAS. In addition, the 1993 legislation increased the centralisation of the curriculum, and of assessment. The Schools Examination and Assessment Council and the National Curriculum Council were set to merge into a new body from 1 October 1993: the School Curriculum and Assessment Authority (SCAA).

The implications for local authorities of the 1988 and 1993 changes were to extend powers of choice to parents,[13] governors and head teachers, to centralise control of the curriculum, and to pass control of the inspection of schools to a new agency. Choice for parents and governing bodies will mean understanding the world of contracts and markets, compulsory competitive tendering and delegated budgets. The accountability of schools to parents for these tasks will become formidable. The responsibility of schools to the wider community raises questions of accountability. This will be provided through information (including publication of examination results in the 'league tables') but not accountability through local authority elections. The government's view, by contrast, was that the representation of parents on governing bodies itself made schools more accountable to the community.

There are also important longer term implications for the structure and role of Local Education Authorities. While in 1993 it was too early to envisage the disappearance of the educational role of local authorities, since they retained certain strategic and regulatory functions, there were already signs of the diminution of their scope. Some local authorities were already considering a merger of their social services and education departments as the majority of their secondary schools became Grant Maintained. Under the 1993 Act local authorities were no longer obliged to establish education committees ('authorities').[14] As well as increased choice for parents, a degree of redress is built into the legislation. Parents have a right of appeal to the local government ombudsman irrespective of the status of the school. This highlights an interesting anomaly. Parents of pupils in Grant Maintained schools can complain to the local government ombudsman about issues over which the local authority has no control. There is a further anomaly in the local authority's position. It was becoming evident in the spring and summer of 1993 that parental dissatisfaction over the 'statementing' of pupils for special needs assessment was causing conflict. And it was unclear where responsibility for these special needs pupils lay, between the FAS and the LEA; this may lead to redress being sought through the courts rather than through approaches to the elected local authority.

There is yet a wider anomaly here. The local authority (with its remaining powers over special needs schooling and excluded pupils) is accountable to the community that elected it. The funding agency, FAS, is accountable to the Secretary of State. It is possible that this body will in time develop its own regional and local bureaucracy, since it is difficult to see it carrying out its functions for all schools from a single central base. This would turn it into a non-elected Local Education Authority. If, alternatively, local authorities were to provide the local bureaucracy, then they would be doing so as the agents of the FAS and the Department. Redress in this situation becomes complex, and again the outcome may be increased attempts to resolve conflicts in the courts.

Both the Funding Agency for Schools and the Welsh Schools Funding Council are unelected quangos with accountability to the Secretary of State. Although they share – and in some areas have total responsibility for – the function of securing sufficient school places, and distribute funds to Grant Maintained schools, they are centrally, not locally, appointed, and have no public accountability to local communities. Education Associations appointed under the FAS remit to deal with 'failing schools' will not be locally accountable either; members of the EAs will be appointed by the Secretary of State.

In the field of education the aim of recent legislation has been to make schools more responsive and accountable, to individual choice on the one hand, and to employers and the wider community on the other. Open enrolment, opting out, LMS, and performance indicators (through the publishing of test results) opened the system to market forces. This was decisive, in the government's view, in raising standards. There is, however, another side to the way choice has been implemented. The widening of parental choice, school autonomy and market forces have combined with increased centralisation to create a fragmentation of responsibility. The Secretary of State has taken on a range of powers which he exercises directly, and can delegate powers to new central quangos whose members he appoints. The FAS is responsible for capital and recurrent grants to Grant Maintained schools, and for sharing, and then assuming, the responsibility for the supply of school places. The Education Act 1993 gave the Secretary of State an active role in removing surplus places by issuing directions to local authorities and to the FAS.

Although increased centralisation over funding, places and curriculum calls into question the autonomy of schools and their governing bodies, Secretary of State Patten stressed, in the debate on the Education Bill in 1993, that belief in such 'self-government' was at the heart of the 1993 legislation.[15] In practice, school governing bodies will face a formidable range of central direction which, unlike the control from former Local Education Authorities, will be more remote. The government's 'enabling' model of local government also fares badly under the educational reforms. The local authority's power to promote and support education in the community is severely curtailed, and may eventually disappear. In the debate on the Education Bill John Patten appeared to recognise that this would be the case. Commenting on a newly introduced clause on the Secretary's powers (not, as in the 1944 Act, 'duties') to promote the education of the people of England and Wales, he said:

> This new clause certainly does not sound the death knell for council control of primary and secondary schools. In effect, schemes of delegated management and self-government have almost done that already.[16]

And although Local Education Authorities would retain certain key strategic responsibilities, notably in the area of special educational needs, they would no longer be the sole, and in some cases no longer a substantial, provider of education.[17]

The reforms, therefore, raise questions of a significant 'democratic deficit': planning and providing for local schools, albeit indirectly, is an important part of what effective community government should be about. Instead, what has been implemented is, in effect, 'consumer democracy'.[18] Not, it should be noted, as it might have been couched in the language of the 1970s, a 'participative democracy'. The language is instructive. The participant, under the traditional understanding, was the citizen; now democratic involvement is that of the consumer. But it should be noted that although accountability will be maintained over time to successive generations of parents, democratic choice will not. Once parents have voted for the school to become Grant Maintained, future generations of parents will not be allowed to reverse that decision, or comment on it.

Housing

A second area in which there have been moves to greater choice and the operation of the market is housing. Legislation has provided for the sale of local authority housing to tenants at discounted prices, for rents-to-mortgage schemes, and for tenants to opt out of local authority control by voting to transfer to alternative landlords. During the 1980s the role of local authorities in social housing diminished significantly: council housing declined from 32 per cent of the UK housing stock in 1979 to 27 per cent in 1987, with a parallel fall in public expenditure on housing. At the same time, housing stress increased: by 1991 the number of people accepted as homeless by local councils was estimated at 180000.[19] The numbers in temporary accommodation had increased steeply by the end of the decade. Between 1988 and 1990 the numbers of homeless households in temporary accommodation increased by 56 per cent in Greater London, 49.5 per cent in the rest of England, and 59 per cent in Wales.[20] At the same time, those without any accommodation, sleeping rough, increased dramatically; particularly in London and other major cities, and among the young. Among the young, homelessness rose as changes in the Social Security system altered eligibility for benefits, and in some cases removed it altogether. Local authorities have no legal responsibility for most homeless single people, but do have a duty towards those who are 'vulnerable'. For other groups, as expected, there was a strong correlation between homelessness and poverty.[21]

Since the 1987 White Paper the government has envisaged a reducing role for local authorities and increased provision by housing associations.[22] The language of the White Paper is again that of casting local authorities as enablers rather than providers. The 1988 Housing Act extends the choices available to council tenants which had been introduced by the 1981 Council Tenant's Charter (which included the right to information, to inspection of personal files and, after the 1984 Housing and Building Control Act, the right to repair; these rights are reaffirmed and extended by the Citizen's Charter provisions for a Council Tenants' Charter published in February 1992) and the right-to-buy legislation of the Housing Act 1980, extended in 1986. The right to transfer to alternative landlords may be exercised individually or collectively (and in the case of blocks of flats and maisonettes, only by the latter method).

In practice tenants' choice has been exercised collectively, though those who did not wish to transfer were not compelled to do so. The Housing Corporation operates the exercise of choice in providing information on which tenants base their decisions. The Housing Corporation also approves landlords who wish to take over public housing. In addition to tenants' choice, local authorities were empowered by the Housing Act 1985, the Housing and Planning Act 1986, and the 1988 Act to transfer some or all of their housing stock to other landlords, including associations sponsored by local authorities for this purpose. Local authorities undertaking voluntary transfer must show that the proposals are supported by tenants, but once the decision has been taken, individual tenants who object cannot stay with the council. Initially, there was considerable controversy over the ballot arrangements used to elicit tenants' wishes: in effect, abstention was counted as acquiescence. Under voluntary transfer, unlike tenants' choice, tenants who vote 'no' are still transferred to the new landlord.

For local authorities, voluntary transfer has additional attractions. First, the stock remains in the rented sector, and is not eroded by right-to-buy provisions. That is, by transferring stock to a housing association, a supply of social housing is maintained. Second, voluntary transfers generate capital resources which the authority can use to build new housing or refurbish existing houses, although these advantages were diminished under the 1993 Housing and Urban Development Act, whereby new Voluntary Transfer Housing Associations (VTHAs) will be required to allow rents into mortgages, thus lowering future capital receipts. The government is also concerned that voluntary transfers have been large-scale to single landlords. In future it is envisaged that stocks will be broken into smaller blocks for transfer, to encourage tenant participation in management and diversity of tenure. The numbers of transfers allowed each year will be limited, and the government will charge a 20 per cent levy on receipts from housing transfers.[23]

This levy is necessary, it is claimed, since it helps to offset housing benefit costs, which switch from the local authority to the Exchequer when stock is transferred.[24]

VTHAs are not the only form of diversity and choice now proposed. An alternative is the transfer of ownership to 'local housing companies'. The idea here is to transfer council housing to a new landlord body as a going concern. The local authority could nominate 30–40 per cent of the directors, and tenants themselves might play a major role as directors. The companies, being in the private sector, would not add to the Public Sector Borrowing Requirement (PSBR). Such companies would be more accountable to tenants and councils than housing associations, with stock being split into several companies to encourage diversity. The companies could operate on an equal footing with housing associations, but allow local authorities to maintain a strategic role in housing. The research of Wilcox *et al.* argues strongly for their promotion on financial, tenants' choice and local authority influence grounds.[25]

The provisions of the 1988 Act also introduced alternatives to local authority control of major regeneration projects of council estates suffering severe physical decline. The Act established Housing Action Trusts (HATs), independent agencies modelled on the Urban Development Corporations, which would be responsible for refurbishing such estates. When refurbishment was complete, the tenants would choose whether the estates would be run by local authorities, housing associations or private business. The 1993 Housing and Urban Development Act reaffirmed that HAT tenants will have the right to return to council ownership once work is finished. The HATs took over responsibility for the landlord function from local authorities, but were expected to involve the private sector in both these functions, and in the refurbishment work. HATs were expected to complete their work over a five-year period.

The effect of the 1988 legislation was initially slight, and the entry of private landlords into the field was limited. In the areas of tenants' choice and HATs, little of the housing stock changed hands, reflecting tenants' fears of future rent rises and security of tenure (under the 1988 legislation, 'approved landlords' under tenants' choice offer 'assured' rather than 'secure' tenancies). It was only in the area of voluntary transfer, where local authorities themselves took the initiative, that property moved out of council control; these transfers moved stock to existing housing associations, and to new ones created for the purpose.[26] Even here there was initial reluctance on the part of tenants to switch landlords.

The 1989 Local Government and Housing Act increased the emphasis on the enabling and regulating role of local authorities. It curtailed local authorities' ability to provide housing by allowing them to spend only 25 per cent of their capital receipts and 50 per cent of other asset receipts; research for the DoE concludes that there is little prospect of further council house-building.[27] One effect of these provisions was to encourage local authorities to consider voluntary transfer of their housing stock, a trend which is likely to gather pace as local government reform is implemented. In addition, the 1989 legislation required local councils to 'ring-fence' their housing revenue accounts to disallow transfers of money from the general rating fund, or vice versa. One result has been that councils, determined to maximise rent income to avoid rent increases, have been taking strong action to evict tenants in rent arrears. Unless those evicted have special needs, they will not normally be offered alternative accommodation. The main effect of the ring-fencing requirements was to force local authorities to budget to avoid a deficit on the housing revenue account. The government's argument was that this would make the local authority more accountable to the tenants as customers. In practice the result has been greater centralisation: government provides a general subsidy (to include the rent rebate element of housing benefit) and has increased control over rent levels and over maintenance expenditure.

All the policies in the housing field were intended to increase individual choice, and make social housing more responsive to market forces. This, it was argued, would improve efficiency and the quality of service delivery. Tenants are encouraged either to leave the social housing market altogether through the right-to-buy provisions, or to seek alternative landlords. Local authorities are encouraged to become enablers rather than providers, and to use the surplus (where available) from rental income to pay for housing benefits for tenants. In effect, tenants themselves are contributing to the relief of poverty by paying some of the costs of housing benefit.[28]

The significant power remaining to local authorities was the statutory duty to house the homeless. This presents problems. In some cases the obligation to house the homeless has been mitigated by the voluntary transfer provisions. Where stock has been transferred to a housing association, local authorities have been able to enter into agreements that enable them to nominate tenants. But where alternative landlords have been established under tenants' choice provisions, some families or individuals may not be acceptable. This could then turn the local authority into the provider of last resort, a residual welfare function. The private rental sector, by contrast, remains marginal. In 1992 privately rented dwellings constituted some 8 per cent of the housing stock, though the government was trying to extend choice through lessening of controls on lettings and through the Business Expansion Scheme of the 1988 Finance Act.[29] Co-operatives offer a further alternative choice of housing, but they also are relatively marginal: there are some 250 common ownership co-operatives in Britain, and a smaller number of various kinds of tenant management co-operatives and estate management boards. In all, Birchall calculates, there are still only about 900 permanent cooperatives of all kinds, covering some 30000–40000 dwellings. In the 1990s the co-operative sector looks set to become incorporated into the much wider movement of tenant participation and control under the tenants' choice and related provisions.[30]

The 1988 legislation strengthened the role of the housing associations by increasing their funding through the Housing Corporation (though Housing Association Grant funding for 1993–5 was subsequently cut substantially) and by increasing the pressure on them to charge rents closer to the market level. One consequence of this trend, however, has been to make some new housing association estates into concentrations of disadvantaged families, since only those in receipt of housing benefit could afford the rents. In 1993 it was estimated that more than 75 per cent of housing association tenants were partly or wholly dependent on welfare benefits.[31] The expanded role for housing associations which the 1988 legislation brought about has, in effect, changed their activities. They have moved away from the areas in which they specialised to become developers of general needs housing. At the same time, their capital grant (the Housing Association Grant) support has been reduced. Whereas in the 1970s housing associations were given up to 90 per cent subsidies, the grant rate went down to 67 per cent in 1993, with a forecast of 62 per cent in 1994. Lower grant means higher rents. Higher rent levels result in more tenants who are dependent on housing subsidies (and the danger of being caught in the poverty trap), and increase the segregation of social housing communities.[32] Housing associations now find themselves managing large estates housing very low-income families with children; these estates then become as prone to problems as disadvantaged local authority council estates.[33]

The trend in housing, as in education, is to greater centralisation and decentralisation. Central control has increased through the government's powers to create HATs, through the requirements to establish and ring-fence a separate housing revenue account, and over housing subsidy. A national quango, the Housing Corporation, has a key role in the operation of the housing association movement, which the government sees as an alternative to former local authority provision. Greater decentralisation occurs through tenants' choice of landlord, voluntary transfer of estates out of local authority control, and diversification to housing associations, right-to-buy, and rents-to-mortgages provisions. In the mid-1990s, however, local authorities remain substantial owners of stock, although the trend to voluntary transfer will accelerate diversity.

A crucial question then becomes that of tenants' rights, and their participation in management; a recurrent theme in the decentralisation and quality issue. The Institute of Housing has issued a guide on Tenant Participation in Housing Management, and housing authorities are anxious to get 'closer to the customer'.[34] To this end some authorities have formal tenant participation agreements with representative tenants' organisations. Other councils have introduced Estate Management Boards, made up of tenants, councillors and cooptees, and controlling an estate budget. The amount of control over rent collection and lettings is negotiable. The DoE's Priority Estates Project has played a major part in promoting Estate Management Boards and similar initiatives, and has encouraged local authority landlords to decentralise.[35] But there is a need to ensure that tenants do not control the allocation of tenancies in ways which would veto 'undesirable' individuals or sections of society. Under the 1993 Leasehold Reform, Housing and Urban Development Act, tenants were given a 'right to manage', but where a Tenant Management Organisation uses local authority management services then these will have to be put out to competitive tender under CCT provisions.[36]

The danger in these developments is again the fragmentation of service delivery, this time in housing services, and of housing associations with weak public accountability. For example, the poor auditing arrangements in some housing associations present a standard of accountability that would be regarded as unacceptable in local government.[37] The enabling role of local authorities will also develop and change: the local authority will have to develop ways of managing housing management contracts, and foster contacts within a wide network of local bodies and professionals. The local authority will also have to explore ways of providing local people with information on their rights, and on the duties of the 'enablers' and 'providers' – the local authority and the social/ private landlords.

Care in the community

The third major area which highlights the issues of consumer choice and diversity is that of care in the community, as established by the National Health Service and Community Care Act 1990. The Act embodied the proposals of the White Paper *Caring for People* and the Griffiths Report of 1988, which had advocated that local authorities be given the pivotal role for care in the community.[38] The objectives as set out in the White Paper were to 'enable people to live as normal a life as possible in their own homes or in a homely environment in the local community'. Although the Act was originally intended to come into force on 1 April 1991, a phased timetable for implementation was subsequently introduced, with the major elements being postponed until 1 April 1993.

The community care provisions gave local authorities the major responsibility for providing, either directly or through other agencies, social care for the elderly, and for people who are mentally ill or have physical or learning disabilities. The local authority providers, including those responsible for day, domiciliary, respite and residential care, organised on either a generic or a client group basis (for example, the needs of ethnic communities[39]), were expected to contract for all services, whether provided by their own units or by private or voluntary organisations.[40] That is, there was particular emphasis on what the 1989 White Paper called the 'mixed economy' of care: a move to contracting services out to tender with private or voluntary agencies. Again, the emphasis is on widening choice, encouraging diversity, and changing the role of public bodies to that of purchasers rather than providers. Welfare pluralism refers to the system whereby social and health care is provided by the plurality of statutory, voluntary, private and informal sectors. Welfare pluralism, however, has not only an anti-statist and anti-bureaucratic thrust but, by the same token, a de-centralist and participatory one also; a theme to which we return below.

Under the new legislation, funding for residential care was transferred from Social Security to local government. The Social Security budget which had covered costs of people in nursing and other homes was phased out, and grant for these purposes was included in the normal local authority grant. This money, like the rest of local funding, was subject to government limits on expenditure, and gave central government greater control of community care expenditure. In 1993 there were fears that local social services were taking over responsibility for community care at a time of severe financial constraints which would not cover needs in spite of additional funding provided for the changes. In the case of mental illness services, however, a specific grant was paid to local authorities. Local social services departments have a duty to assess the needs of any person they believe requires community care; they may then provide service themselves, or contract with another agency to do so. Local authorities must publish a community care plan, and set up both an arm's-length inspection agency for all premises in which community care services are being provided, and a statutory complaints procedure.

Community care was established as a means of widening choice and options through services provided by the private, voluntary and not-for-profit sectors. This widening of choice, by extending the use of alternative organisations, was seen as a viable and cheaper alternative to hospital care. In so doing, however, it ignores three key problems of the care agenda. The first issue is the need to recognise that much of the care to dependent people is provided not by public or voluntary sources but by family and friends, often under severe constraints, in an informal system. A second problem surrounds the cost of residential care. In recent years Social Security payments have fallen below the costs of providing residential care, and independent homes have been heavily subsidised by families and charities. This puts publicly financed individuals in non-state homes at risk, and conflict arises over whether local authorities should bear the top-up costs. Residents in independent homes, while they are eligible for Income Support, can still suffer problems, since this support is means-tested. Such problems mean that in practice, for many people, effective choice will be extremely restricted. The third problem of the community care agenda arises out of the statutory requirement on local authorities to provide individuals with assessments of their needs, even if there is no money to meet them. The issue of redress may then become, as in the changing education scene, one where people will resort to action through the courts over unmet needs.

In spite of these difficulties, the new proposals were seen as a means of giving positive encouragement to the integration of local services, cutting across agency boundaries and providing a multi-disciplinary approach.[41] Such an approach would focus on partnership between statutory and voluntary bodies, and direct attention away from bureaucratic hierarchies of professionals to more collaborative arrangements. And whereas in the past social services, like health, had been mainly producer led, the separation of purchasing from provision required a major change in organisational culture (see below). In practice a major outcome of the new arrangements has been to place an increased emphasis on networking skills across a wide range of responsibilities, involving close working between health and social services. These responsibilities have arisen not just in community care but in the effects of the Children Act 1989, which came into force in October 1991. The Children Act stresses that children should be cared for within the family wherever possible, that assessment of need should be given, and that care should be provided by partnership with parents or carers.

The complexity of the local network of care was further increased by the fact that while district authorities were not social services authorities, they did have responsibilities in the housing field for such matters as sheltered housing, adaptations, care and repair schemes; and over day centres, meals on wheels, and so on, which will become increasingly important for sustaining care in the community. Monitoring the quality of care in a situation where the local authority is purchasing services from a wide range of bodies and collaborating with others becomes a complex procedure, as the 1987 White Paper had conceded.

Quality and redress: the Citizen's Charter

The extension of the market of choice and diversity which underlay the education, housing and community care legislation of the late 1980s and the 1990s was matched, in the government's view, by a need to ensure that services were of high quality and responded more effectively to consumer demand. The Citizen's Charter has been criticised, however, as a superficial and marginal exercise, a weak means of anticipating the EC Directive on Consumer Rights. Indeed, it was said, the judicious placing of the apostrophe exactly marked its individualistic, anti-collective stance. A more fundamental criticism is that it is about passive consumerism rather than active citizenship. From this perspective the provisions of the Charter and the language of customer and citizen are instructive.

The themes of the Citizen's Charter were quality, choice, standards and value. In the words of the 1991 White Paper, the rationale is to 'raise quality, increase choice, secure better value, and extend accountability'.[42] These objectives would be achieved through competition, contracting out, publication of information, performance targets, complaints procedures and improved means of redress. A new standard for the delivery of quality would be published by the government – the Charter Standard – and those public services that met the standard would be awarded the Chartermark.

The Citizen's Charter proposals laid down that individual charters for all public services would be published. In the case of local authorities, the government's perspective is implicitly enabling, in support of choice and wider consumer participation:

> The real task for local authorities lies in setting priorities, determining the standards of service which their citizens should enjoy, and finding the best ways to meet them. By concentrating on these strategic responsibilities they will enable their communities to enjoy higher standards, more choice, better value for money and a greater degree of involvement in the decisions which affect them. The key

tools by which we seek to achieve this transition are competition and accountability.[43]

Where standards were not met and complaints were upheld, it was not assumed that redress would necessarily involve compensation. In the last analysis the most effective form of redress was the right of exit: the choice of an alternative source of service.[44] Where competition was absent and a market solution was unavailable, then alternatives would be provided not only through setting standards and monitoring performance, but through greater use of contracting out of services and the strategy of the purchaser–provider split.

Part one of the Local Government Act 1992 dealt with the Citizen's Charter provisions, in the four areas of local authority performance standards; auditors' reports and recommendations; publication of information by the Audit Commission; competition. The Audit Commission was given new powers to direct authorities to collect and publish information to assist in comparing standards of service. The resulting information would be published. Local authorities were required to make formal responses to auditors' reports and recommendations. Central to the whole strategy was the idea of national league tables of performance. Some charters would be set nationally; specifically the parents' charter for education and the tenant's charter in housing. For other areas, local authorities would publish service standards. In the area of competition, the 1992 Act gave the Secretary of State power to make regulations to define conduct as competitive or anti-competitive.

Throughout the White Paper and legislation, however, the concept of the citizen is a narrow one. Empowerment of the individual is mainly through access to information and complaints mechanisms. Although powers are given to individuals, there are no *legal rights* to services. There is no sense in which the Citizen's Charter embodies or promotes civic rights that could be codified and enforced; its concern is, rather, with consumer protection. Also absent is the requirement to seek the views of the community as a whole, or the democratic representation and balancing of conflicting interests and demands. The aim is not a charter of rights but contracts of services. That is, the Charter, despite its name, is a consumer protection charter.

But quality of services has to address questions of equality and equity (levels of income, personal mobility, disability, discrimination, for example), both between and within groups and over time. The Citizen's Charter, that is, should be seen within the wider framework of the need to revitalise democracy through much greater freedom of information and enforceable rights. The Citizen's Charter and the specific charters for particular services, moreover, offer little help on how to obtain legal redress if basic standards are not met, and the position is not improved by the financial constraints faced by Citizens' Advice Bureaux, and by the legal aid restrictions introduced in 1993.

The question of standards and information as a means of improving user satisfaction with services is not confined to the Citizen's Charter proposals of 1991. Labour and the Liberal Democrats argued that the Charter was derivative of ideas long suggested by them. The Labour Party had launched 'At Your Service' proposals for local authority service standards in April 1986, followed in April 1989 by the *Quality Street* proposals, and later by proposals for a Quality Commission, which included the idea of a system of quality audits for local services. Speaking in the November 1991 Citizen's Charter debate in the House of Commons, opposition spokesman Chris Smith used the language of rights and accountability: the rights of users, customers and electors; and the accountability of local authorities for budgets and services, by ensuring that a proportion of every council is elected each year.[45] At local level, a number of councils (in York, Lewisham, Milton Keynes and elsewhere) have produced their own charters or contracts for standards of service; for example in refuse collection. Local authorities have pioneered charters, public service agreements and customer complaints systems. Some of these agreements – the York Citizen's Charter for example – include the civic rights and entitlements of citizens as well as concern for standards of service to consumers. Typically, local charters include information, targets, points of contact, and details of complaints procedures. The Liberal Democrats, who had published *Citizen's Britain* in 1989, also took the view that rather than a Citizen's Charter the government's proposals were a public service consumer's charter; their vision was for a society with genuine freedom of information, a Bill of Rights, decentralisation and a fair voting system. Again, the language is that of citizen, rather than consumer, rights.[46]

Quality and performance

A central feature of the Citizen's Charter proposals was the emphasis on competition, to be achieved through performance indicators and their publication nationally, and through an extension of contracting out of services, through the Compulsory Competitive Tendering (CCT) provisions. Local authorities have been statutorily required since 1980 to subject their services to competition. The Local Government Planning and Land Act 1980 introduced competition into building and highways construction and maintenance. The Local Government Act 1988 extended the provisions to most other local authority blue-collar services. The 1988 Act barred 'non-commercial considerations'; that is, contract compliance, and other practices designed to encourage contractors to hire local labour or people from disabled or disadvantaged groups. By early 1993, 85 per cent of the work had been awarded to in-house bids.[47] In 1991, to support the principles set out in the Citizen's Charter, the government issued the Consultation Paper *Competing for Quality.*

In the government's view, the benefits of CCT extended beyond cost savings. It separated client and contractor functions, improved monitoring procedures, and thus enhanced accountability. There was now scope, the government believed, to extend CCT to professional services.[48] The 1992 legislation modified the provisions of the 1988 Act to extend competitive tendering into professional services. Ninety per cent of the work in all services would be subject to CCT, in a phased manner, by April 1997.[49] These professional services would cover a wide range of activities, including theatre and arts management, construction services (architecture, surveying), housing management (under the Housing and Urban Development Act 1993), financial, personnel and legal services. By the beginning of 1993 a number of councils were signing contracts – or outsourcing, as it was being called – for managing financial services of various kinds. Internally, this meant that individual local authority departments become customers or clients of external contractors providing, for example, payroll or pensions administration. But the 1992 Local Government Act has wider implications. It gave the Secretary of State powers to issue regulations requiring local authorities to comply with government guidance on what constituted anti-competitive behaviour. In effect, this makes local authorities the agents of the state in deciding who will provide local services.

CCT raises important questions about accountability and choice. The consumer may have to wait a considerable time before a council can be pressurised through the ballot box to change the tender and/or the provider. The separation of councillors from responsibility for service provision removes a direct link between service users and elected members. The frontline services of education, housing and social services have depended on close relations between members and officers, guiding both policy and implementation. Under CCT local people may find that their councillor can do little to make changes or provide redress when things go wrong. That is, democracy and accountability are potentially diminished, since the local authority does not control, except through the contract system, the services for which it bears responsibility; its role is to act essentially as proxy for the real client, the user.

Additionally, extending CCT to the core activities of local authorities – in finance, personnel, administration and legal services – will create an increasingly complex internal market which may reduce, rather than improve, efficiency of operation. It will certainly increase the fragmentation of management and responsibility, making local councils reliant on a patchwork of core service inputs with a reduced overview of service delivery. Traditional departmental hierarchies will alter under the internal market arrangements that divide service provision into purchaser and provider. The climate is that of the contract culture, and of compulsory pluralism of service provision. And insisting on a clear client–provider split is problematic when in fact, in 1993, the bulk of work was still carried out in-house by Direct Service Organisations. If this changes under the 1992 legislation, the situation alters markedly. The core activity remaining to the local authority would be the production of the budget and accounts, specifying services to be provided, arrangements for contracts, setting and monitoring standards – and, of course, responsibility for the democratic process of elections.

It is also argued that CCT may have achieved cost savings, but has done so at the expense of substantially diminished pay and worsening conditions of service for employees. Controversy over employees' rights at transfer, under the Transfer of Undertakings

(Protection of Employment) Regulations 1981 (TUPE), were tested in the European Court under the 1977 European Community's Acquired Rights Directive. The Court's decisions appeared to imply that where a transfer of an undertaking takes place, the contractor inherits the employees and their current terms and conditions. But TUPE still did not mean, it was argued, that the contractor could not make staff redundant, or alter conditions in the longer term. This controversy remained unresolved in autumn 1993.[50]

The debate on quality

Contracting out services in the interest of efficiency and competition operates within a framework of an increased focus on quality. The new managerialism seeks closer attention to the needs of the consumer: a more responsive administration than the perceived rigidities of former 'unaccountable' bureaucracies as criticised by both right and left. The point here is that questions of efficiency cannot be divorced from those of quality; the drive to performance indicators instituted by the government and operated through the Audit Commission must refer to quality as well as quantity. Performance measurement not only provides essential information to councillors and officers, it is a key part of accountability.

Those involved have argued that performance measurement which relies on quantity only, on the presentation of 'league tables' in what are criticised as crude and limited forms, is not sufficient. Effectiveness as well as efficiency is crucial, and it is this which is central to accountability. In spite of these reservations over the complex methodological problems involved in devising measures for use in areas such as education and social services, performance measurement now forms a recognised element of the new managerialism, as well as being statutorily required.

Quality is an elusive term. Broadly, it refers to the processes which ensure that services actually meet the needs of users. This raises questions both about who the users are, and about how their needs are identified. More specifically, quality refers to the degree to which a good or service meets its specification or, more actively, the extent to which it is fit for the purpose for which it is intended.[51]

Quality control ('conformance to specification') and quality assurance ('organisational capacity', or 'building-in' quality systems) emphasise these aspects. In practice, the operation of CCT has meant that local authorities are paying particular attention to the use of quality assurance systems under the British Standard for quality assurance (BS 5750), as well as devising their own data for use in performance measurement.

Services, however, are much more difficult to manage for quality than are products. Services are susceptible to resource constraints, changing needs, and non-standard and discretionary levels of provision. In addition, in the public domain values differ, and it is precisely the role of governing authorities to mediate conflict and balance competing interests and demands. For those who actually deliver services, similar issues may arise, involving the use of discretion and evaluation of competing demands. Quality, that is, is about judgement: about levels of service, the effectiveness of outcomes, and who is to define the user's needs and satisfactions. And how is 'need' to be assessed and evaluated? How is 'unmet need' to be incorporated into measures of performance? In the past these judgements have been exercised through a 'top–down' approach, dominated by professionals; the new managerialism emphasises devolved management, 'control by contract' and the 'empowerment of the customer'.[52] These in turn imply the need to examine the total organisational culture rather than the narrower issue of performance measurement.

In the consumerist approach, quality comes from empowering the individual as consumer. That in turn implies some redistribution of power in favour of users of services. But this suggests an individualist bias which neglects groups and the wider community, and favours present and directly involved consumers rather than future or inarticulate or apathetic ones. Moreover, user groups can be regarded as special and sectional interests, with little thought for the wider community. The trend to 'government by contract',[53] by contrast, emphasises service output that can be specified and measured. The main exemplification of this is the use of performance indicators that emerged from the Citizen's Charter initiative.

Local authorities are required by Section 1 of the 1992 Local Government Act to publish the performance indicators in a local commercial newspaper (i.e. not an in-house journal), and to make them available for inspection by local electors. The Audit Commission will publish national summaries from spring 1995. The government hoped that such measures would enable the public to judge quality. The Audit Commission has acknowledged that this is problematic, since quality is hard to define and there are few agreed quality standards. In future the Commission intends to carry out research into user views on what constitutes quality. The Commission also recognised that there were issues of equality, but did not address these directly. It hoped to consult both the Equal Opportunities Commission and the Commission for Racial Equality to see if suitable equality indicators could be developed. The questions of who has access and how appropriate services are to particular groups (including the elderly and the needy) remain problematic.

Initially the Audit Commission proposed 189 indicators covering 14 service areas. This was then reduced to 84 covering 11 service areas for the first year of the scheme's operation.[54] Local authorities, however, already have their own measures; the Audit Commission's indicators will have to be incorporated into these existing measures. To some degree this has been recognised by the Commission in that the measures include indicators which ask authorities to relate performance to local standards. Others argue that if performance is to be related to local needs and objectives, then what is needed are Quality Audits, by which the public can be involved in the process of service planning and delivery.[55] A number of local authorities have adopted this approach, incorporating views of users, councillors, frontline staff, and community groups. Thus Quality Audits are a more participative and pluralistic approach which goes beyond narrow cost considerations.

The fundamental problem, however, still remains: how far consumer rights can help individuals to obtain quality. The consumer is a complex amalgam of citizen-as-user and citizen-as-customer. Although right and left have different perspectives on the definition of consumerism, there is widespread agreement that quality must be judged from the point of view of those who use services. Where differences occur, these relate to the view of the right that quality is best pursued through competition; while to those on the left the emphasis must be on the wider community context and on democratic accountability.

Quality and choice: bringing the citizen back in

The delivery of services cannot be considered outside the context within which consumer needs and citizen voices operate. The rationale of public services is not the satisfaction of individual demands, but meeting needs collectively defined within a framework of public policy. The result is that, as Prior, Stuart and Walsh put it, 'In the public service, public purpose and user or customer needs have to be balanced.'[56] The local arena is a forum for community demands as represented by the elected council. Local authorities, in turn, ensure a plurality of decision centres within the unitary state. In this situation, accountability assumes a multiplicity of forms: to users, to customers, to electors, and to community as potential or future users.

Within this context the search for quality and choice becomes a matter of process as well as performance measures. On the one hand, there are arguments in support of direct user democracy; that is, the involvement of clients and consumers in the planning and delivery of services.[57] On the other, this direct involvement is also promoted through participation in decentralised structures. To this end, the theme of decentralisation and participation, which has been stressed in earlier chapters, is a fundamental aspect of the search for quality and choice. The focus on decentralisation has two aspects: the changes in management culture, and citizen inputs into the planning and delivery of services. Both have given rise to flatter forms of organisational structure in which personnel and budgetary powers are devolved to unit- or neighbourhood-accountable centres. Decentralisation allows a multidisciplinary approach, ease of access, and flexible response to user demands.

The development of these decentralised forms can be thought of as a spectrum: from schemes involving users in, for example, tenant management arrangements, to neighbourhood organisations concerned with a broad range of issues and having some form of representative mandate. In addition, the networking and contracting which service provision now entails must be accompanied by greater consultation through neighbourhood groups, and by promoting pressure group representation on local committees more seriously. The difficulty has been that provisions for CCT, opting out and performance indicators have obscured the debate on the cogency of decentralisation, to groups or to areas, as an effective means of ensuring real user inputs. What is needed is to build networks with community groups and decentralisation of service provision. To be effective, however, such changes call for the devolution of responsibility and accountability: political and managerial decentralisation must go hand in hand.[58]

If consumerism is to be anything more than cosmetic then it must, as the public service orientation of Stewart and Clarke and others stress, emphasise services *for* the public rather than *to* the public. This then encapsulates both the customer for whom services are provided and the citizen to whom the local authority is accountable. In the public sector what is crucial is not imperfect choice within surrogate markets, but political control. Services are consumed on a collective, not merely an individual, basis, and it is only through political control that accountability can be exercised. It is in this context that decentralisation has been advocated as increasing both consumer and citizen democracy.

In the local arena, decentralisation has three important dimensions: devolving power from the centre to the periphery of an organisation; coordinating services at area level; combining administrative with political involvement.[59] Where services have devolved responsibilities to frontline staff, user and client participation can make an important input to service delivery. Much will depend on the organisational culture of that service, and the extent to which users can effectively challenge official decisions, particularly over priorities and unmet needs. At area level, local authorities have used a variety of mechanisms – one-stop shops, 'little city halls', area committees – to bring together the administration of a number of services. The third form of decentralisation involves an important political dimension. Local authorities have set up neighbourhood forums, local councils or committees, on which elected representatives and other community members sit. In this form, decentralisation encourages community participation in decision-making, and brings accountability into sharp focus: infusing representative democracy with direct democracy, as Hambleton puts it.[60] The aim of these decentralisation mechanisms is to improve quality in ways which genuinely involve both the customer and the citizen, but people will not take part unless there is strong infrastructure supporting different forms of participation and an organisational climate of negotiation.[61] There are now extensive examples from local authorities of good practice in all these three forms of decentralisation: area offices, direct user input, and extensions of representative democracy.[62]

Conclusion

The call for greater decentralisation highlights the argument that 'government by contract' and the consumerist movement are marks of the vacuum that now lies at the heart of local government. The centralisation of powers to ministers and national quangos, and the decentralisation of choice to individuals as parents, tenants and users of services, is in danger of bypassing the elected local council. There is a paradox here. Empowering people in the search for quality and choice has little to say about the role and power of elected representatives, and can imply decentralising power away from them to individual users and groups.[63] By contrast, as Rhodes has put it, local government is about more than service delivery; it is a means of creating a pluralist society by which individuals gain political experience outside Parliament. It enhances citizenship by enhancing participation.[64]

Rather than focusing so exclusively on choice and performance measurement, more consideration should be given to enhancing democratic processes to foster choice through the ballot box and direct input from individuals and groups. From this perspective, introducing proportional representation would be much more effective than the extension of CCT. The opposite argument is that the choice exercised by parents, tenants, or clients needing community care ensures genuine accountability. The choice the individual makes helps to shape services, and in this sense the local authority's monopoly over the direction of policy is diminished.

It is participation which empowers people. It is this concept of empowerment – empowerment as participation – that lies at the heart of citizenship, not just the exercise of individual choice in relation to specific services. But as Taylor and Benington note: 'the role of local government in empowering and politically developing individuals and communities is not an inherent characteristic but a goal whose attainment requires a committed and self-critical approach from local politicians and officers'.[65] That is, it is a matter of political will, not of structures. Moreover, the question then arises: does the apparent consensus that quality of service is the prime purpose of local government itself call into question representative local democracy?[66]

There are some interesting pointers in this direction. Suggestions have been made that powers over service delivery could be given directly to separate agencies at neighbourhood level which bring together, for example, social services and health in the provision of community care. Indications of this thinking may be found in the National Association of Health Authorities and Trusts (NAHAT)'s report *The Future Direction of the NHS*, where Ham and Appleby suggest that integrated contracting bodies could be created to cover both health and social care. Primary care 'businesses' would provide a one-stop shop for patients and clients, and would operate under contract to an integrated commissioning agency.[67] Education Secretary John Patten has also envisaged integrated agencies by which, for example, Neighbourhood Watch schemes could become the model for what he termed care associations and environmental associations. Central funds would be distributed directly to those associations that were able to demonstrate the most effective service provision, and these bodies would take over responsibility from local authorities.[68]

The debate on citizens and consumers, on markets and choice, has neglected the role of the elected member and representative democracy. As Rhodes argues, democratic accountability could be strengthened by a series of measures, including greater accessibility to meetings and information, use of referenda, and seeking ways to increase turnout in local elections.[69] The emphasis on quality and performance measurement is not an end in itself but part of the context in which the political process can be revitalised and the role of the elected member strengthened. The strengthened councillor role involves both taking up advocacy for the communities and for constituents, and taking a more strategic stance for the overall performance of services. It is councillors who set strategy and review performance. As quality agents, councillors have two roles. At the centre of the authority they set strategy and targets; in the ward or neighbourhood they join with constituents and frontline staff in assessing outcomes. This in turn has consequences for internal committee structures at central and neighbourhood level, and the mechanisms for performance monitoring, complaints and redress. The emphasis shifts to civic leadership on the one hand – representing the community – and to working with others in a pluralistic local network on the other.

In the consumerist perspective the local council is seen as promoting (if not directly providing) the delivery of services to individuals. It is essentially a depoliticised perspective which ignores the governance role of local authorities: the representation of and responsibility to the community, and the promotion of collective well-being. A key element in local authorities' governance role is to mediate and balance interests; that is, to judge as well as to respond. The need is for democratic pluralism, not just welfare pluralism. In democratic pluralism people, both individually and in groups, can express views, make demands, become involved, and seek redress. To this end the accountability and responsiveness of services would be improved by seeking user views through participation as well as through survey questionnaires, as in the Audit Commission's research plans. Needs not only require articulation, they also demand the setting of priorities. Negotiation over priorities, in the light of equality and equity, lies in the political domain. This has become more, not less, important as local authorities share governance with a range of private, voluntary and not-for-profit organisations.

What has emerged in the legislation in education, housing and community care since the mid-1980s is rather different. Increased centralisation to ministers and quangos, and decentralisation to individual consumers, have marked an attempt to marry consumer sovereignty with state regulatory power. This amounts to a 'new moral and political order of individual rights and public accountability of government to consumer choice in the market-place'.[70] As such, as Ranson argues, it is a – flawed – moral order of individual self-interest in the marketplace. Ultimately, the consumer and the citizen should not be seen as antithetical concepts. Services need to be accountable to individuals and communities in both a political and a direct sense. Services, that is, must be accountable both to the needs and the demands of users, and nurture a common well-being: the consumer within the community of citizens is the goal.

Notes

1. A.O. Hirschman, *Exit, Voice and Loyalty: Responses to decline in firms, organisations and states* (Cambridge, Mass.: Harvard University Press, 1970).

2. *The Citizen's Charter – Raising the standard*, Cm 1599 (London: HMSO, 1991).
3. See, for example, A. Richardson, *Participation* (London: Routledge & Kegan Paul, 1983); N. Boaden, M. Goldsmith, W. Hampton and P. Stringer, *Public Participation in Local Services* (London: Longman, 1982).
4. T.J. Peters and R.H. Waterman Jr, *In Search of Excellence* (New York: Harper & Row, 1982).
5. J. Stewart and M. Clarke, 'The public service orientation: issues and dilemmas', *Public Administration*, vol. 65, 2, 1987, pp. 161–77.
6. K. Walsh, *Marketing in Local Government* (London: Longman, 1989).
7. G. Jones and J. Stewart, 'Champions and pioneers', *Local Government Chronicle*, 12 March 1993, p. 13.
8. Department of Education and Science, *Technical and Vocational Education Initiative (TVEI) England and Wales 1983–90* (London: HMSO, 1991).
9. In 1993 it was announced that the 'City' label attached to existing CTCs would be dropped, so that the initiative could cover all areas.
10. For an analysis of the scheme, see G. Whitty, R. Edwards and S. Gewirtz, *Specialisation and Choice in Urban Education: The City Technology College experiment* (London: Routledge, 1993).
11. In practice, of the first group of successful applicants for registration as inspectors, 60 per cent were based in local authorities, with the rest from private consultancies: *Ofsted Corporate Plan 1993–94 to 1995–96* (London: Ofsted Publication Centre, 1993).
12. Registered inspectors are trained and selected by Ofsted; once registered, inspectors compete for contracts to check schools.
13. The position of voluntary aided schools, 85 per cent of whose capital costs came from central government and all their running costs from local authorities, remained largely unchanged, although they were encouraged to opt out of local authority control. In 1992 there were 1875 Church of England schools, 1817 Roman Catholic schools, 17 Jewish and 4 Methodist. The issue of voluntary aided status for Muslim schools remained problematic. Muslim private schools began to apply for state support only in the 1980s, when the need to reduce surplus state school places had already become imperative; in 1992 there were still no voluntary aided Muslim schools.
14. P. Thomas, 'The educational circle completed', *Local Government Chronicle*, 30 April 1993, p. 13.
15. *House of Commons Debates*, vol. 220, 2 March 1993, col. 159.
16. *ibid.*, col. 162. The clause had been described in the press as marking the death knell of local authorities.
17. *ibid.*
18. S. Ranson and H. Thomas, 'Education reform: consumer democracy

or social democracy?', in J. Stewart and G. Stoker (eds), *The Future of Local Government* (London: Macmillan, 1989), pp. 55–77.

19. J. Greve, *Homelessness in Britain* (York: Joseph Rowntree Foundation, 1991); S. Wilcox, *Housing Finance Review 1993* (York: Joseph Rowntree Foundation, 1993).

20. Greve, *Homelessness in Britain*, p. 7.

21. National Audit Office, *Homelessness – A report by the Comptroller and Auditor General* (London: HMSO, July 1990); for government initiatives on homelessness, see Greve, *Homelessness in Britain*.

22. Department of the Environment/Welsh Office, *Housing: The government's proposals*, Cm 214 (London: HMSO, 1987).

23. S. Wilcox with G. Bramley, A. Ferguson, J. Perry and C. Woods, *Local Housing Companies: New opportunities for council housing* (York: Joseph Rowntree Foundation, March 1993), pp. 19–21.

24. R. Vize, 'Levy on housing transfer receipts kept to 20%', *Local Government Chronicle*, 29 January 1993, p. 5.

25. Wilcox with Bramley, Ferguson, Perry and Woods, *Local Housing Companies*.

26. *Inquiry into British Housing: Second report June 1991* (Chaired by HRH The Duke of Edinburgh KG, KT) (York: Joseph Rowntree Foundation, 1991), p. 23. By 1993, five estates had voted in favour of HATs since the scheme began in 1988: in Hull, Waltham Forest, Liverpool, Castle Vale, Birmingham, and Bow, Tower Hamlets.

27. D. Mullins, P. Niner and M. Riseborough (Centre for Urban and Regional Studies, University of Birmingham), Department of the Environment, *Evaluating Large Scale Voluntary Transfers of Local Authority Housing: An interim report* (London: HMSO, May 1992), p. vii.

28. *Inquiry into British Housing: Second report June 1991*, p. 22. Administration of housing benefit by local authorities was severely criticised for delays in processing claims, thereby putting at risk some of the most vulnerable tenants; see National Audit Commission, *Remote Control: The national administration of housing benefit* (London: HMSO, 1993); *For Whose Benefit?* (London: National Association of Citizens' Advice Bureaux/Shelter, April 1993).

29. B. Hayward and J. Turtle, *Business Expansion Scheme Survey of Tenants*, Department of the Environment (London: HMSO, 1991).

30. J. Birchall, 'Housing co-operatives in Britain', Department of Government Working Papers No. 21 (Uxbridge: Brunel University, 1992), pp. 6–10; J. Birchall, 'The hidden history of co-operative housing in Britain', Department of Government Working Papers No. 17 (Uxbridge: Brunel University, 1991). See also D. Clapham and K. Kintrea, *Housing Cooperatives in Britain: Achievements and prospects* (Harlow: Longman, 1993).

31. M. Simmons, 'Gimme shelter', *The Guardian*, 30 April 1993.

32. *Inquiry into British Housing: Second report June 1991*, pp. 80–1.

33. D. Page, *Building for Communities: A study of new housing association estates* (York: Joseph Rowntree Foundation, April 1993), pp. 3–7, 26–31.

34. Institute of Housing, *Tenant Participation in Housing Management* (London: Institute of Housing, 1989).

35. G. Hollis, G. Ham and M. Ambler (eds), *The Future Role and Structure of Local Government* (Harlow: Longman, 1992), Chapter 3, 'Housing: continuing challenges and new opportunities', p. 48.

36. *Competing for Quality in Housing: Competition in the provision of housing management. A consultation paper* (London: Department of the Environment/Welsh Office, June 1992). Similar provisions were also envisaged for Scotland. See also *Tenant Involvement and the Right to Manage: A consultation paper* (London: Department of the Environment/Welsh Office, December 1992). The CCT process in housing management will begin in April 1994, and the contracts themselves will be timetabled to come into operation progressively from 1996 to 1999.

37. The National Audit Office reported that over the period 1987–8 to 1992–3 only half of the housing associations had submitted their accounts to the Housing Corporation on time; see *Housing Corporation: Management of housing associations* (London: National Audit Office, 1993).

38. *Caring for People: Community care in the next decade and beyond*, Cm 849, Department of Health (London: HMSO, November 1989); Sir Roy Griffiths, *Community Care: Agenda for action* (The Griffiths Report), (London: HMSO, 1988).

39. For consideration of some of the issues relating to ethnic communities, see 'The black community and community care', *Community Care Comment: 2* (London: Local Government Information Unit, nd [c. 1990]).

40. House of Commons Social Services Committee, Eighth Report, Session 1989–90, *Community Care: Planning and cooperation*, HC 580–1 (London: HMSO, 17 July 1990).

41. Audit Commission, *Making a Reality of Community Care* (London: HMSO, December 1986).

42. *The Citizen's Charter: Raising the standard*, Cm 1599 (London: HMSO, July 1991), p. 4.

43. *ibid.*, p. 34.

44. *ibid.*, pp. 47–9, 50.

45. Chris Smith, *House of Commons Debates*, vol. 198, 15 November 1991, col. 1351.

46. Malcolm Bruce, *House of Commons Debates*, vol. 198, 15 November 1991, col. 1366.

47. Audit Commission, *Realising the Benefits of Competition: The client role for contracted services* (London: HMSO, 1993).

48. Department of the Environment, *Competing for Quality – Competition in the provision of local services. A consultation paper.* Cm 1730 (London: HMSO, November 1991), pp. 22–5. Local authorities had been using internal agreements to govern relations between departments – that is, between providers and users of central support services *within* the council's administration – in order to ensure that users were paying for the support services they used. See *Agreeing on Quality?: Service level agreements* (London: Association of Metropolitan Authorities/Convention of Scottish Local Authorities/Birmingham City Council, 1991).

49. CCT was affected by local government reorganisation, which altered boundaries and status. Councils in the first two tranches of reorganisation were allowed to suspend CCT for up to thirty months; in Wales, this period was extended to two and a half years.

50. For an analysis of the issues involved, see *Transfer of Undertakings (Protection of Employment) Regulations 1981, Acquired Rights Directive 1977*, LGIU Special Briefing No. 43 (London: Local Government Information Unit, February 1993).

51. K. Walsh, 'Quality and public services', *Public Administration*, vol. 69, 4, Winter 1991, pp. 503–4.

52. P. Hoggett, 'A new management in the public sector?', *Policy and Politics*, vol. 19, 4, 1991, pp. 243–56.

53. *ibid.*

54. Audit Commission, *Charting a Course* (London: HMSO, 15 December 1992).

55. I. Sanderson, 'Quality, strategic planning and performance review', in I. Sanderson (ed.), *Management of Quality in Local Government* (Harlow: Longman, 1992), pp. 93–117. See also M. Hodge, *Quality, Equality, Democracy: Improving public services*, Fabian Pamphlet 549 (London: Fabian Society, September 1991).

56. D. Prior, J. Stewart and K. Walsh, *Is the Citizen's Charter a Charter for Citizens?*, Belgrave Paper No. 7 (Luton: Local Government Management Board, 1993), p. 31.

57. For a comprehensive analysis of client and user involvement, see P. Beresford and S. Croft, *Citizen Involvement: A practical guide for change* (Practical Social Work Series) (London: Macmillan, 1993).

58. L. Gaster, 'Quality, decentralisation and devolution', in Sanderson (ed.), *Management of Quality in Local Government*, pp. 41–65.

59. R. Hambleton, *Consumerism, Decentralization and Local Democracy*, Working Paper 78 (Bristol: University of Bristol School for Advanced Urban Studies, March 1989), pp. 6–8.

60. R. Hambleton, *Urban Government in the 1990s: Lesson from the USA*,

Occasional Paper 35 (Bristol: Bristol University School of Advanced Urban Studies, 1990), p. 126.

61. For a discussion of these quality issues, see N. Pfeffer and A. Coote, *Is Quality Good for You?*, Social Policy Paper No. 5 (London: Institute for Public Policy Research, 1991).

62. G. Stoker, 'Decentralization and local government', *Social Policy and Administration*, vol. 21, 2, Summer 1987, pp. 157–70; V. Lowndes and G. Stoker, 'An evaluation of neighbourhood decentralisation', *Policy and Politics*, Part I, vol. 20, 1, 1992, pp. 47–61; Part II, vol. 20, 2, 1992, pp. 143–52; P. Hoggett and R. Hambleton (eds), *Decentralisation and Democracy* (Bristol: University of Bristol School of Advanced Urban Studies, 1987).

63. Hodge, *Quality, Equality, Democracy.*

64. R.A.W. Rhodes, 'Developing the public service orientation; or let's add a soupçon of political theory', *Local Government Studies*, vol. 13, 3, May/June 1987, pp. 63–73.

65. M. Taylor and J. Benington, 'The renewal of quality in the political process', in Sanderson (ed.), *Management of Quality in Local Government*, p. 165.

66. *ibid.*

67. C. Ham and J. Appleby, *The Future Direction of the NHS* (Birmingham: National Association of Health Authorities and Trusts [NAHAT], 1993).

68. 'Patten spells out citizen power', *Local Government Chronicle*, 12 February 1993, p. 4.

69. Rhodes, 'Developing the public service orientation'.

70. S. Ranson, 'Education', in N. Deakin and A. Wright, *Consuming Public Services* (London: Routledge), 1990, p. 193.

CHAPTER 9

CONCLUSION: CITIZENSHIP, COMMUNITY AND DEMOCRACY

Citizens and the local arena

Citizenship and community are contested ideas which have acquired a central part in the debate on life in the modern city. The local arena provides a framework for the exercise of individual and group participation, but it can do so only if significant decisions are taken at local level. This in turn depends on the existence of decision-taking structures, and on the powers and functions of local bodies. The exercise of citizenship, however, does not necessarily imply a system of local self-government. There are two opposing perspectives here. To those on the right, the main argument has been that citizen empowerment is achieved through devolving choice to individuals: as parents, school governors, tenants, clients. Such empowerment is truly democratic, since it allows genuine choice and renders services accountable both to those who use them and to the wider community. In the 1990s, however, some on the right have appeared to be reconsidering the bases of cohesion in society. In what seemed to be a rejection of Margaret Thatcher's assertion that there was 'no such thing as society', David Green of the Institute of Economic Affairs asserted that the challenge now was to identify a sense of community or solidarity that was compatible with freedom. Green's suggested model is of a 'civic capitalism', based on free-market ideas but with an emphasis on solidarity and mutal consideration – but founded on voluntaristic, not state, initiatives. Similarly, John Gray's *Beyond the New Right*, while affirming a reduced role for government as the umpire of market capitalism, also focuses on what he sees as the human need for local roots and strong forms of common life.[1]

To those on the left, consumer choice has gone hand in hand with significant increases in centralised power – over funding, standards, assessment, and the range and nature of services to be provided. Centralisation and individual choice leave, it is then argued, a vacuum at the heart of local democracy. Who is to speak for the community, for the common good? It is the representative local authority that has the legitimate position of balancing interests, representing the community and providing leadership, and ensuring equity among individuals and groups, and over time.

The debate on citizenship in the local arena has not been confined to a concern with enhancing the powers and rights of the users of services. The strains and conflicts of city life have commanded increased attention. The controversy over the existence of an underclass, the continued problems of urban regeneration, and the mitigation of urban unrest have all been the subject of policy initiatives. These initiatives – in welfare, inner-city redevelopment, and programmes to combat crime and disorder – have remained fragmented between different government departments, and between local government and a variety of unelected public agencies or quangos. There is no concerted urban policy, but a series of separate and frequently time-limited programmes. The network of intergovernmental and inter-agency provision makes it very difficult to produce an overall strategy for the urban economy, or for the delivery of services.

The neoliberal view is that no such state-led plan is necessary. And while targeted initiatives to promote economic regeneration are appropriate, the ultimate objective is to restore responsibilities to the market, to individuals and families, and to voluntary organisations. This 'urban policy' is founded on privatism, actively promoted by political decisions; in Barnekov, Boyle and Rich's words: 'the public choice of privatism is the dominant characteristic of contemporary urban policy in both the United States and Britain'.[2] That is, as Chapter 8 has suggested, the moves during the 1980s in Britain towards 'enabling' local authorities, and towards the individual exercising choices in the market-place, themselves form a purposive urban policy of multi-agency provision and consumer sovereignty.

The 'problem of the cities'

In the 1960s it appeared that a new approach to British urban policy had emerged with the rediscovery of poverty, and the initiatives designed to address concentrations of immigrants. The result was a policy of urban aid and programmes directed at the social problems of the 'inner city', in contrast with the universalism and national standards of the founding years of the postwar welfare state.

From the mid-1970s onwards the emphasis changed again, to a belief that the problem of the cities was a problem of economic and physical decay which could be solved by leveraging private investment into regeneration projects. King argues that there have been two sorts of rationale in urban policies. The first facilitates private investment; it is compatible with the *laissez-faire* approach of the Thatcher years, and the emphasis on the removal of state regulation. The second attempts to address the social and political consequences of urban decline, including the dangers of disorder and economic crises. The former rationale of urban policy is more powerful in the long term, while the latter has been influential for only short periods.[3] In practice there are now calls for an amalgamation of the two. As Robson puts it, the need is for 'cross-departmental and long-term urban policy which is more genuinely targeted to the deprived and which more effectively links housing and transport with economic development'.[4]

The problems of the cities, though they are frequently cast in economic terms, have a wider base. In particular, the political structures and processes of local affairs have come under strain as governments have sought to shift service provision from the state to deregulated and market-led organisations. The future of the citizen as part of the self-governing community, however, is dependent on the future of the city as *polis*: as a political and civic arena with local government as both provider and enabler, and as the setting for a renewed civic culture and civic pride. The alternative is the dissolution of the city, with the flight of the more prosperous to the suburban and 'rurban' hinterland, leaving a disadvantaged and increasingly ghettoised population at the city core and on peripheral housing estates.

If this were to happen, the scenario of the future might be of divided cities in which middle-class neighbourhoods were protected by private security firms, alarmingly akin to vigilante groups, while no-go inner-city ghettos with high crime levels were controlled by armed police. The private security industry, for its part, has called for clear guidelines to govern the growing number of security patrols employed by residents to guard their neighbourhood, to avoid the possible development of private vigilante schemes. Reporting on these trends, Brian Robson, adviser to the Department of the Environment, has been critical of the short-term and uncoordinated nature of urban policy, with its proliferation of agencies. The cutbacks in Urban Programme funding and the suspension of the third round of City Challenge, announced in the 1992 Autumn Statement, occurred, paradoxically, just as evidence was emerging that inner-city policies were enjoying a degree of success. The result, Robson warned, might be a choice: the self-confidence of European cities as they coped with change, or the ghetto and its violent crime evident in many American inner cities.[5]

Urban policy in the 1980s fostered city projects that have achieved success in their own terms, including a wide range of regeneration schemes for central areas. But these areas are too often surrounded by decay and dereliction; the result has been an increased polarisation in conditions and life chances. It is the well-being of the whole city which is at issue. The key to sustainable cities is the now-familiar list of local action with its themes of empowerment, devolved decision-making, and partnerships between the public, and the private and voluntary, sectors. Otherwise cities will continue to haemorrhage economically and socially, and city-centre dynamism will remain surrounded by social and economic squalor.

The economy of the cities, however, has changed dramatically in the last 20 years. Cities are no longer the locus of production but of consumption, and the major attractions of leisure, the arts, research and other high-value skills provide a continued rationale for urban life. At the same time, the reverse side of regeneration has led to large new single-use areas like the Isle of Dogs in London Docklands, driven by the pension funds and the big institutional investors. Their vision of the contemporary city is based on a misconception: the massive single-use areas have no street-related activities, with the result that these developments become alienating places. The cities' real need is for mixed use and development.

In this situation the local authority is the only entity which has a commitment to the area as a whole, and an overview for its economic well-being; and the local authority is still the only strategic authority in the planning sense. At the same time the response of local people to these strategic overviews of regeneration is ambivalent. They may welcome attempts to encourage inward investment, but at the same time call on the local authority to defend the community against developers and business. Incoming investment, for its part, is looking for an infrastructure which includes education and training, research and quality of life. The burden for managing this situation has fallen to local authorities because of the lack of an effective regional dimension, particularly in England; and also because of the question marks surrounding the revision of county structure plans consequent on the reform of local government. The vacuum caused by the lack of a regional dimension has in part been filled by subregional consortia. These may take the form of collaboration for economic purposes or joint boards, agencies and other working arrangements which arise as a consequence of local government reform. Nevertheless, the city-wide authority remains the vital key, providing the leading 'governance' role at the centre of a network of partnerships and of decentralised, participative processes.

The city's position in the regional and national context is legitimised by the diversity and pluralism fostered by place. The 1990s are seeing an increasing emphasis on the need to sustain the benefits of plural democracy to counteract the centralising trends of nationally appointed and controlled quangos. There has been an erosion of constitutional pluralism: thirty years ago local government was responsible for about a third of public administration; that is now severely curtailed. This increased centralisation has been aided by the fact that local councils now raise only around 15 per cent of their revenue from local taxation; and capping has become virtually universal, since councils are, in effect, capping themselves. The results are an even tighter central control, and diminished local accountability. There is a need, therefore, for improved accountability, beginning with a system of locally determined taxation related to locally determined expenditure. To strengthen the position of local government, a case has also been made for local authorities to be given general competence powers, taking ideas from the Scandinavian 'free commune' and elsewhere, and promoting a much wider notion of 'enabling' than that favoured by Conservative governments. Local government must be real government; not administration or minimalist facilitation, but both enabler and provider.

Inclusion or exclusion?

The economic and political problems of the cities highlight the question of the extent to which all can share equally as citizens in the life of the cities. The polarisation of rich and poor, of affluent and decayed neighbourhoods, and of those with secure jobs and those with no job or casualised employment, has generated a debate on dependency and powerlessness. Although the concept of the underclass is contested, there is concern with the exclusion and isolation of those whose life-chances and lifestyles threaten to make them non-citizens. A wider but related concern has been with the 'dependent' – those whose reliance on state benefits, arguably, is debilitating, going beyond a monetary relationship into a behavioural and attitudinal one. The dependency relation is a power relation; in recognising this, it is necessary to reaffirm the centrality of our mutual interdependence as active human participants in a common endeavour.

Mutual interdependence as a corollary of citizenship faces another difficulty: the argument that the notion of community is a pernicious myth which has nothing to do with city life. For significant numbers of people, it is argued, cities are not communities but staging posts, providing leisure facilities, hotels, restaurants, business meetings; and their outer edges act as the setting for home-centred activities. In the electronic age the centuries-old rationale for cities is vanishing. People and employers find it cheaper to move work elsewhere, and residents depart. If nothing is done to make cities safer and more attractive, their decline will mean an increasingly polarised population of rich and poor, with a deterioration of public services and increased racial tension. Divisions will also grow as prosperous places increase in prosperity, and their housing becomes unaffordable to those people who are needed to maintain services. Solutions have to be found in long-term planning, but such a perspective has been out of fashion for over a decade. On the contrary, the neoliberal influence on policy appears to be leading to a residual welfare state on US lines, with its well-recognised effects of widening income and areal disparities, and adverse implications for individual mobility, access and choice.

The changing local scene

The reform of local government which is set to take place in the second half of the 1990s raises interesting issues of community and representation. The number of local authorities is being reduced, with the corollary of fewer elected representatives, making Britain even further out of line with the situation in continental Europe. This reduction occurs on top of the other trend of the early 1990s, that of an increasing non-elected governing elite, Stewart's 'new magistracy'.[6] The issue here is not just the appointed membership of quangos – in health, school governing bodies, Training and Enterprise Councils, and the like – but the question of their openness to the public and the press, and their answerability to the local community, as opposed to their – weak – accountability to ministers and Parliament.

At the same time, the government's conception of the enabling authority, which has the strategic function of controlling the contracts of privatised services, means that questions of size and comprehensiveness of function are no longer key issues. Local authorities of this regulatory kind can be small or large; they can purchase services individually or in consortia, or contract with each other to supply services. The difficulties here are again in the area of accountability and control. The experience of the joint boards and committees set up following the abolition of the metropolitan counties in 1986 suggests that professionals gain in influence while board members lack real political control, so that meaningful accountability declines.

The changing structure of local government is progressing alongside internal changes in the provision of services. The Compulsory Competitive Tendering provisions have introduced a purchaser–provider split which seeks to inject the benefits of market competitiveness into local services. This, it is argued, enhances consumer choice and improves standards. At the same time, CCT and the opting out of schools and public sector tenants from local control provide more effective, and therefore more genuine, accountability to individuals who actually use services. The right has argued that far from producing a 'democratic deficit', this increases democracy. The analysis in Chapter 8 showed that the effect of internal changes in the provision of services has been to increase both centralisation and particular forms of decentralisation. The powers of Secretaries of State and national quangos have increased, and certain powers of control or influence have been devolved away from local councils to parents, school governors, council tenants, and service users.

The argument, then, is that this creates a vacuum at the heart of local democracy, with a diminished role for local authorities as the focus of the wider common good. If local authorities are to move beyond their traditional role as machines for the delivery of services, and avoid becoming, as government wishes, a clearing house for contracted-out services, then their political role as democratic bodies needs to be enhanced: representing, empowering, negotiating and mobilising, as Benington and Taylor put it.[7] To work towards these objectives, the processes of local councils need to be more open and transparent, as does the work of individual councillors. The councillor role should not be confined to that of consumer advocate or watchdog, though this will be an expanding area of work; it should be deliberative as well. To this end councillors need more support, just as participating individuals and groups do. But supportive services should not be seen solely in terms of salaries for a small group of members forming the executive; this would be divisive.

The introduction of quasi-markets and opting out has taken place in a changing climate of management in which quality has dominated the agenda across the political spectrum. The search for quality has focused on the Audit Commission's stress on the three Es: economy, effeciency and effectiveness. Statutory requirements for performance indicators, published locally and in national league tables, and Citizen's Charter provisions for information, access and redress of complaints, are one aspect of the changed management culture. But there have been very different emphases on how quality might be improved, notably by greater decentralisation to neighbourhood and to client groups, and a greater stress on participatory rather than representative democracy at the localised level. The outcome of these moves to markets and contracting out has been a move from local authorities founded on principles of bureaucratic hierarchy to networks and partnerships between public, private and voluntary sectors.

The city in the international context

Fundamental economic restructuring at the global level has meant restructuring at the level of the city and the community. Economic restructuring within cities has taken place in three main ways: as a result of branch plant closure, relocation to suburbs or further afield, and changing skills and labour markets. During the 1970s and 1980s cities declined as centres of production, and traditional industrial employment showed a marked downturn. Production decisions are now made on an international rather than a national basis. State intervention in this restructuring has been through incentives to business, and through regeneration initiatives involving central–local and public–private partnerships.

The effects of global economic restructuring are evident in the changes to labour markets. There have been substantial shifts to part-time working and increases in both low- and high-paid service sector jobs. These changes have affected employment migration, household formation and housing. The results have been a polarisation both within cities and between cities and expanding small and medium towns and rural areas, and very uneven economic development. These movements in turn have destabilising effects on neighbourhoods, which undergo a cycle of change and decay; on community life, with the potential break-up of long-standing institutions and organisations; and on local politics.

Global restructuring has affected local and regional economies, and had a spatial effect on downtown development. Prestige projects, leisure, arts and retail attractions have all been used to lure a mobile executive class back into major urban areas. The obverse of these developments is the existence of areas of abandoned plant and decay. The essential element in community politics, then, becomes the extent to which networks of people in communities can combine to produce forms of organisation leading to the effective

regional and national level. It is accountable to residents as voters, consumers and clients. As local governance, local authorities rest on and promote an active citizenship. As Clarke and Stewart express it: 'Local authorities as local government must not merely accept the rights of citizens, but should seek to enhance them. In enhancing them they are enhancing the basis of their own existence.'[10]

At the same time, however, this representative democracy is no longer judged as self-justifying. It must be infused with participative democracy, involving decentralisation of services and the input of groups and neighbourhoods. In expanding the avenues of involvement it must be recognised that participation rates may in practice be low, and that they are strongly correlated with social indices, particularly with levels of education. The result is then elitist domination, not expanded participation: such participation is inegalitarian.[11] Moreover, participation and control at localised neighbourhood level may reinforce these disadvantages. Poorer groups and poorer areas gain a degree of self-direction, but remain disadvantaged compared with richer areas and groups. Without an overall strategy and resources, participative democracy reinforces the status quo. It is also the case that people in disadvantaged areas may dismiss consultation and greater 'involvement', since their primary demand is for adequate services competently delivered. To combat these difficulties, suitable structures, and positive support, must be provided to encourage individuals and groups to take part when and if they wish to do so, and to sustain their involvement beyond the initial protest or demand. The argument is not that people must or will be involved, but that means should exist to ensure that they can. It is here that the divergence of approach between right and left reflects the dilemma of the emerging ideology. The right argues that it is precisely the self-government of schools, of welfare pluralism, of consumer choice, that widens involvement and democratic accountability. The left believes that this empowerment of the individual is deficient. It is an inadequate account of democracy because it demotes the legitimate interest of the wider community, ignores problems of equality, and replaces the citizen with the consumer.

Democracy articulated as process and structure is crucial. The key questions are: what structures and procedures exist to facilitate people's involvement in decisions, provide them with adequate information, and ensure the quality and equity of those decisions?

One danger of the contract culture, for example, is that avenues of complaint and redress may become more, not less, complex. The Citizen's Charter provisions require local authorities to set up formal complaints procedures, and make them widely known. At the same time the complexities of responsibilities, as we saw in Chapter 8, in relation to education, may make recourse to the courts more likely; a form of redress that is dependent on access and finance. Contracting out of services to private or not-for-profit bodies may remove these services from the remit of the local government ombudsman, again lessening avenues of redress.

In this context, both citizen and consumer need more information. For the latter, it can be argued that the emphasis on quality, the use of charters and performance indicators, the requirements that local councils, and schools, produce more information, has highlighted the growing awareness of the need. For the citizen, there is a need for a better range as well as depth of information: rights to information in relation to services; more data and explanations (what do the indicators mean?); diverse sources of information, through radio, television and newspapers. It could also be argued that in order to increase information, changes in electoral systems are needed, with moves towards proportional representation, annual council elections, the reporting back of ward representatives and committee members.

What must be avoided in exploring all these avenues is arrival at a situation where quasi-market choice is seen as an alternative to involvement in decisions. Participative democracy should infuse, not replace, representative democracy; both are needed in a multi-layered, pluralistic society. There is also a need for the views, demands and choices of the user as well as the citizen, and the encouragement of the participation of service users. This raises the crucial question: to what extent can we talk about empowerment, when we in this country are subjects, not citizens, and rights are not codified? This must be set in the wider context of the Constitution, and it has been argued that the quickest way to establish citizen rights would be to incorporate the European Convention of Human Rights into domestic legislation as the first step towards the creation of a Bill of Rights, including freedom of information. In Britain citizenship takes the passive form of subjects rather than the Aristotelian active concept of those who take part in the public life of the polis, and exercise both rights and duties.

But even though citizenship is not protected in a written Constitution, its expression through civic action can still be defended. Although participation in practice suffers from a number of defects, including apathy, elitism and potential sectionalism, that is no reason for rejecting the Mill tradition. As Rhodes puts it, emancipation through citizenship provides the 'noble aspiration' of local government, and a justification of its public service orientation.[12]

Most importantly, in conjunction with the infusion of participatory democracy, representatives still need to provide civic leadership. The suggestions for the reform of the internal management of local authorities, with opportunities for experimentation with different forms of executive leadership and committee structures, has potential benefits for representative democracy. The existence of a form of 'cabinet' executive and the reduction of the number and size of committees would speed decision-making, and could arguably attract more people into public life. A more high-profile 'cabinet', or even a directly elected Chief Executive, might also stimulate greater public interest and higher electoral turnout. If such initiatives were to be taken, then safeguards should be introduced to prevent any collective executive becoming a closed cabal. A number of processes could be used, including Question Time and scrutiny committees on the lines of the House of Commons Select Committees. Additionally, councils should consider holding open meetings and forums, not just at civic centre level, but in different neighbourhoods and with a range of groups and interests.

Two views remain key elements, though not necessarily polar opposites, of the debate on people and cities. One view, put forward by Osborne and Gaebler in *Reinventing Government*,[13] is that we are living with outdated public systems created during the industrial age, which need to be replaced with decentralised, more entrepreneurial and responsive public organisations. The key themes are empowering, encouraging competition, meeting the needs of the customer, and investing in prevention, not cure. The other view is that both municipal socialism and neoliberal ideology, with its materialist individualism, are inadequate in the revitalisation of a civic culture. The real problem is how to combine both public and private solutions in an era when municipal institutions are under threat, and a sense of civic achievement is difficult to foster. The essential requirement is to put the *polis* back into urban policy. The prescription of de Tocqueville, writing in 1835, retains a resonance for the late twentieth century:

> Yet municipal institutions constitute the strength of free nations. Town meetings are to liberty what primary schools are to science; they bring it within the people's reach, they teach men how to use and how to enjoy it. A nation may establish a free government, but without municipal institutions it cannot have the spirit of liberty.[14]

Notes

1. D.G. Green, *Reinventing Civil Society* (London: Institute of Economic Affairs, 1993); J. Gray, *Beyond The New Right* (London: Routledge, 1993).
2. T. Barnekov, R. Boyle and D. Rich, *Privatism and Urban Policy in Britain and the United States* (Oxford: Oxford University Press, 1989), p. 232.
3. D.S. King, 'The state, capital and urban change in Britain', in M.P. Smith and J. R. Feagin (eds), *The Capitalist City: Global restructuring and community politics* (Oxford: Basil Blackwell, 1987), pp. 222–3).
4. B. Robson, 'The enduring city: a perspective on decline', in B. Robson (ed.), *Managing the City: The aims and impacts of urban policy* (London: Croom Helm, 1987), p. 20.
5. B. Robson, Presidential Address, Institute of Geographers' Annual Conference, January 1993, as reported in S. Abbott, 'Inner cities "face choice of gun law or regeneration" ', *The Independent*, 6 January 1993; B. Robson, 'Power-driving the cities', *The Guardian*, June 1993. (In summer 1993, Professor Robson's address had still not been printed in the *Transactions of the Institute of British Geographers*. This was a consequence of the fact that the report had not been released by the Department of the Environment, a matter which has been commented on by the editor of *Transactions*. See R. Lee, 'The presidential address 1993', *Transactions of the Institute of British Geographers*, vol. 18, 2, 1993, p.165.)
6. J. Stewart, 'The rebuilding of public accountability', in J. Stewart, N. Lewis and B. Langley, *Accountability to the Public* (London: European Policy Forum, 1992).
7. J. Benington and M. Taylor, 'The renewal of quality in the political process', in I. Sanderson (ed.), *Management of Quality in Local Government* (Harlow: Longman, 1992), pp. 184–5.

8. J.R. Feagin and M.P. Smith, 'Cities and the new international division of labor: an overview', in Smith and Feagin (eds), *The Capitalist City*; p. 30).

9. R.A. Dahl and E.R. Tufte, *Size and Democracy* (Stanford, Calif.: Stanford University Press), 1974, p. 140.

10. M. Clarke and J. Stewart, *Choices for Local Government for the 1990s and Beyond* (Harlow: Longman, 1991), p. 66.

11. P. Bachrach and A. Botwinick, *Power and Empowerment: A radical theory of participatory democracy* (Philadelphia, Penn.: Temple University Press, 1992), p. 23.

12. R.A.W. Rhodes, 'Developing the public service orientation; or let's add a soupçon of political theory', *Local Government Studies*, vol.13, 3, May/June 1987, p. 67.

13. D. Osborne and T. Gaebler, *Reinventing Government: How the entrepreneurial spirit is transforming the public sector* (Reading, Mass.: Addison-Wesley, 1992).

14. A. de Tocqueville, (ed. P. Bradley), *Democracy in America Vol. 1* (New York: Vintage Books, 1945), p. 63.

INDEX OF NAMES

INDEX OF SUBJECTS